Routledge Revivals

Leisure and the Changing City 1870 – 1914

By the late nineteenth century, the city had become the dominant social environment of Britain, with the majority of the population living in large cities, often with over 100, 000 inhabitants. The central concern of this book, first published in 1976, is to assess how successful the late Victorians were in creating a stimulating social environment whilst these developing cities were being transformed into modern industrial and commercial centres. Using Bristol as a case study, Helen Meller analyses the new relationships brought about by mass urbanisation, between city and citizen, environment and society. The book considers a variety of important features of the Victorian city, in particular the development of the main cultural institutions, the provision of leisure facilities by voluntary societies and the expansion of activities such as music, sport and commercial entertainment. Comparative examples are drawn from other cities, which illustrate the common social and cultural values of an urbanised nation. This is a very interesting title, of great relevance to students and academics of town planning, Victorian society, and the history and development of the modern city.

Leisure and the Changing City 1870 - 1914

Helen Meller

First published in 1976
by Routledge & Kegan Paul Ltd

This edition first published in 2013 by Routledge
2 Park Square, Milton Park, Abingdon, Oxon, OX14 4RN

Simultaneously published in the USA and Canada
by Routledge
711 Third Avenue, New York, NY 10017

Routledge is an imprint of the Taylor & Francis Group, an informa business

© 1976 Helen Meller

All rights reserved. No part of this book may be reprinted or reproduced or utilised in any form or by any electronic, mechanical, or other means, now known or hereafter invented, including photocopying and recording, or in any information storage or retrieval system, without permission in writing from the publishers.

Publisher's Note
The publisher has gone to great lengths to ensure the quality of this reprint but points out that some imperfections in the original copies may be apparent.

Disclaimer
The publisher has made every effort to trace copyright holders and welcomes correspondence from those they have been unable to contact.

A Library of Congress record exists under LC control number: 76383866

ISBN 13: 978-0-415-84213-6 (hbk)
ISBN 13: 978-0-203-76293-6 (ebk)
ISBN 13: 978-0-415-84216-7 (pbk)

LEISURE AND THE CHANGING CITY, 1870-1914

H. E. MELLER
Department of Economic and Social History
University of Nottingham

ROUTLEDGE & KEGAN PAUL
LONDON, HENLEY AND BOSTON

*First published in 1976
by Routledge & Kegan Paul Ltd
39 Store Street,
London WC1E 7DD,
Broadway House,
Newtown Road,
Henley-on-Thames,
Oxon RG9 1EN and
9 Park Street,
Boston, Mass. 02108, USA
Set in 11 on 12 pt Linotype Granjon
and printed in Great Britain by
Willmer Brothers Limited, Birkenhead
© H. E. Meller 1976
No part of this book may be reproduced in
any form without permission from the
publisher, except for the quotation of brief
passages in criticism*

ISBN 0 7100 8430 7

CONTENTS

PREFACE ix

1 INTRODUCTION 1
   I   The 'modern' city 1
  II Leisure and the city 5
 III Civilization and social citizenship 6
 IV Civilization and 'the social question' 11
   V The social and cultural environment of cities 16

2 BRISTOL IN THE LATE NINETEENTH CENTURY 19
   I   The physical growth of the city 19
  II Physical condition of the city 25
 III The condition of the people 31
 IV Social change in city and suburb 35

3 THE CITY AND ITS CULTURAL INSTITUTIONS 40
   I   Cultural activities in Bristol in the early nineteenth century 42
  II The civic 'cultural renaissance' of the 1860s and '70s 48
 III Cultural activities 1875–98 62
 IV The 'municipalization' of cultural institutions 65

4 BRISTOL'S LEADING CITIZENS –
   A GOVERNING ELITE? 72
   I   Philanthropy and the élite 74
  II Religion and the governing élite 77
 III Bristol's town council 85
 IV Case studies of the élite 91

CONTENTS

5 MUNICIPAL FACILITIES FOR LEISURE AND PLEASURE — 96
I The development of public libraries — 100
II Municipal provisions for recreation and sport — 109
III Contribution of municipal experience to a greater demand for town planning — 117

6 THE 'CIVILIZING MISSION' TO THE POOR — 122
I The 'civilizing mission' and the YMCA in the mid-century years — 126
II Socio-religious work in the 1860s — 130
III Penny readings and the beginnings of mass cultural entertainment — 134
IV The response of socio-religious workers to urban growth — 138
V New developments at the YMCA — 145
VI The social experiment of Clifton College Mission — 149

7 SOCIO-RELIGIOUS PROVISIONS FOR LEISURE 1890–1914 — 161
I Temperance work and the provision of leisure facilities — 163
II Leisure provisions for young people — 169
III Provisions for education outside the formal school system — 175
IV Developments in adult education — 189
V The social work of religious missions — 194

8 URBANIZATION AND LEISURE – THE SECULAR CULTURE OF CITY AND SUBURB — 206
I Popular amusements of the people — 206
II The Labour movement and leisure — 214
III The passion for music — 219
IV The pursuit of organized sport — 225

9 SOCIAL DEVELOPMENT AND THE CITY — 237
I The socio-religious response — 237
II Leisure and social change — 241

ABBREVIATIONS — 253

NOTES — 255

SELECT BIBLIOGRAPHY — 279

INDEX — 295

LIST OF ILLUSTRATIONS

PLATES

1 J. Storrs Fry 1826–1913   *between pages* 149–150
2 Mark Whitwill 1826–1903
3 H. O. Wills 1828–1911
4 Lewis Fry 1832–1921
5 Bristol Art Gallery 1905
6 Bristol Art Gallery, Interior
7 Jacobs Wells' Swimming Bath 1884
8 Close up of city coat of arms, Jacobs Wells' Swimming Bath
9 Central Reference Library, Bristol, built 1906
10 Interior of Central Reference Library
11 Bristol Museum and Library 1871
12 The People's Palace 1892
13 A cycle rally in Clifton 1886
14 The Industrial and Fine Arts Exhibition 1893
15 The Bristol YMCA, by S. Loxton
16 Clifton College Mission to St Agnes, Men's and Boys' Club
17 St Agnes Working Men's Club Committee

DRAWINGS

Bandstand in park	*page* 55
Museum interior	82
Open air swimming bath	111

LIST OF ILLUSTRATIONS

Bristol Boy Scouts	142
St Philips Free Library, and Branch Library Reading Room, Interior	183
Music hall	221
Park scene	244

Drawings by S. Loxton, from the manuscript collection at the Bristol Reference Library

I should like to acknowledge with many thanks the generous help of Mr Geoffrey Langley, County Reference Librarian, with the selection of these illustrations. Plates 1-4, 6-12, 15-17, and the S. Loxton drawings, are published with the kind permission of Bristol Reference Library. Plates 5, 13 and 14 are published with the kind permission of Reece Winstone.

PREFACE

The purpose of this book is to explore the social and cultural environment of a large city at a time, in the nineteenth century, when cities had become the dominant, social environment of the nation. How successful were the late Victorians in carrying out a stimulating social environment from the unpromising material of a large industrial city? Such a theme demands a focus, since it can be all-embracing. This study is limited in two ways: to a manageable context, an individual city, in this instance the city of Bristol; and second, to the attempts made by those citizens who responded in a specific, self-conscious way to this challenge by providing leisure and cultural facilities.

This is a narrow framework, particularly as it excludes the largely undocumented day-to-day experiences of the majority of citizens, which make up an important part of the social environment. But it does make possible a closer study of the link between the growth and changing physical form of nineteenth-century cities and the social responses that were made to it. The choice of Bristol for a case-study has no further significance than its size. All large cities of more than 100,000 population were becoming transformed by 'modernizing' factors, so that they all shared common elements of change, whatever differences were to be found in their economic structures. Thus the history of Bristol can provide an insight into the social response to a changing urban environment of more general significance than the local context.

This study contains much material from a doctoral thesis submitted to the University of Bristol. It gives me great pleasure to record my warmest thanks to Professor William Ashworth, who acted as my supervisor for the thesis, and whose constant encouragement and creative criticism have been of inestimable value to me, both then and now. I have especially to thank him and Professor Sidney Pollard for reading the manuscript and for offering so many helpful comments. Many other people have given me much help and advice. I should like to express my deepest gratitude to Mr Patrick McGrath for his attempts, made from his great knowledge of Bristol's history, to help me avoid errors of fact; to Dr B. W. E. Alford for his kind response to my queries about Bristol's economic structure; and to Mr Large and Mr Sherborne and other members of Bristol University, particularly the library staff, who have offered me much advice and encouragement. My thanks are also due to Professor H. J. Dyos, for his encouragement and suggestions on the best ways of utilizing the thesis for a book; and to Professor J. P. Cole, for his advice on the historical geography of large towns.

In addition, I should like to thank those who helped me so much in the early days of my research, particularly the Reference Librarian at Bristol Central Reference Library, Mr Langley, and Miss Ralph, the City Archivist at that time. I should also like to thank the Librarian of Clifton College Library and the Secretary of the Bristol Trades Council, Kingsley Hall. To the librarians, or their assistants, in the sample of towns of 100,000 or more inhabitants in 1881, whom I visited or wrote to with lengthy queries, I am most grateful. They are too numerous to name individually, but their help has been vital in enabling me to generalize, at some points, with more conviction. The range of source material used in this book has been indicated, as far as possible, in notes and a select bibliography, though the present economic stringency has forced these to a minimum.

Finally my very grateful thanks are due to family and friends, and to my colleagues, at Sheffield University (1966-8), and at Nottingham University, who have all helped me in many different ways. In the task of producing the manuscript for publication, I have to thank Mrs Valerie Glass for her help with the sketch maps. Above all, I have to thank Mrs Gwen Parker who, undaunted by my constant revisions, has typed the manuscript with great skill and speed, contributing more than she realizes to its final production.

August 1975   Nottingham

I
INTRODUCTION

One of the most remarkable social changes in nineteenth-century Britain was the congregation of the majority of the population into large cities. Such a development was unprecedented, though other areas of Europe and the USA were undergoing a similar transformation by the end of the century.[1] No one doubted that the Industrial Revolution had brought material advantages, however unevenly distributed. But had urbanization brought parallel social and cultural riches to those now forced to live in cities? In the new relationships brought by mass urbanization, between city and citizen, environment and society, there was a need to create new living patterns, as a means of collective social stability and as a means of promoting individual fulfilment. Traditional customs and mores became eroded, and the challenge for the late Victorians was to replace them with the assets of city life, freedom of choice, mobility and a wider range of social and cultural experiences.

I THE 'MODERN' CITY

The proportion between the rural and town population of a country [wrote one American observer of these processes[2]] is an important fact in its interior economy and condition. It determines, in a great degree, its capacity for manufactures, the extent of its commerce and the amount of its wealth. The growth of cities commonly marks the progress of intelligence and the arts, measures the sum of social enjoyment, and always implies excessive mental activity, which is sometimes healthy and useful, sometimes distempered and pernicious.

In England, the point of no return was reached in 1851, when the census revealed that the population was equally divided between town dwellers and country dwellers. Each subsequent census showed an increase in the proportion of urban dwellers: 61·8 per cent in 1871, 72·05 per cent in 1891, and 80 per cent in 1911, with the large towns of more than 100,000 population taking a dominant share of that increase.

This development of large cities, however, was not only a matter of scale. There were also qualitative changes which, *in toto*, were transforming city life. These changes have been described as the process of modernization and, in the period 1870 to 1914, they were speeded up so that all large cities were becoming 'modern' cities. The historical forces generating this transformation have been summed up by Professor Handlin.[3] He suggests that 'modern' cities sprang 'from three profound and interrelated changes in the society external to them – the development of the centralized national state, the transformation of the economy ... and the technological destruction of distance.'[4] The prototype of such a city was London in the sixteenth and seventeenth centuries. In the nineteenth century, however, when the first group of provincial towns (Manchester, Liverpool, Leeds, Birmingham and Bristol) reached and surpassed the 100,000 mark in population; and in the mid-century years, when the second group (led by Sheffield, Wolverhampton, Newcastle upon Tyne, Bradford, Salford and Stoke on Trent) did the same, these interrelated factors gained greater strength in transforming them into 'modern' cities.

In many ways, the two decades of the 1860s and '70s marked a transitional stage in this trend. For instance, the significance of the first factor, the 'centralized national state' in relation to cities in the nineteenth century, lay largely in administration. The evolution of a new relationship between central and local government was a long drawn-out process, interspersed with elements of economic theory, social experience, and much social prejudice. But in the late 1860s and early '70s an attempt was made to clarify the relationship and put it on a business footing. Basic elements in this activity concerned the Poor Law, public health, housing, education and town improvements. There was a cluster of government reforms, indicating new levels of responsibility and contact, particularly the Sanitary Commission of 1869-71 and the setting up of the Local Government Board, the 1870 Education Act and the codification of public health legislation in the 1875 Act. The Torrens and Cross Acts of 1868 and 1875 initiated a new response to slums and the era of by-law housing, even if they were not generally applied and their results were to be seen largely in a few striking examples. However, the greater regulation of housing, road improvements, cleaning, paving and lighting of streets, policing, provision of water and sewage disposal, and refuse collecting had, in aggregate, a considerable impact on the physical environment of the 'modern' city.[5]

The second factor, the transformation of the economy, was also at a formative stage in the 1860s and '70s, in its impact on the physical shape of the city. It was not only that the changes brought by the Industrial Revolution were now being more extensively implemented than before; from the 1870s, wider economic forces were increasingly transforming land use in the centres of large cities. By then, Britain and the British economy had become the central pivot in the extending activities of a world multilateral economy.[6] The physical impact of such a development was felt first in London, the world's financial and commercial centre, in the ports and the cities engaged in major export trades. But the growing flow of imports and exports and the increasing sophistication of commercial activity had repercussions which were experienced by all large provincial centres.

Central areas were mainly cleared of residential building and manufacturing activities, and the space left was quickly utilized for offices and warehousing for commercial enterprises and related services. Factors such as the increase of food imports contributed significantly to a revolution in wholesale and retailing methods, with the establishment of centrally controlled nationwide networks. Two new retailing techniques, the chain store and the department store, were both developed in the late Victorian period.[7] They became part of a new pattern of relationships between city and citizens, the latter now largely banished to the residential and industrial suburbs. The centre became on the one hand, the working environment for mainly white-collar workers, on the other, the source of services such as shops and amusements. The total exile of citizens from central areas was not complete, as pockets of residential buildings did remain, situated either between the centre and outer suburbs, or trapped by physical barriers such as railway lines.[8] These tended, especially on the east side of cities, to be slums, created by soaring land values and the inability of lower income groups to pay higher rents or to move to the suburbs.

Suburbs, of course, were a crucial feature of the 'modern' city and their development was related, not only to economic growth, but also to technological advances in transport. This introduces the third 'profound change', the technological destruction of distance, to have a dramatic impact on the city. The main-line railway system had been completed, more or less, by the 1860s. It had had considerable impact on many cities as lines were thrust through to the centre, destroying areas of slum housing and encouraging extensive road improvements for better access to the station. But transformations in local transport were to have even more far-reaching effects on everyday life.[9] The suburban train and tram, introduced largely in the 1870s, made a clear division between work-place and residence available to the majority of the population. The establishment of shopping and entertainment services in the centre depended on better local transport. The technological destruction of distance made people more mobile within the city and also away from it. Seaside towns, spas and holiday resorts began to grow enormously from the 1860s, fed by new supplies of tourists on holiday trains.[10]

All cities of 100,000 or more inhabitants were profoundly affected by these developments in the half century before the First World War. Since these cities were also absorbing a greater proportion of population growth than small towns and rural counties, the experiences of modernization must have been similar for a large proportion of the population. This is not to say that all large cities were similar. Lewis Mumford's universal 'Coketown' has been attacked by Professor Asa Briggs for reasons which are supremely valid.[11] Each town or city is a complex organism with variations in economic and social structure, social institutions and traditions; and it is these very differences which are crucial to an understanding of historical development. But city boundaries are not city walls. The impact of the modern industrial city, the reaction of its inhabitants to life in the city, to the search for happiness, are universal themes which those in Britain, and other industrialized, urbanized nations, had to explore.

II LEISURE AND THE CITY

The study of leisure activities provides a unique insight into the responses made to the challenge of social development in the city. The concept of leisure, however, is not an easy one to handle. Leisure is not simply an adjunct to work. As Elias and Dunning point out:

> The pleasurable satisfaction provided by leisure activities tends to be treated as an end – to the end of giving relief from the strain of work and of improving man's capacity for it. However, if one asks, primarily, what the function of leisure is for work, the possibility of discovering what its function is for men tends to be obscured.[12]

This latter possibility is the one most relevant to a study of social development, or the 'civilizing' process. Since the function of leisure for society at large was undergoing rapid transformation in the late Victorian period, deliberate attempts were made to redefine its function. The creation of an urban civilization which would meet the full emotional, intellectual and recreational demands of a nation, could only be the product of conscious, deliberate thought.

In the 1860s and '70s realization of this fact was becoming far more widely experienced as the numbers now living in cities grew. Few would have disagreed with W. S. Jevons, writing in the *Contemporary Review* of 1878: 'As society becomes more complex and the forms of human society multiply, so must multiply also the points at which careful legislation and continuous social effort are required to prevent abuse, and to secure the best utilization of resources.'[13] The potential of life in a 'modern' city could not be realized without effort. But the direction of that effort has sometimes obscured the nature of the 'civilizing' process. Instead of social development in new circumstances implying a higher level of potential experience for everyone, what was sometimes more evident was the considerable pressure exerted on the masses to make them accept their lot.

Such an emphasis highlights the political element present in any conscious and deliberate attempt to initiate social change. In the year of revolutions, 1848, in the *Communist Manifesto*, Marx and Engels rage against all those working for social adaptability;

the economists, philanthropists, humanitarians, improvers of the condition of the working class, organizers of charity, members of societies for the prevention of cruelty to animals, temperance fanatics, hole and corner reformers of every imaginable kind ... [who] want all the advantages of modern social conditions without the struggles and dangers necessarily resulting therefrom.

This middle-class effort to control the direction of social change can be 'summed up in the phrase: the bourgeois is a bourgeois for the benefit of the working class.'

But regardless of who wielded the political power, it remained a vital fact that a modern, industrialized, urban society had to evolve new social conditions within which to operate. Marx's 'modern social conditions' were in a constant state of development. Eric Lampard writes: 'Urbanization itself may be regarded as the organizational component of a population's achieved capacity for adaptation.'[14] By this he means two things. The ability of the community to adapt itself to changing economic circumstances and to continue increasing its economic wealth; and second, the ability to evolve a new social order able to understand and exploit the latest economic and technological developments to the fullest *social* as well as economic advantage. Given the economic, social and political inequalities of mid-Victorian society, vested interests were bound to try and shape the evolution of the new social order to their own advantage. But social change in the 'modern' city was not so easy to control. The assets of city life, the greater freedom, mobility and social aggregation of large numbers, militated against any simple, easily controllable pattern of development.

III CIVILIZATION AND SOCIAL CITIZENSHIP

In fact, even amongst those with a similar class background, there was little unanimity on the pattern that future social development should take. Civilization was a theme with a wide variety of possible interpretations. Could it be defined by contrasting rural life and values with city life and civilization? Or did it refer to the formal view of cultural experiences, the pursuit of the liberal and visual arts?

Or was it a far more pragmatic and pervasive influence altering social relationships and behaviour in a never-ending process of social change? These were questions without answers. But one thing was clear, in the historical context of mass urbanization, what happened in each large city was more than a matter of local concern, it was part of the national response to the challenge of civilization.

> The central and significant fact about the city [wrote Geddes and Branford], is that it functions as the specialized organ of social transmission. It accumulates and embodies the heritage of larger units, national, racial, religious, human. On the one side is the individuality of the city – the sign manual of its regional life and record. On the other side are the marks of the civilization, in which each city is a particular element.[15]

The use of leisure and the provision of facilities for leisure and pleasure thus gained a new significance from the mid-century years. The provision of cultural facilities devoted to the formal concept of Liberal Culture, for instance, sometimes became the spearhead of an attempt to salvage the reputation of the city. Many contemporaries considered that the modern city had destroyed the traditional values of English society. Pugin, Ruskin and William Morris were riding the crest of an anti-urban wave in their championship of medieval buildings and medieval towns in harmony with the countryside and rural life.[16] The affluent middle classes built their suburbs with extravagant amounts of land for each house as if they were really in the countryside, or at worst, some country town.[17] The cardinal sins of the modern city were the total ugliness of its environment and the destruction of a sense of community, that nub of nineteenth-century social thinking, because of the enormous numbers of citizens now segregated in different residential suburbs according to economic status. As Disraeli wrote in *Sybil*: 'There is no community in England: there is aggregation, but aggregation under circumstances which make it rather a dissociating than a uniting principle.'[18]

Ideas on what constituted fellowship, neighbourliness and a sense of community, supplemented by idealized conceptions of the past were important for shaping ideas on what to do to improve the city in the late nineteenth century.[19] The anti-urbanism of the affluent middle-class suburbs was counterbalanced by a new concern shown by these same middle classes as private benefactors or municipal councillors to make the centre of their cities both more impressive and beautiful. The models were the great cities of the ancient civilizations. The method was the municipalization of certain cultural institutions, libraries, museums and art galleries, which were then housed in magnificent buildings. As Canon Barnett wrote in 1890 (echoing the words of Birmingham's civic gospellers, a quarter of a century earlier) the idea was that the city would 'catch and raise the thoughts of men, as in the old days the thoughts of their citizens were caught by ... Florence and Venice.'[20]

The involvement of the municipal council in the cultural life of the city developed alongside the extension of its authority, with the reorganization of local government.[21] But institutions of Liberal Culture did not mark the extent of its activities. Local councils became sucked into the amorphous but persistent movement in search of 'neighbourhood' and 'community' which was such an important issue in the late nineteenth century.[22] Indeed, before practical considerations of resources limited the possibilities, there was much debate over the optimum size for a local government body, since it was considered that local government should be a 'community' activity. In the 1870s strong arguments were put forward in favour of the parish as a viable local government unit as it had some semblance of a genuine local community. When the matter was finally decided in favour of a single local authority in cities of over 100,000, it was hoped that the principle of democratic representation on the council would retain the interest and reflect the wishes of all citizens.

It became the duty of councillors of specific wards to respond to those wishes, and to fight for the provision of social amenities for their local communities. The result was a new awareness of the relationship between the environment and social life. Stimulated by the increasing provisions for public health and education, many local councils responded by extending their vision of what was possible under these heads. As a reporter on the *Western Daily Press* wrote in 1895:

The larger provincial towns are ... laying out parks and playgrounds using in fact, municipal funds to increase the pleasure and health of the community. It would be difficult to estimate the value of this development ... town life was often neglected in the craving of what was understood as utility ... the future of life in large cities may be contemplated with the assurance that it will be brighter, sweeter and more rationally enjoyable ... the municipal evolution which is taking place is rendering local authorities more appreciative of the necessities of modern life and more anxious to adopt improvements that will add to the happiness of the communities they represent.[23]

Such optimism in view of the fact that the east ends of most cities had not changed much by 1895 (and were rarely brighter and sweeter) is only explicable in terms of contemporary thinking on citizenship and community, which reached a peak in the last two decades of the century. T. H. S. Escott, writing in 1897 on the subject of the *Social Transformation of the Victorian Age,* devotes a whole chapter to what he describes as 'Social Citizenship as a Moral Growth of Victorian England'.[24] The key word here is 'moral'. Social citizenship had strong overtones of a religious crusade. It filled the vacuum left by the increasingly obvious fact that the churches and chapels were never going to evangelize the urban masses. What exactly was meant by 'social citizenship' was never quite clear, but definitions of considerable ingenuity and subtlety were put forward by religious leaders and philosophers. For Canon Barnett, for instance, 'social citizenship' was the very essence of social life. The modern city he believed, with some imagination, could be made into the Ideal City.[25] What was needed was leadership and financial resources from the rich, who could devote themselves to the welfare of their city which, with their support, could become an almost independent unit in the national state. The moral impulse which would stimulate the affluent, the benefit to the poor of a well-run city, and the provision of a rich cultural existence, would create a new experience of urban living, a higher civilization.

Philosophers, intellectuals and statesmen worked on the theory of 'social citizenship' without Canon Barnett's immediately practical objectives in mind. Their work was part of an attempt to give a political meaning to the theory of equality. Typical of the kind of definition of citizenship that found favour was that given by James Bryce in his lectures, published 1909, entitled *Hindrances to Citizenship*. He wrote:

> Each member of a free community must be capable of citizenship. Capacity involves three qualities – Intelligence, Self-control and Conscience. The citizen must be able to understand the interests of the community, must be able to subordinate his will to the general will, must feel his responsibilities to the community and be prepared to serve it....[26]

The political implications of this attitude were spelt out by T. H. Green. His politics of conscience was a desperate attempt to create a moral base for a palpably unequal society. The spoils and riches of the few could be justified by their social conscience and sense of duty. The salvation of society was equal social citizenship. Green wrote:

> In spite of a fundamental identity of interests between employers and workmen ... there always will be, there always must be, antagonisms of interest; and these can be met only by moral ideas appropriate not to the feudal, but to the citizen stage. Men's rights will clash, and the reconciliation must come through a higher gospel than the gospel of rights – the gospel of duty....[27]

As a self-generating propaganda campaign, 'social citizenship' was highly successful. It was preached from the pulpit, written about in the press, penetrated many social organizations down to the humble evening classes at the local board school where the course 'Duties of the Citizen', given on a voluntary basis by leading citizens, was a hardy perennial.[28] Patrick Geddes, pioneer British sociologist and town planner, was able to capitalize on this propaganda to underpin his theory of civics and his approach to town planning. The success of the Regional Survey Associations, promoted by Geddes,[29] an important influence on early town planning practice in Britain, was fed by people steeped in ideas of 'social citizenship'.

As in the settlement movement and other attempts, more consciously orientated towards community building, the supply of voluntary labour and support was unfailing.

IV CIVILIZATION AND 'THE SOCIAL QUESTION'

Such a response, however, cannot be explained by ideals of civilization alone. The circumstances which helped enormously to stimulate it, bring one close to the heart of social reaction to the modern industrial city. The fact was that the city was now universally recognized as the centre of modern social problems. Whereas Manchester and Liverpool, for instance, in the early Victorian period had provided horrifying evidence of deterioration in social conditions and huge social problems, their experience was considered exceptional rather than the rule. Now every large city was involved. This was a vital shift which permeated all social responses to the city in the late Victorian period.

Centrally placed, in whatever approach to the 'civilizing' process was adopted, was the need to respond to the social problems of Want, Ignorance, Idleness, Squalor and Disease.[30] Since these problems were concentrated, particularly in the more central areas of cities, it was possible to relate them to more than the lack of moral fibre of the poor. The utilitarian response to poverty of the 1834 Poor Law Amendment Act was beginning to be questioned now that the conditions of the urban environment were better understood. It was recognized that social conditions could act like a vice-grip on the lives of the poor, the very relief of destitution posing a moral problem for the worthy poor from which there was no escape.[31] For those with a concern for civilization, 'the social question' took on a new and more urgent form.

The 'social question' was a convenient term which was used to cover all social problems, mainly remarkable for the distance it put between social problems and the members of Respectable Society, of whatever class or creed. The approach of the Social Science Association, founded in 1857, specifically to hold annual congresses in large cities, where aspects of the 'social question' could be discussed more thoroughly, underlined this distinction.[32] The 'social question' referred to the social conditions suffered or perpetrated by those who belonged outside the pales of civilization. The actual term was coined around 1840 to refer to the undermass of the population, particularly those in large cities whose lives, it was suggested, must be nasty, brutish and short. Their emancipation was to form the major plank of the new urban society.[33]

The core of the 'social question' was the conquest of mass poverty and the preparation of the proletariat for full citizenship by means of education, moral training and welfare programmes. Initially, however, what was not always apparent to those working on ways of achieving this, was the nature and extent of poverty and the social and political implications of bringing the 'undermass' within the mainstream. Over time, these implications became more obvious and provided setbacks and a severe test of the social intentions of the reformers. But also by that time, economic development had greatly transformed the basic factors influencing the 'social question'. These factors need to be outlined briefly.

The mid-Victorian economy for all its rapid growth rate and success as 'the workshop of the world', relied heavily on large pools of casual labour which were easily expendable, and easily replaced.[34] But the late Victorian period witnessed important changes in this respect. Greater sophistication in the techniques of manufacturing, new industries, and the growth of tertiary industries were creating an occupational structure leading to a trend away from casual labour to semi-skilled and skilled work; though at the same time, many skilled artisans were losing their status in the face of technological changes.[35] The overall result, however, of economic changes in the period 1875–96 on the lives of the working classes, was a marked rise in real wages. The cheap food imports of this period were to bring the British working classes one of the most direct benefits they had yet received from the promises inherent in the Industrial Revolution. Such developments were to make major inroads into the problem of poverty and the undermass though, of course, it by no means eliminated large-scale poverty. The poverty cycle, outlined by Rowntree in his study of York at the end of the century, still brought very large numbers of the working classes into poverty at some time in their lives.[36]

Indeed, this last discovery, from the scientific surveys of Booth and Rowntree, was completely confusing to the body of opinion that had been used to discussing the 'social question' at the meetings, for instance, of the Social Science Association (dissolved finally in 1886). Instead of the 'undermass', the unknown lost souls beyond the pales of civilization, there was the startling revelation that the experience of poverty was not confined to them, but affected the lives of the working classes, hitherto distinct in the minds of the social reformers. The shock of assimilating this information however, was left mainly to the Edwardians, who could feed on the spate of social surveys undertaken to emphasize these facts.[37] Only after the turn of the century did the revelations of the 1880s become widely understood. Social responses were usually some way behind the pace of economic change.

For the first generation facing mass urbanization in the 1860s and '70s, the facts of poverty were relatively unknown. In the circumstances it was perfectly possible to approach the 'social question' in a theoretical way, particularly to relate it to the other pressing problem, the process of civilization. It was even possible to argue, not that the 'civilizing' process could only follow after the elimination of poverty, but that the 'civilizing' process could result in the elimination of poverty. Such a possibility opened up all kinds of approaches to the 'social question'. Social scientists, social and cultural reformers, philanthropists, anyone indeed, who took a serious view of future social development and their responsibilities as citizens, could engage in a wide variety of activities under the impression that they were contributing to an overall solution to the 'social question'.

The result was a growth of concern about the 'social question', coupled with a remarkably theoretical approach. Reformers rarely identified themselves with the objects of their concern. But it was not only the class element which produced the unrealistic approach and the overriding interest in civilization and social relationships. It was possible for the most radical thinkers of the day to consider that the 'civilization' of the undermass was the most important aspect of the 'social question'. By the mid 1860s, the ideas of evolutionary positivism had become widely diffused amongst the educated public, and provided, as J. W. Burrow writes:

> an intellectual resting place, a point of repose at which the

tension between the need for certainty and the need to accommodate more diverse social facts and more subtle ways of interpreting them than the traditional certainties allowed for, reached a kind of temporary equilibrium.[38]

For a brief moment there was a confrontation of equal strength between the traditional, conservative views of society and the new radical insights into the process of change, being pioneered by sociologists, philosophers and thinkers. Out of the friction between the two was to come 'the flame of creativity manifest in new insights, new perspectives, and new ideas'.[39] Such a flood of new vision however, was to have a practical outcome. At the centre of the new developments lay the concept of evolution and the question arose of equating evolution with progress. Influential thinkers such as Herbert Spencer and J. S. Mill were prepared to be optimistic in outlook and support the idea that progress was inherent in the process of evolution,[40] though Mill justified this by developing a theory of progress. The task of political theory as he now saw it 'was to supply, not a set of model institutions, but principles from which the institutions suitable to any given circumstances might be deduced.' The criterion in any given case should be 'what great improvement in life and culture stands next in order for the people concerned, as the condition of their future progress, and what institutions are most likely to promote that'.[41]

For those whose interest focused on the city, 'improvements in life and culture' seemed immediately related to social and cultural reforms. The problem was, which institutions were likely to promote social evolution? For Matthew Arnold, the starting point was culture. Culture was the elevating force teaching us 'to conceive of true human perfection as a *harmonious* perfection developing all sides of our humanity.'[42] He wanted cities to be cultural centres, to be endowed with institutions of Liberal Culture, particularly universities.[43] So intent was he on this vision, that whilst he admits in *Culture and Anarchy* that 'our pauperism increases more rapidly than our population', he suggests what is needed is more culture.[44]

Social evolution and the pursuit of culture had profound attractions for others who started from a very different vantage point. These were the people concerned about the Two Nations and the complete breakdown in communication and contact between rich and poor. The idea developed that cultural unity might be a socially cohesive force when all other factors, including the physical form of the modern city, were tending to tear society apart. This idea was to reach its fullest development in the 1880s, but it first gained recognition in the 1860s and '70s.[45] Under the influence of theories of social evolution, the idea of trying to raise the level of civilization as a way of solving the 'social question' struck a deep chord of response. The problem was not the objective, but the practical means for setting about achieving it. It was a question of looking around and deciding where to begin.

W. S. Jevons, the economist, writing in 1878, decided to begin on popular amusements.[46] On his return from abroad he was horrified by the contrast in behaviour between the orderly people of the Scandinavian and Low Countries and the populace of England. It led him to write: 'Among the means towards a higher civilization, I unhesitatingly assert that the deliberate cultivation of public amusements is a principal one... popular amusements are no trivial matter but one that has great influence on national manners and character.'[47] Social behaviour was an indication of a higher civilization and thus, in Jevons's view, the reform of public amusements was a perfectly legitimate way to combat the 'social question'. He was not alone in his belief. Public holidays were institutionalized in 1871 with the establishment of Bank Holidays and attempts were made to divert the public from vulgar amusements to the more elevating. Here technology was on the side of the reformers since such possibilities as cheap holiday excursion trains to country and seaside were a wholesome influence now within the reach of many.

But by chance, the idea of providing wholesome diversions was found to have far greater potential as a means of encouraging the 'civilizing' process than had ever been realized before. The powerful Temperance movement, whose main objective was to transform social behaviour, had begun to appreciate that this was vital to the success of its mission.[48] Its energies were directed towards providing alternative amusements to the pub and to cleaning up the music halls. The greatest asset of this approach was its ability to attract a response from the normally unresponsive. Such a possibility as this was not wasted on other voluntary groups dedicated in some way to improving social life and conditions amongst the urban poor. Religious missionaries and provincial philanthropists found themselves working more towards a concern over the use of leisure as a means, initially, of making contact with the poor. From there it was but a step to the conviction that an improved social environment was the key to the solution of the social problems of the city.

It was a response which penetrated most religious and philanthropic organizations devoted to social work. There was room in this activity for the emotions so firmly held in check by the COS philosophy.[49] From its foundation in 1869, the Charity Organization Society had strongly reaffirmed the principles that poverty was caused by the moral failings of the individual and that indiscriminate charity aggravated the situation, further demoralizing the poor. In providing for the social life of the poor, the callous calculations over the distribution of relief could be forgotten in enthusiasm for making social contact and improving the social environment. Charles Kingsley, in typical Christian Socialist vein, wrote:

> For it is this human friendship, trust, affection which is the very thing you have to employ towards the poor and to call up in them. Clubs, Societies, alms, lending libraries are but dead machinery, needful perhaps, but, like the iron tube without the powder, unable to send the bullet forth one single inch.[50]

V THE SOCIAL AND CULTURAL ENVIRONMENT OF CITIES

The question that the historian has to ask however, is how far did all this activity shape the social life of the city and widen the social and cultural experiences of the urban masses? The fact is that hopes of social development and the pursuit of an ideal of happiness was by no means limited to city councillors, philanthropists and socio-religious workers. All migrants, making their way to the city, had raised expectations that they might find a freer and fuller life than they had known before, even though their incentive for migration was economic opportunity. In these circumstances the use of leisure and the facilities for it gained a deeper significance.

The pursuit of popular pastimes was a sensitive indicator of this.[51] The growth and modernization of cities and the greater degrees of social discipline now enforced by magistrates and the law were bound to transform the nature of popular pastimes. But many activities became transmuted, not destroyed. One of the most outstanding examples of this was the development of organized sport. The evolution of the modern game of football for instance, has been studied by sociologists as an indication of social change and an insight into social development.[52] The astonishing fact that the most urbanized nation in the world was to lead the world in introducing or redefining sports and pastimes, reinforces, once again, the creativity of the period 1870–90 in pioneering new ways of seeking recreation and leisure.

In practical terms, social reformers concerned with leisure activities had to face competition from popular pastimes, including sport, as well as the age-old social attractions of the inns and public houses. Mass urbanization also encouraged the commercial exploitation of leisure, which was to reach new levels of invention and sophistication. The cheap press, music sheets, mass-produced musical instruments, the development of new techniques in theatre and music hall were products of technical invention which were to revolutionize urban leisure activities.[53] These developments did not lead necessarily in the direction of a higher civilization, as envisaged by many social reformers. The links they had believed in, between the use of leisure, cultural activities and a higher civilization, refused to materialize.

But their response had an impact far greater than might have been expected, since they were responsible for building social institutions, putting their ideas into permanent form with bricks and mortar and, in many cases, endowing these institutions with financial resources for their future survival. This institutional framework was then able to develop and to influence significantly, the future social development of the city. The 'modernization' of large cities coincided in many instances with the period of greater local influence of a socio-economic élite, whose degree of concern about the 'social question', though varied, was often profound. Since they made the decisions about town improvements and their wealth supported the voluntary organizations dedicated to social improvement, the experience of city life, for the generations first exposed to mass urbanization, owed not a little to them.

The process of civilization, even the elements within that process, defy definition. But the ensuing chapters are devoted to the attempts made to shape the urban environment, through institutions and activities, to meet the potential of a 'civilized' life for society and the individual. The late Victorians in their advocacy of the 'civilizing process' uncovered a range of social needs relating to different groups within society, of all ages. They were pioneers in meeting the challenge of the social consequences of mass urbanization.

2
BRISTOL IN THE LATE NINETEENTH CENTURY

The first task, in an investigation of the relationship between environment and society, is to establish what kind of environment had evolved in the late Victorian city, in this instance, the city of Bristol. Nineteenth-century Bristol was not a typical product of the Industrial Revolution; and both the city's economic structure and population growth remained largely atypical of the national trends for large cities. In the first half of the century this was particularly the case, as the city lived through the losing battle with Liverpool to be the major port on the west coast. Its size in 1851, of 137,328 inhabitants, which made Bristol the sixth largest town in England, was due to its former importance as a port and the lead it had built up, particularly in the late eighteenth century, over other provincial towns. In the second half of the century the city remained amongst the top ten largest cities, running seventh in 1901. Now, however, Bristol was no longer the very atypical large city that it had been, as gradually, it began to experience economic and social changes of a nature broadly similar to other large towns. Some of these changes will be outlined below.

I THE PHYSICAL GROWTH OF THE CITY

One of the clearest indications of the 'modernizing' process at work in the city is to be found in changes in its physical structure. Since Bristol escaped any major disaster of fire, bombardment or destruction (before the twentieth-century blitz), its physical structure evolved over the centuries, according to the economic and social factors then at work. Changes occurred continuously, but the pace

LEISURE AND THE CHANGING CITY

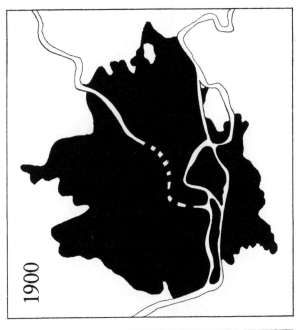

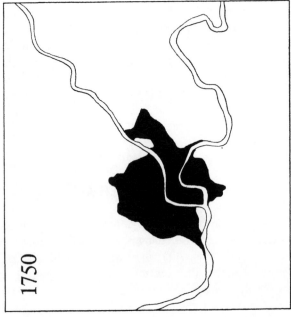

of change became quite unprecedented in the nineteenth century. This was most obvious in terms of growth (see the sketch maps of Bristol at 1750 and Bristol at 1900). Changes in scale however, were supplemented by extensive changes in land use, harbour facilities and developments in transport.

Transformations in these respects had taken place in the city's periods of prosperity,[1] and had been of increasingly important dimensions from the late seventeenth and early eighteenth centuries. At the beginning of the eighteenth century, Bristol had become the largest city and port in the kingdom outside London.[2] Wealth from the slave trade, the West Indian trade and other mercantilist ventures was lavished on the city's infrastructure, in both its public and private sectors. Bristol Bridge was re-built and the roads and thoroughfares leading to it straightened and widened. A number of new public and commercial buildings were erected, such as a Council House and Exchange; and the trade and commercial guilds, such as the Coopers and the Society of Merchant Venturers, built themselves new halls in the classical style.

The main speculative building boom however, occurred after 1785 with the growing mania amongst builders for constructing elegant houses for the affluent, largely in Clifton.[3] But areas still within the city boundaries were also affected. The Unitarians, who at that time could number most of the city's aldermen amongst their congregation, built themselves a new chapel in Lewins Mead. The Royal Infirmary was begun, and areas to the west of the Cathedral, Park Street, Great George Street and Berkeley Square were developed. The newly established parish of St Paul, with a new parish church, was built up and there were extensive building operations in the Kingsdown area. All did not go smoothly and there were several crises and collapses of the market. But this Georgian-style development boom spilled over into the first decades of the nineteenth century, transforming the medieval city plan and creating new focal points of social life.

However, all this development was dwarfed by the scale of change which took place in the nineteenth century. In the period up to 1914 there were four boundary changes (1835, 1895, 1897 and 1904), extending the area of the city from 4,879 acres to 17,004 acres. Changes in the physical structure of the city became related to the two most significant trends being experienced, in differing degrees,

TABLE 2.1 Bristol urban cluster (i.e. built-up area)

Boundaries	1861	1871	1881	1891	1901	1911
Ancient city	66,027	62,806	57,479	55,549	45,836	
Added 1835	88,066	119,890	149,395	166,029	178,177	
City of 1835	154,093	182,696	206,874	221,578	224,013	
Added 1895–1930	22,076	33,425	53,534	74,827	115,137	
City of 1904	176,169	216,121	260,408	296,405	339,150	357,173
Added 1935	2,800	2,900	3,100	3,100	3,400	4,900
City of 1935	179,000	219,000	263,500	299,500	342,500	362,000
Fringe	11,000	11,800	13,800	17,500	22,500	25,000
Total	190,000	231,000	277,500	316,000	365,000	387,000

by all large British cities. These were changes in land use in central areas, particularly from residential uses to commercial and business uses; and growing population densities in the city's peripheral areas (see Table 2.1).[4]

The ancient central area of the city did not increase its rate of growth in the first half of the nineteenth century and from the mid-century actually declined, first relatively, then absolutely. In the early decades the fastest growing areas were those to be incorporated into the city in the 1835 boundary extension. But the rate of growth even there, was declining by the mid-century and the new areas of fastest growth were to be found in outer rings around the city, which were substantially incorporated into the city in 1895, 1897 and 1904. Yet these extensions were not taken far enough to include the areas growing fastest in the period 1901–11 which were an outer ring, not brought into the city until 1935. The city's fastest growth rate therefore took place in three major spurts in concentric rings round the city, fom 1861 to 1881, 1881 to 1901, and 1901 to 1911.[5] (See sketch map of land and use in Bristol at 1880.)

Accompanying these periods of growth were changes in the physical structure of the city, giving it attributes which were more recognizably 'modern'. It gained a modern transport system; a commercial centre; an industrial eastern region and suburbs, which tended to divide residents into social groups. The main-line Great Western Railway had actually reached Bristol in 1841, and the station was sited to the east of the city. This further encouraged the

BRISTOL IN THE LATE NINETEENTH CENTURY

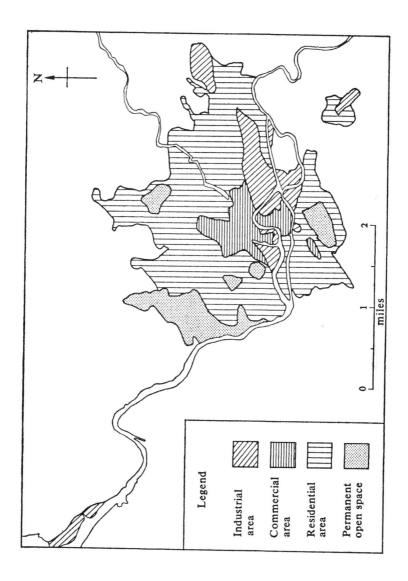

development, apparent since the 1830s, of an industrial area to the east of the city. By the 1870s and '80s the new districts, Easton and Eastville, provided the city with an example of a working-class industrial and suburban area of the kind commonly found in large cities since the Industrial Revolution. Bristol witnesses to the Royal Commission on the Housing of the Working Classes in 1884,[6] however, stressed that such developments were quite a recent phenomenon in Bristol.

At the same time though, other areas such as Bedminster and Totterdown were undergoing similar developments, and by the turn of the century, Brislington and Mangotsfield. With this type of industrial and working-class development in the eastern sides of the city, the more affluent citizens withdrew, to the north and west, in their search for social exclusiveness. Clifton, since the building booms of the eighteenth century, had been the most exclusive residential district near Bristol. After the incorporation of the area into the city in 1835, the work of the Georgian developers was completed with a controlled in-fill of large Victorian villas. Control was exerted by geographical and economic as well as social factors. Land available for development in Clifton was limited to the north by the Downs, preserved as an area of outstanding natural beauty by a private Act in 1862, and to the west and south by the Avon gorge and the curve of the river. This made land expensive, and property developers were thus anxious to preserve the social exclusiveness and expensiveness of the area. The result of their work was to create a large, fully developed, middle-class residential district which contained, not only the houses, but also the educational and leisure institutions suitable for a middle-class way of life.

Clifton provided the complete environment for Bristol's wealthier citizens, largely independent of the older city itself. This was a transformation of emphasis of considerable importance, which had taken place mainly between the 1835 boundary extension and the 1870s, when the process was virtually complete. However, since the development of Clifton was limited, not all the affluent could live there. For those with middle-class aspirations but fewer financial resources, there were the highly respectable residential areas of Kingsdown, Cotham and Redland. Then, as these areas became fully developed and thus ceased to be on the suburban frontier, fresh developments were made on the other side of the Downs to Clifton, further north to Stoke Bishop and Westbury-on-Trym. For the very favoured few, whose fortunes were multiplying in the second half of the century, even Clifton did not provide adequate scope. In 1867 I. K. Brunel's suspension bridge over the Avon was opened, making possible the development of some very large houses with spacious gardens on the other side of the Gorge. By the 1890s some of the wealthiest families, such as some members of the Wills family, had reached the ultimate in social exclusiveness and had moved out into country houses in Somerset and Gloucestershire.

Thus the urban plan of Bristol in the nineteenth century shows a degree of change unprecedented in its long history. It was not only a matter of size. There were important changes in the use of land within the city, with the centre losing population and gaining instead offices and warehouses; the development of industrial and residential suburbs, and the segregation of the classes. These changes were due to forces which were transforming all large provincial cities in this period and making them recognizably modern. The topographical evidence shows that Bristol in the late nineteenth century was becoming a 'modern' city.

II PHYSICAL CONDITION OF THE CITY

The growth of the city in the nineteenth century led to an aggravation of the usual urban problems of public health, housing and traffic congestion which were to contribute to the expansion of local administrative duties and closer links between central and local government. Bristol, on the whole though, was fairly slow compared with other big cities, in responding to the need to control these problems more comprehensively. In 1850 Bristol was the third most unhealthy city in England with a death rate of one in twenty-eight. But then Bristol had been a very large city long before the Public Health Movement, and the failure of the city to expand substantially in the first half of the century helped to disguise the need for action. The facts were beginning to be revealed, first by the Bristol Statistical Society in the late 1830s, whose members carried out careful surveys of housing and the standards of living in selected poor areas of the city; and second by the investigators sent by the Royal Commission on the Health of Towns in the early 1840s.

These latter, Sir H. T. De La Beche and Dr Lyon Playfair, in their *Report on the Sanatory Condition of Bristol,* 1845, outlined the situation in the city. They made three important points. They emphasized that the worst conditions were to be found in the most ancient parishes in the city, particularly Temple, Bedminster, Redcliff and St Thomas.[7] These areas had been gaining in population in the early nineteenth century. Since they were already closely built over, more people meant overcrowding, and overcrowding led to a deterioration of conditions. The situation was thus acute, but confined largely to specific areas. Second, the provision of public services, especially a sewerage system and a water supply, was markedly defective. There were no water-cleansed sewage pipes in poor areas. Where a drain existed, it often simply fed the stagnant waters of the floating harbour with untreated sewage. As for the water supply, the commissioners sternly wrote: 'Viewed as a sanatory question, there are few, if any, large towns in England in which the supply of water is so inadequate as Bristol.'[8]

But the future was not all bleak. The third point made by the commissioners concerned Bristol's natural potential for healthiness. The city's worst conditions were confined to the oldest areas and Bristol had no counterpart, at that time, of the acres of slum dwellings being built in Liverpool and Manchester and other great cities. The city was also fortunate in its air. Public health reformers of the early 1840s mistakenly believed that air pollution was the primary cause of disease. Though Bristol did have 'works evolving noxious vapours or much smoke', these were situated in the eastern districts, in the lee of the prevailing westerly winds which could thus sweep cleanly through the city. The commissioners concluded:

> As the climate is salubrious, and poverty not peculiarly severe, we can only look for the cause of the unhealthy state of the city in the neglect of proper sanitary conditions. We have seen these to be, bad drainage and sewerage, deficient supplies of water, bad structural arrangements of streets and dwellings, and overcrowded state of the population. These are, in a great measure, removable causes, and most of them are within the recognized province of legislation.[9]

This, of course, was the conclusion that they were hoping to come to from the outset. Their report was part of the great propaganda campaign, mounted by Chadwick, to prove the need for more public health legislation.[10] Yet even if their conclusions were largely predetermined, their investigation was important as a pioneering attempt to assess the physical condition of the city. Subsequent events were to prove that their faith in legislation was, to put it mildly, over-optimistic. Bristol was never in the forefront of cities adopting the great legislative and administrative changes of the second half of the nineteenth century which were to transform the duties of local government.[11] But in three key areas, changes were taking place which fundamentally altered the city's physical condition. Decisions were made, though often in a fumbling and half-hearted way, to improve the environment by undertaking street improvements, by providing a higher standard of public health services and finally, at least by recognizing that the housing of the working classes was an urgent problem.

Much of the initiative however, in all these areas came from private individuals. An Improvement Committee of the Town Council was only set up in 1840 when a private citizen had left a bequest of £10,000 for the purpose. Since the council was preoccupied with other matters, particularly the docks, the plan put forward by the Committee in 1845 was quietly shelved for twenty years.[12] But by 1865, certain improvements began to appear vital. The narrow, inconvenient and dangerous streets between Bristol Bridge and the railway station at Temple Meads were obvious cases. They were swept away and replaced by the broad Victoria Street (at the cost of several acres of slum dwellings). Bristol Bridge itself was now, once again, too narrow and needed widening, and different parts of the city were still cut off from one another by toll bridges. All this was remedied in the late 1860s and early '70s and other improvement plans carried out. The Hotwells Road, leading to the docks, was widened and straightened; the 'malodorous Frome', tributary of the Avon on the east side of the city, was arched over (though a suitable drainage system for the river was not worked out and there was extensive flooding in eastern areas of the city in 1889 and 1892); finally, new roads were built mainly to connect new suburbs with the city centre.

As for public health measures, the town council was equally reluctant to undertake much expensive work, but gradually the pressures mounted, forcing it to take some action. A rather inadequate system of sewerage was built in the 1850s, but the attempt to cut down expense was thwarted when a completely reorganized system had to be paid for at the end of the century. The water supply was left to private enterprise. Competition between the Society of Merchant Venturers (who owned most of the local wells) and a private water company did not, however, lead to the speedy advent of an adequate supply. They both promoted bills in parliament, and parliament decided in favour of the waterworks company. However, an adequate and constant water supply to all parts of the city, all the year round, was only achieved for the first time in 1882. By 1914 Bristol remained one of the very few large cities where the water supply was still in the hands of a private company.

Under pressure from the ignominy and fear of being the third unhealthiest city in 1850, the town council did decide to adopt the 1848 Public Health Act and set up a Sanitary Authority in 1851. This meant that the city acquired a number of permanent officials, particularly a Medical Officer of Health, who were able, collectively, to do something to improve the physical environment. Inspecting nuisances, isolating fever cases, exhorting the council to clean, light, pave and surface streets, cumulatively had a considerable impact on the city from the 1860s and '70s. Such developments were largely responsible for the city gaining the hard, sharp, straight lines of street and pavement, characteristic of the 'modern' city. Dr Davies, Bristol's Medical Officer of Health though, was no militant reformer in favour of indefinitely extending the responsibilities of local government. He performed his duties conscientiously and his frequent publication of mortality figures, showing the wide discrepancy between rich wards and poor wards in the city, roused the social conscience. However, he saw his role in terms of ensuring minimum standards of public health, not advocating the maximum benefit that collective action might bring.[13]

For this reason, perhaps, little was done in Bristol to control the most crucial element in the relationship between environment and society, housing, particularly the housing of the urban poor. Bristol did not adopt either the Torrens or Cross Acts of 1868 and 1875. Widespread concern about the housing of the working classes only became apparent in the early 1880s, when it had become a national issue as well as a local scandal. The Sanitary Authority in the city set up a sub-committee to look into the matter in 1887. But decisive action was difficult when even the guidelines set down in the 1890 Housing Act, the outcome of the deliberations of the Royal Commission, provided no easy solutions to the housing problem.[14] It had become obvious that good housing could not be created merely by legislation. Bad housing was directly related to poverty. Improvements would require additional financial support beyond the economic capacities of the poor in Bristol. In 1890 a new pressure group composed of philanthropists and town councillors was formed, the Bristol Committee for Promoting the Better Housing of the Poor. The town council was induced to adopt some by-law regulations on building in the course of the 1890s. But the impact of all this concern on the physical environment of the poor was very limited.

Most of the destruction of slums in the city had occurred in the course of the street improvement schemes of the council. There had been no attempt to rehouse those who were evicted, apart from the efforts of private philanthropists. One group had set up an Industrial Dwelling Company in the 1870s; the Misses Winkworth had organized another scheme, on Octavia Hill lines, for tenants in Dowry Square, Hotwells; and three tenement blocks of 'improved' dwellings were built in Jacobs Wells Road. They were hardly enough, in total, to make any impact on the housing problem. The council had provided a model common lodging house in 1905, but this was a very limited response, and by 1907 and 1908, the plight of the poor was investigated in two more reports, one local, one national. The 1907 Report was from the local Bristol Housing Reform Committee, sponsored by the Trades Council. The 1908 investigation was part of the national enquiry by the Board of Trade into working class rents, housing and retail prices.

These two reports provide between them the best evidence of the physical condition of the city in the Edwardian period. The Board of Trade Report, with its perspectives modified by its national coverage, was relatively optimistic. The overall statistics for overcrowding in Bristol were 'slight when compared with the conditions in some other large centres of population.'[15] Rents were lower than in London, but then so were the average wage rates. With an occupation structure that was extremely varied, Bristol did not experience wide-scale destitution with the vagaries of the trade cycle.

But there was a hard-core of poverty, and those unfortunates who suffered because of it had been harried from district to district by the modernization of the city.

In the centre of the city there was now a 'nucleus consisting almost entirely of business houses and public offices or institutions'. The poor had been pushed into the transitional area between this centre and the more affluent residential suburbs. The city slums were fewer perhaps, but still well defined, to the north and west, and to the south in Bedminster, in the narrow streets and courts which huddled beside the river. The conditions to be found in these areas though, were the exception rather than the rule. The real norm of Bristol working-class housing was to be found in the newer developments in Bedminster, Easton and St George. 'The great bulk of working class dwellings conform to two general types – the small plain-fronted house built direct from the pavement, and the larger house with bay windows and a small forecourt.'[16] As far as standards of housing went, both these types were considered reasonable.

The local Report from the Bristol Housing Reform Committee had a different purpose which made it less optimistic. It concentrated on the plight of the urban poor which was desperate, even if the problem was confined largely to specific districts. It tried to show that it was a mistake to think in terms of a hard-core problem. 'Under the present system, while houses in the poorer districts are being condemned or closed, whole areas in the suburbs are arising which, from lack of a definite policy, will soon become little better than slums.' The writers of the report had reached the understanding that control over the physical environment was not a matter of simply eliminating abuses. A constant process of urban renewal was needed which involved 'a comprehensive housing policy for the whole of Bristol'.[17]

These ideas were receiving wider recognition now that a town-planning movement promoted, amongst others, by housing reform bodies, was gaining wider publicity.[18] It was to lead to a conception of housing and planning which went far beyond the adoption of minimum standards for the housing of the poor. But the vision of the future that was inherent in the first town planning act of 1909 was not born in Bristol. The natural endowments of the city, its established traditions, and the comparatively late development of working-class suburban areas meant that there had been less response to the idea of environmental control for the future than in other large cities. But at least by the end of the century the city did have a civic administration and a network of services designed to counteract the worst health hazards of large-scale urbanization and to improve the condition of the physical environment.

III THE CONDITION OF THE PEOPLE

Environmental change was accompanied by extensive social changes. The problem however, is determining the nature and extent of these changes in the absence of hard data. Evidence about real wages, income distribution, and patterns of consumption, working conditions and hours of work, is either non-existent or patchy. The problem is made particularly acute by the fact that the economic structure of the city was not shaped, initially, by the forces unleashed by the Industrial Revolution, and yet the city was able to support an expanding population. This was a combination which was in many ways unique. Bristol's vital social statistics tend to reflect those special circumstances, rather than the commoner trends to be found among the northern industrial cities of comparable size.

This is particularly evident in relation to population growth and migration to the city. The doubling of population between 1801 and 1841 was relatively modest compared with the 'shock' cities of the Industrial Revolution, which grew between 40 per cent and 50 per cent in the decade of fastest growth 1821–31.[19] In the second half of the century there was a general slowing down in growth rates, partly because the size of large cities now made such growth rates an impos-

TABLE 2.2 Population growth in Bristol in the nineteenth century

1801	61,153	1861	154,093
1811	71,433	1871	182,696
1821	85,108	1881	206,874
1831	104,408	1891	221,578
1841	125,146	1901	339,150*
1851	137,328	1911	357,173*

* Boundary changes

sibility, and partly because the fastest growth was taking place on the periphery of cities, not always included within the city boundaries. The fastest growing areas tended to be smaller industrial towns or suburbs of large towns,[20] and once again Bristol did not fit, or have examples of either of these categories.

Probably the main reason why Bristol's population growth followed such an individual pattern lies in the city's modest ability to attract migrants. The hinterland of the city was largely agricultural and there were no dramatic 'push' or 'pull' factors to encourage migrants to the city. In fact, the city was remarkable for the smallness and unusual age distributions of its gains by migration.[21] The increase in population in the Bristol area after 1871 was almost wholly the consequence of natural change rather than migration.[22] Whilst there were decades when there were strong inward flows of migrants, such as the 1860s which produced a net gain of some 17,000–18,000; other decades actually experienced a net loss by migration, for example the 1880s and 1900s, when Bristol appears to have been only a staging post in the migratory flow.

The result of these migratory patterns was to ensure that the city never experienced any sudden influx of destitute immigrants, such

TABLE 2.3 Intercensal rates of population change (%)

Decade	Bristol cluster	Gloucester and Somerset less cluster	England and Wales
1801–11	21·6	11·1	14·0
1811–21	18·3	17·2	18·1
1821–31	21·8	13·0	15·8
1831–41	19·1	7·5	14·3
1841–51	10·0	2·3	12·7
1851–61	11·5	1·6	11·9
1861–71	22·3	3·1	13·2
1871–81	20·3	−0·4	14·4
1881–91	13·7	0·6	11·7
1891–1901	14·4	1·5	12·2
1901–11*	5·7	4·0	10·9
1801–1901	388·7	72·7	265·8

* Figures 1901–11 relate to the city administrative area, and to Gloucestershire and Somerset less the city.

TABLE 2.4[23]
Bristol intercensal growth by natural increase and net migration

	1861–71	1871–81	1881–91	1891–1901	1901–11
Natural increase	12·3	16·5	14·8	13·3	11·5
Net migration	10·0	3·8	−1·1	1·1	−5·8
Total	22·3	20·3	13·7	14·4	5·7

as the Irish to be found in Manchester and Liverpool. The agent carrying out the two surveys on the poor for the Bristol Statistical Society in the late 1830s, was specifically asked to obtain information from the poor on their place of origin. In the larger survey, covering more than one-fifth of Bristol's population, only 8·4 per cent were Irish, 2·8 per cent Welsh. This lack of ability to attract longer-distance migrants and yet at the same time to support a five-fold increase in population in the course of the century, indicates a mixed economic performance. It was obviously better than those towns, such as Bath, Chester, Colchester, Great Yarmouth and Norwich, which failed to grow at the national rate of population increase.[24] Yet it was by no means a performance indicating new levels of wealth and prosperity. Wages were, on average, lower in Bristol and there were numerous examples of widespread use of out-of-date technology, for example, in the manufacture of boots and shoes, depressing the competitive edge of the city's industries.[25]

Contemporaries believed that the crucial factor in the local economy was the port. Yet the inadequacies of the port were obvious in the early decades of the century as Liverpool raced ahead. By a curious irony, the most advanced ships in the world were built in Bristol in the late 1830s and '40s, I. K. Brunel's 'Great Eastern' and 'Great Britain'.[26] The latter, however, was unable to pass through the lock gates, holding the water of the floating harbour (completed in 1809), thus dramatically highlighting the inadequacies of the docks for larger, steam-powered vessels. The town council took over the city docks in 1848, and in 1884 eventually acquired the new docks developing at Avonmouth and Portishead to service larger ships. But this resurgence of the city as a significant port had little impact on its industrial structure and employment. The source of the port's commercial prosperity, in the late nineteenth century, lay in imports and not exports; of all the large ports in England, Bristol did the most one-sided business. Between 1887 and 1913, the city's trade only grew a very little faster than that of the country as a whole, which was a poor showing when compared to the other great ports.[27] The port developed largely as a centre for importing grain, fruit, dairy produce, cattle, and also some naphtha and petroleum. It was not the outlet for an export-orientated industrial hinterland.

An explanation of the ability of the city's economic structure to support a growing population must thus be sought elsewhere. Contemporaries were impressed with the growth rates achieved in the luxury trades such as cocoa and chocolate making, tobacco and cigarettes, and stationery and paper products. These industries brought their owners, the Frys, the Wills and the Robinson families much wealth. But the work-force employed in these industries was only a small proportion of the total. Indeed, there was no single overwhelmingly dominant source of employment in the city, as is revealed by the lists of occupations in the decennial censuses. An impression builds up, supported by other circumstantial evidence, that the city's economic structure was made up from numbers of small businesses and industries, providing mainly the goods and services for which there was a demand in a large city like Bristol. There were firms manufacturing household furniture, coaches and vehicles, millinery, corsets and tailoring, boots and shoes, and household products such as soap, and brush making.

Some larger-scale industrial activities to be found in the city included shipbuilding (on a modest scale), light engineering, printing, chemicals, a corrugated iron works (the largest in the country), and brass and bell foundries.[28] Employment for women was limited. Corset manufacturers and milliners employed female labour, and Bristol's unsuccessful cotton mill at St Lukes provided a demand for labour, but at very low wages. Best opportunities for women were to be found in the modern factories of the luxury trades where, for instance, in Robinson's factory in 1895, a cardboard-box-making machine created employment for an extra 2,000 women in three years. The huge majority of working women found employment in domestic service.

The increasing commercial activities and the development of retail trading in the city centre did create some employment opportunities at lower levels for those with a modicum of education. By the end of the century, some women gained employment as office or shop assistants. Commerce, banking, insurance and the law, all well established in the city, provided good opportunities for educated young men. Meanwhile for the uneducated, there were the docks and general labouring, or work in all the activities concerned with the transportation of both goods and people. There was plenty of employment in this latter category in a city like Bristol, where ideas on the rational location of industries were slow to develop. J. S. Fry's chocolate factory provides an outstanding example, as it expanded enormously in the late nineteenth century and yet was sited in the centre of the city with no direct rail or water communication. The railway had helped Bristol to become an entrepôt for the south and the west, and there were employment opportunities as substantial changes took place in the marketing, wholesaling and retailing processes. Bristol boasted the largest covered goods yard in the country by the twentieth century.

Thus the overall impression of employment opportunities in the city is distinctly varied. The major industries of the Industrial Revolution, coal, iron and steel, textiles and heavy engineering had a small place in the city's industrial structure. Yet there were some industries undergoing technological changes, and steam power was far more widely used by the end of the century. The numbers employed in these more 'modern' industrial units were, however, a minority of the total work-force. For the majority, working conditions were only changing gradually. If, however, the material standard of life of the working people of Bristol is compared to that to be found in other large cities, as in the pages of the 1908 *Board of Trade Enquiry into Working Class Rents, Housing and Retail Prices*, then conditions in these respects in Bristol do not appear to be markedly different from elsewhere.

IV SOCIAL CHANGE IN CITY AND SUBURB

The social environment of the city changed considerably over the course of the nineteenth century; and such changes were a significant aspect of the 'modernizing' process being experienced by all large cities. Unfortunately, in the case of Bristol even less is known about these changes than about the economic structure of the city. However, as the city grew, its citizens were being increasingly segregated into suburbs, based on class and wealth, and this profoundly affected social attitudes towards the city. In the absence of data on family structure and kinship, social mobility and class, not much detailed analysis can be made. However a few comments might be hazarded on the effect of this suburbanization on Bristol's middle classes, who were to provide the leadership and resources devoted to improving the social environment of the city.

A key starting point for this is the special relationship that existed between Clifton, the middle-class suburb *par excellence,* and Bristol. Clifton was the counterpart of Broomhill in Sheffield, The Park in Nottingham, or Edgbaston in Birmingham. But it had one important difference. It was more than a mere suburb. Clifton in fact, had developed separately from Bristol as a town in its own right, especially in the late eighteenth and early nineteenth centuries when it was a fashionable watering place. Its Regency houses had provided a charming, stylish and acceptable milieu for the impoverished lord, the Indian 'nabob', the retired army officer, the gentleman of leisure, the professional or literary man, and all the other variations to be found in the British upper classes.[29] The manor of Clifton was owned by the Society of Merchant Venturers, whose wealth and prestige was second to none in the city.

The result of this illustrious past was to create a tradition in which Clifton society became a symbol of the social aspirations of the rising middle classes, as they moved from the centre of Bristol. The strength of feeling generated by these aspirations and the separateness between Bristol and Clifton can be illustrated by some political pamphlets written anonymously in the 1860s. In one, the writer complains that

> It is not an uncommon thing to hear residents of Clifton who draw from the trade of Bristol the money which they there expend ... talking, in the true spirit of 'snobs', of Clifton having become quite vulgar since 'the tagrag from Bristol have taken so much resort to it'.[30]

The point he makes, which was to be made in another pamphlet, was that since Clifton had been developed fully, it was no longer so exclusive.

There may have been, and doubtless was a time, when Clifton was essentially a place of resort, its residents being only occasional ones and probably ... members and connexions of the Aristocracy proper. But is it so now? or do even our 'Merchant Princes' as we term them, tenant its palatial abodes? The answer must be, No. The greater bulk of the residents have derived their means from, or are now engaged in the busy commerce of the City: retail tradesmen in the larger streets, cashiers, bank managers, lawyers, surgeons, clerks and accountants.[31]

In other words, the professional and commercial classes whose prosperity and number were increasing rapidly in the late Victorian period.

The development of Clifton (and the other middle-class suburbs) did have a decisive effect on class consciousness. An absurd example is cited by the pamphlet writer, who overheard a conversation of a Clifton lady who 'boasted of being "of a county family" and declared that "she could not think of associating with Bristol people" while all the time she was herself, the daughter of a retail shopkeeper in Clare St.'[32] Matthew Arnold's Philistines had arrived and were panting for recognition. In this context the significance of the founding of the public school, Clifton College, in 1862 becomes evident and the reasons for the power and influence wielded by the headmaster of that institution. Such aspirations also indicate the source of some of the social power of leading families, whose wealth and position pushed them into pre-eminence. It was the segregation into class-bound suburbs too, which explains why poorer areas of Bristol had to be virtually rediscovered in the 1880s; and why some people, within Clifton society, were to react strongly against all that it stood for, and to devote their entire energies to the causes of the Bristol working man.[33]

One thing stands out, however, about Bristol's middle classes, and that is they seem to have had a far stronger influence on the civic life of Bristol than was common in other large cities. Of course, political and economic power was largely in the hands of a dominant middle-class élite in all cities at this time. But Bristol's middle classes appear to have exercised a social influence which was unprecedented. It is possible that this middle-class influence was due to the relative numerical strength of the middle classes in

Bristol. There is no way of assessing the figures absolutely accurately. But there is evidence which strongly suggests this strength. In the 1908 Board of Trade Report, if Bristol is placed with the two towns most closely related to it in size, the proportion of population given as belonging to the professional and commercial classes is significantly greater in Bristol than in other cities of comparable size.

	Professional: 1,000 population	*Commercial:* 1,000 population
Sheffield	14:1,000	19:1,000
Bristol	21:1,000	25:1,000
Bradford	16:1,000	20:1,000

There is no doubt that Bristol's economic structure was likely to provide a good number of employment opportunities for the middle classes.

Further evidence of the strength of the middle classes in Bristol can be deduced from figures and statistics relating to domestic service (since the incidence of domestic service is a good indicator of class). In comparison with the two towns closest in size to Bristol in 1901, Bradford and Sheffield, the figures for Bristol are 36:1,000; for Bradford 18:1,000; for Sheffield 28:1,000. In the case of Bradford, this could illustrate the strength of alternative sources of employment for women. But this was certainly not the case for Sheffield where the number of occupied women was low. The conclusion has simply to be that there was a greater demand in Bristol.

Evidence to support this theory can be tentatively put forward from census returns on the proportion of males to females in different areas of the city. A study of the census returns from 1871 to 1901 of the municipal wards reveals certain areas where a high proportion of the population were women, a surplus which was more than likely to be made up of an army of female domestic servants. In 1871, in St Michael's ward (which included part of Redland and Gotham area), females made up 61·6 per cent of the total; in Clifton ward, they formed 60·9 per cent, District ward 59·0 per cent; when the overall average number of females in the city was 53·4 per cent of the total. In 1901 the picture is similar. By then the excess of females in the city as a whole was 53·9 per cent. In Westbury it was 63·3 per cent, Clifton 61·0 per cent, St Michael 60·5 per cent. When Matthew Arnold talks of the middle classes of Sheffield as the upper ten thousand, it is probably safe in Bristol to at least double that number. Bristol of all the large cities of comparable size had probably the largest contingent of middle classes.

3
THE CITY AND ITS CULTURAL INSTITUTIONS

It is tempting to define 'culture' in relation to the city, in Addison's verse, as a process:

> To make man mild and sociable to man
> To cultivate the wild licentious savage,
> With wisdom, discipline and the liberal arts
> Th' embellishments of Life.[1]

At least such a definition would have appealed to many social reformers of the 1860s and '70s, who liked to think of culture as a social force to unite the burgeoning middle classes; as a 'civilizing' influence on the poor, and as additional illustration of Western supremacy over the world.[2] In the mid-century years, in the afterglow of the huge success of the Great Exhibition of 1851, it was easily possible to believe that Britain's growing influence on world trade and economic development could be paralleled by the cultural influence of a magnificent civilization. At that time, Britain was by far the most urbanized nation in the world.

John Addington Symonds, addressing an audience at Bristol's foremost cultural association, the Bristol Philosophical Institution, in 1861, outlined the challenge. As England now has wealth, health and safety,

> in this safety and retirement, all works of peace should flourish, all science, philosophy, literature and art should culminate – all that tends, in the immortal words of BACON 'to the glory of the Creator, and to the relief of man's estate'.[3]

Such a sentiment was to echo and re-echo in council chamber and committee room, in public institution and private drawing room, in all the major cities in the last third of the century. Outward manifestations of it were to be found everywhere, such as the message of the 'civic gospellers' in Birmingham, projecting that their city might one day become the 'home of a noble literature and art' like Florence and other cities in the Italian Renaissance.[4] It was found in the ambitions of the University Extension movement and in the increasing number of towns adopting the Free Libraries and Museums Acts and acquiring art galleries. The most urbanized nation must be the most 'civilized'.

There was thus a stimulus to the provision of cultural and educational facilities from idealistic projections of a great civilization which was reinforced, on a more mundane plane, by practical considerations of diffusing new knowledge. Yet the form of these organizations and their success or failure depended not so much on worthy objectives, as their ability to reflect social developments and social aspirations. The organized, formal, cultural life of the city was the froth, the superstructure of social change. Institutions, established and organized on a voluntary basis, clearly reflected the social power of those responsible for their growth.[5] Cultural pursuits could provide an acceptable social milieu, where changes in economic power could be socially recognized, where the parvenus could meet the old élite.[6] Such institutions were neutral ground, largely outside the realms of religion and politics. Membership of cultural clubs and societies could, and did, cut across such social barriers, creating a sense of unity amongst the socio-economic group who belonged to them.

In the course of the century much faith was pinned on extending this feeling of unity to social groups beyond the élite. Support for the concept of cultural unity between all classes grew as the divisive social tendencies of economic change, the creation of Two Nations, became ever more apparent. The attraction of the idea for the élite was, that if some compromise had to be made to secure a peaceful future, then it should be made in the social and cultural sphere, rather than the economic. Yet even this was difficult. The concept of cultural unity rested on the idea of equal opportunity for all to share cultural experiences. Such a question posed the double problem of the availability of resources to develop cultural facilities on a wide enough basis and the need to persuade all social groups to participate.

The concept of cultural unity was an intellectual ideal which appealed most to the professional classes. In the 1860s and '70s, they were still a small group, as the only professions with accepted social status were the clergy, doctors, lawyers, artists and writers, and those concerned with superior educational institutions, particularly public schools and the Universities of Oxford and Cambridge.[7] In Bristol this group was deeply involved in the cultural institutions of the city and they were largely responsible for the concerted effort that was made to put flesh onto the bones of the idea of cultural unity. They had one powerful argument at hand. Cultural institutions developed in the city, and the city could provide the context for experiments in social equality. The inhabitants of a large city were but one large community and equal opportunities for all could be provided by civic institutions, equally available to all.

Promoting this idea and working out its implications was the most important development in the cultural life of the city. The rest of this chapter will be devoted to an analysis of these changes in the main cultural institutions of Bristol. Yet the contribution made in Bristol to the cultural life of the future was neither unique, nor even particularly remarkable. Other large cities, such as Manchester, Birmingham and Leeds achieved more at an earlier date. Each large city though, however individual its own record, was contributing to a fresh, practical definition of a national civilization. Bristol itself entered the nineteenth century in the somewhat unique position of having developed civic cultural traditions of a pre-industrial age. The transformation of those traditions in the course of the century, however, provides a clear illustration of the local response to changes taking place on a national level.

I CULTURAL ACTIVITIES IN BRISTOL IN THE EARLY NINETEENTH CENTURY

There is no doubt that Bristol, in the late eighteenth and early nineteenth century offered a rich variety of cultural experiences. Its wealth, its established institutions, the elegance of Clifton with its mineral drinking waters and reputation for healthiness, and the beauty of its natural surroundings, made the city both a desirable and fashionable place to live. But the city provided an environment in which people could respond individually to cultural activities rather than collectively in civic institutions. Cultural activities were spontaneous, personal, and usually, informally organized, since the educated world which supported them was small and well known to each other, though in relation to other cities, it was probably the largest outside London. The major difference between Bristol and the northern towns of the Industrial Revolution was its cosmopolitanism, again second only to London, and the fact that people came to Bristol to enjoy its amenities rather than to make their fortunes.

However, by the late eighteenth century, new forces were at work which would ultimately transform the cultural institutions of the city. The central influence was the different responses made to the acquisition and diffusion of knowledge. Much was due to the Evangelicals, Nonconformists, merchants, businessmen, doctors and school-masters, who all found an increasing imperative to improve facilities for education, which collectively generated a new concern over the development of cultural life of the city. It was a complex process, but in Bristol at least, there were two factors which were outstanding. These were the impact of Evangelical thinking on social behaviour, as outlined by the work of Hannah More; and the dedication of the Nonconformists in the city to education. A few sentences, of course, can hardly do justice to the impact of the Evangelical Revival on attitudes to leisure. But Hannah More's two major publishing breakthroughs, her *Thoughts on the Manners of the Great* (1788) aimed at the rich, and her *Cheap Repositary Tracts* of the 1790s for the poor had repercussions which continued to ripple and eddy through all levels of society. The emphasis on the moral basis of social behaviour, the duty of the rich and leisured classes to set a wholesome example in the conduct of their lives, and the exhortation for all to dedicate themselves to moral and intellectual improvement, bred a self-consciousness about the use of leisure which had not been there before.

These ideas gained an especially favourable response from a small group of men in Bristol, most of them leading Nonconformists. The city had built up a reputation particularly in the late eighteenth and early nineteenth century, for its excellent educational institutions. The school run by Dr Lant Carpenter, minister of Lewin's Mead Chapel, was widely famous, as was the Grammar School, the Rev.

Seyer's school and Dr Swete's school in Redland, amongst many others. These schools not only attracted scholars from all over the country, they also supplied the city with a group of men, dedicated to education and sympathetic towards the ideas of the Evangelicals. Educationalists and clergy however, were joined by a third small group. This was the medical profession, strengthened by the foundation of the Bristol Medical School.

In some ways though, it is misleading to split this small professional group into different occupational groups. They were closely interconnected by religion, family and friendship. For instance, Dr Estlin ran a particularly famous school in the city. His son was John Bishop Estlin, destined to become a great surgeon. His daughter married J. C. Pritchard, a physician who became one of the founder members of the Bristol Institution. Pritchard's life-long friend was Dr John Addington Symonds, a doctor trained in Edinburgh, who came to lecture at Bristol Medical School and was to contribute enormously to the cultural life of the city. These men, with some Evangelical members of the Church of England, such as the Harford family and the Pinneys, provided the nucleus for the first selfconscious attempt to provide civic cultural institutions, dedicated to cultural diffusion and bringing the educated together.

In 1811 a major scheme was put forward to provide a Literary and Philosophical Institution in Bristol.[8] This was not an original idea, but merely an attempt to bring Bristol into line with developments taking place elsewhere. Literary and Philosophical Institutions were established in many provincial cities in the late eighteenth and early nineteenth centuries, some of the earliest being Birmingham, Leeds, Sheffield, Liverpool and Manchester. The movement gained national status with the Royal Institute of London, founded in 1799 for the purpose of diffusing new knowledge of useful mechanical inventions and improvements. This had become a matter of considerable concern since Telford, Stephenson and other pioneers gave little thought to making their activities matters of general knowledge.[9]

In Bristol, there was some delay before the building of an institution was put in hand, as not enough people thought that the wide diffusion of the new knowledge was important. But the Mayor, at last, was called upon to lay the foundation stone in 1820, and the classical-style building in Park Street, equipped with a lecture room and decorated by the sculptures of the local artist, E. H. Baily, quickly took form. It was to provide a great stimulus to the small group of men, already concerned about the cultural life of the city, who threw themselves into a massive spate of organizing, forming societies for all kinds of cultural pursuits. The Institution was run by a committee whose task it was to make the facilities available to as many societies as possible.

The most important organization, which was promptly formed, was a Literary and Philosophical Society. This Society was to remain the central point of the cultural life of the city for most of the rest of the century since it contained, as well as the small group, numbers of leading citizens. Nearly all other cultural organizations recruited their members from this parent society. In the first four years of its existence in the early and mid 1820s, the Literary and Philosophical Society took its objective of diffusing knowledge seriously, and series of lectures were held on scientific and technical subjects.[10] Collecting information and making it known were key activities and Bristol was one of the earliest of the provincial cities to establish a Statistical Society, encouraged by the developments of the 1830s in the collection of evidence by Royal Commissions and the work of William Farr as Registrar General. The first meeting of the Statistical Society was held at the Bristol Institution in 1836 and its members, including Charles Pinney and Dr Addington Symonds, embarked on plans to investigate social conditions in the city. The investigation of the natural world was taken up with equal enthusiasm and seriousness of intention. The Bristol Microscopical Society, amongst other scientific societies, setting particularly high standards. This society fined its members ten shillings if they failed to produce an original paper at its meetings.[11]

The small group, the Harfords, Dr Symonds, Dr Pritchard, Mr Pinney, the Estlins, the Carpenters, set themselves a hard pace. The signs are that it was beyond their time and resources to maintain it, since a Bristol-based *West of England Journal of Science and Literature* established in 1835, had folded by 1836. Yet support was forthcoming in 1836, when the British Association for the Advancement of Science held its fifth annual congress in the city.[12] After a shaky start, this Association, which drew its strength from the Literary and Philosophical Societies of provincial cities, was to become an important instrument in the mid-century years for the diffusion and exploration of new knowledge and ideas.

The problems which had bedevilled its establishment, however, were to emphasize a dimension of its activities which remained a feature of its annual congresses. This was the social element. Literary and Philosophical Societies were voluntary institutions with exclusive rules, limiting membership usually to the already privileged and educated. Further, they were 'civic' institutions in that their membership cut across religion and political divisions and included men from different professions and occupations. The British Association managed very successfully to instigate an element of competition between the societies in different cities, since it would only elect to hold its annual congress in a town where there were signs of organized cultural activities. Once a city had gained acceptance of an invitation, however, no effort was spared to make the congress socially memorable. In the round of banquets, dinner parties, musical soirées and outings, the activities of the British Association touched the lives of many more people than the small group initially responsible for the activities of the local Literary and Philosophical Society.

These developments led to a widening of Literary and Philosophical Society activities to include cultural activities of the more pleasurable kind, especially of music, and an interchange of ideas and experiences from one city to another. Both these aspects can be illustrated by the foundation of one of Bristol's most famous musical societies, the Bristol Madrigal Society.[18] It was formed after a course of lectures at the Institution in 1836, by Edward J. Taylor, Gresham Professor of Music at Oxford, and formerly a citizen of Norwich, where he had organized a choral society and had been a strong advocate of the Norwich Music Festival, finally established in 1824. The strength of Nonconformity in Bristol perhaps inhibited a similar development at that time, but Taylor's detailed description of sixteenth-century madrigal singing kindled the enthusiasm of a small group who were already in the habit of meeting for musical evenings at the home of a surgeon, Mr Bleech. In the mid-century years, the Madrigal Society built up its reputation and its two public concerts a year became important social events. The success of the society was partly due to an increasing interest in organized musical societies from this period. Mostly choral, but with one or two devoted to instrumental music, this was the formative period for Bristol's musical life, and numerous societies such as the Bristol Vocal Society, the

Choral Society, the Philharmonic Society, the Classical Harmonists and the Orpheus Society became established.

However, the small group largely responsible for the more serious cultural pursuits were not so easily waylaid. Time not devoted to the acquisition of knowledge for their own benefit (and Dr Symonds was in the habit of rising at six in the morning to improve his Greek for two hours before breakfast and a hard day's labour)[14] was spent on the diffusion of knowledge to others. In the early days of the Institution in 1824, a lecture had been held for Bristol artisans to instruct them in the workings of the steam engine and the following year, a Mechanics Institute had been established. However, the activities at this Institute over the decades became largely social, so the small group made another effort in 1844, in the wake of the initial successes of the Trades Early Closing Association. Their aim was to reach the mechanics or weekly journeymen, who would benefit now from regular periods of free time, to ensure that the time should be spent profitably. The Bristol Athenaeum was founded at a meeting presided over by the Mayor; Mr Charles Pinney was made President, and Dr Symonds became one of the principal lecturers in the winter courses designed for cultural improvement.

But Symonds and friends found little dedication here, any more than they had done in the Literary and Philosophical Society, where serious cultural pursuits were largely kept going only by their own efforts. The subsequent history of the Athenaeum was one of slow but steady decline, in spite of efforts to organize courses and visits from lecturers such as Charles Kingsley and Charles Dickens.[15] The ailing institution finally received a blow from which it was never to make a full recovery, when, in the early 1860s, an attack was made on its Nonconformist bias. A Church of England clergyman accused the Athenaeum of 'teaching infidelity and atheism' in the city, because Mr Estlin of the famous Unitarian family had been discussing comparative religion, with special emphasis on the Indian religions, with his class. This event showed that a civic, cultural ideal was still a long way off, a fact reinforced by the decline of the Literary and Philosophical Society itself in the mid-century years. Dr Symonds's son, John Addington Symonds, who was to have a literary career and to become famous for his studies of the Italian Renaissance, lectured for a while at the Bristol Institution, and he gave as his inaugural lecture in 1861, a progress report on the Institution in the decade 1851-61.

The first point he made was fairly gloomy. The number and range of activities organized at the Institution were far less now than formerly. Further, the original aims of diffusing scientific and technical knowledge had scarcely been met; by far the greatest demand being for activities in the arts, especially music and literature. But even these activities had been limited by two crucial factors, shortage of resources and shortage of educated manpower. The Institution had been in financial difficulties as far back as 1836, since members' subscriptions had not been adequate to cover expenses, whilst the responsibility for the organization, administration and support of much cultural activity had fallen on the shoulders of a pitifully small number of people.

The bright point of Symonds's lecture however, was to highlight a major success of the Institution in a social sense. This was that support for societies and activities had come from a cross-section of citizens, regardless of political and religious affiliations. Symonds gives an analysis of the occupations of the 74 individuals who had given their services free to the Institution in the decade 1851-61 to prove his point. The list breaks down as follows: there were 19 medical men, 13 clergy and ministers, 11 gentry, 8 educationalists, 7 lawyers, 5 scientists, 3 architects, 3 literary gentlemen, 3 in commerce and 2 military gentlemen. The activities at the Institution had provided the basis for the integration of social groups within the city formerly without the means, or possibly the desire, for intercommunication. By 1861 the process had not gone all that far. But the framework for future integration amongst the city's upper classes had already been laid.

II THE CIVIC 'CULTURAL RENAISSANCE' OF THE 1860s AND '70s

The period 1865-75 was an extremely formative one in English social life. On a national level, vital changes were made in important areas closely affecting the daily lives of more people than ever before. For those concerned with education and the cultural evolution of urban civilization, the need for change seemed necessary and urgent. The spread of elementary education and thus literacy, and the cultural experimentation of the first half of the century had led to a lively appreciation of the cultural dimensions of urban society. Matthew Arnold, in his great polemic, *Culture and Anarchy,* was even prepared to put forward the view that the greatest threat to the social security of the future was a lack of 'culture'.

He started from the premise that the central ideal of English life was 'that passion for doing what one likes'.[16] Dividing society into the Barbarians (the aristocrats), the Philistines (the middle classes) and the Populace (the rest), it was, he maintained, easy to see that the Barbarians, with their great estates, had plenty of room to hunt, fish and shoot and behave as barbarically as they pleased; whilst the Philistines, with their social inhibitions and strict religious observances had little time for pleasure anyway. Thus doing what one likes 'had been convenient so long as there were only the Barbarians and the Philistines to do what they liked, but to be getting inconvenient, and productive of anarchy, now that the Populace wants to do what it likes too'.[17] He proposed that a group of dedicated men should work to bring a new cultural dimension to the lives of all classes, since such a dimension would create a social consensus and voluntary social control, thus averting the otherwise certain prospect of anarchy in the future.

There were a small number of people ready to listen to his ideas, among them the group in Bristol who had concerned themselves with the fortunes of the Bristol Institution. They found a powerful new ally in the person of the young Rev. John Percival, appointed in 1862 at the age of twenty-eight, as headmaster for Bristol's newest educational venture, the public school, Clifton College. The impetus he was to provide in organizing cultural activities gathered momentum in the decade 1865–75 and the city underwent a virtual 'civic renaissance'. The entire future of the main cultural institutions of the city during the next half century and beyond were fully mapped out in these years. Percival found, in Clifton, that he was working in a favourable environment. Traditions of social integration between Anglican and Nonconformist had been nurtured in the cultural activities held at the Bristol Institution; and the Literary and Philosophical Society provided a strong social base amongst Bristol's upper classes.

However, finding the means and the support for developing the cultural life of the city was not easy. Arnold's vision of culture might have the passion of a moral crusade, but it was no blueprint for practical action. Besides, there were a number of serious ambiguities in the Arnoldian concept of 'culture' which could lead to confusion. It was given such comprehensive dimensions that it could appear to be the solution to social and political problems. Arnold writes: 'culture looks beyond machinery, culture hates hatred, culture has one great passion, the passion for sweetness and light.'[18] Raymond Williams has justly commented that such a view of 'culture' with the emphasis on the spirit and the importance of knowing rather than doing, seems at times: 'very like the Dissenters' Salvation: a thing to secure first, to which all else will then be added.'[19] But there was one advantage of this ideal of 'culture' as the blessed state. All men and all women equally had the right to share it, as all men and all women stood equally before God on the Day of Judgment.

Such was the fundamental belief of the young Rev. John Percival, steeped in the Arnoldian faith, and ready to sear the prejudices of the provincial society in which he found himself, with 'sweetness and light.' His successor at the school wrote of him: 'he saw that the upper classes of our provincial towns were fettered by traditional immobility. This class also wanted light and ideas and expansion and were ready to respond if an opening appeared.'[20] Percival was determined to make that opening the cultural life of the city, involving the development of institutions for all classes and groups in society, including women. Thus the paradoxical situation arose in which Percival devoted his working life to forming an élitist educational institution to transform the social and cultural values of the ruling class; and at the same time, he devoted his extra-mural energies to organized attempts to create cultural facilities amongst all citizens. In his view, the élitist nature of the school did not erect a social barrier; rather the school was to be a central powerhouse radiating support and manpower to the cultural institutions of the city.

The Arnoldian vision of 'culture' in fact, released a powerful new intellectual force behind the development of cultural institutions. To the early nineteenth-century concern about fighting ignorance and brutality using education as a positive measure of social control,[21] was added new dimensions, the pursuit of culture as a socially cohesive force, and the pursuit of culture on a personal level as the means towards an individual's personal fulfilment. Such concerns broke social barriers. Amongst the first to feel the impact were middle-class women. The elevation of women had become a central tenet of the Positivist creed, since Auguste Comte had written on the need for women to have 'equality' in marriage and parenthood. But the problem was how to bring about such 'elevation' in the social context of a male-dominated world, since all that could be hoped for, according to the most advanced scientific views of the day, was an enlargement of the sphere in which women's sex-determined mentalities could operate. The pursuit of Liberal Culture seemed an ideal solution. It could only lead to improvement in character and understanding without disrupting the framework of a woman's life within home and family. Indeed, it could only make her a better companion for her husband and a cultural influence on the home.

The Liberal Culture ideal applied of course, only to the womenfolk of the affluent classes. But it contributed very much to the breakthrough in women's education which took place largely in the 1860s. Bristol was no exception to this trend. The Endowed Charity Commissioners had freed some philanthropic resources for the purpose of developing schools of secondary education in the city for both boys and girls. Yet the strength of the Liberal Culture ideal amongst leading citizens meant that the outlay in secondary education for girls far exceeded what was available from these resources. The new schools, Clifton High School, Redland High School, and others, had a conscious social purpose fully appreciated by their boards of governors.[22] Their course of studies were to be exactly the same as those of the boys' schools, largely based on the study of the classics, though with some study of modern subjects such as history, mathematics and the natural sciences. The social accomplishments, the French master and the dancing master, formerly the pride of female educational establishments, were duly spurned.

In 1868 Percival took this new departure to its logical conclusion by founding an Association for the Promotion of Higher Education for women. He was widely supported and lecturers at the Bristol Institution, all male, since serious cultural organizations were exclusively male, gave lectures for women under the auspices of the Association. The effect on the daughters of Clifton Society was traumatic. Elizabeth Sturge, one of the earliest students, has left a description of the impact of the Association. She rightly points out, of course, that Bristol was not unique and

> the movement for the higher education of women was now taking shape in various ways; notably in the colleges which were founded at Oxford and Cambridge. There were, however, large numbers of young women, anxious for opportunities of improvement who could never hope to become students at either of them.[23]

Social immobility for upper middle-class womenfolk in provincial cities was notorious, since leaving home was usually only possible with marriage. But Miss Sturge continues to describe how the Association brought to the homebound, 'sweetness and light'. There were courses on a great variety of subjects, study was usually unsystematic but enthusiasm was boundless.[24] Reading courses were taken, and essays written, though handed in under a pseudonym, 'such was the dread', says Miss Sturge, 'of having your name known in such a connection.'

Lack of self-confidence and uncertainty about social roles seems to have been a common phenomenon amongst young women at this time. They clung to their classes at the Association for reassurance. Caught up in the evolution of suburban society and the new social and cultural values of their class, the only definite thing about their future lives was that they were likely to be quite different from those of their mothers' generation. Josephine Butler caught the mood when she wrote in 1869,

> The present distress [amongst women] must to some degree be reckoned among the phenomena of a transition period in society ... it is a crisis which calls for action; for it is evident that a readjustment of man's and women's fields of work and in some degree of their manner of life, must take place in order to restore the equilibrium of society.[25]

For the middle-class women of Clifton, the concept of Liberal Culture gave them both a new purpose and a new social role. Intelligent and forceful women like Emily Sturge, trapped socially by spinsterhood and social immobility, could in her private life at home, refuse to fritter away time on what were considered normal female pursuits. Instead, she spent her time in intellectual study, and her aunt commented: 'She had little fondness for the minor occupations which make, or used to make, a part of most women's lives.'[26]

This degree of enlargement in women's activities though, had a wider impact on the cultural life of the city than the personal satisfaction of individuals. In the period 1865–75, women had an impact on cultural activities which was to sustain the liberal cultural crusade well beyond the exciting days of the 1860s. The Association for the Higher Education of Women had a direct influence on transforming the proposal for a new college of science and technology into a university college in 1874; and it was the continued support of women students which provided the base for the future development of the arts faculty of that institution. Mrs Alfred Marshall, wife of the first college principal, a Newnham student herself, did all she could to encourage women to attend study courses.

As Sherborne and Cottle have pointed out in their history of the university, few of the women were interested in more than improving their after-dinner talk.[27] But the few who were, found that these educational facilities gave them a new ability to contribute to the wider social and educational problems facing the city at this time. One or two broke new ground, such as Emily Sturge, who got herself elected as the first female member of the Bristol School Board in 1879. But it was becoming accepted that women's sphere of activity, especially for those of intellectual standing, could be extended outside the family to social and educational work. Such work was considered after all, to be closely related to the kind of demands met by women in the family.

Social work particularly, was considered suitable, especially since the 1860s cultural diffusion was added to the other philanthropic activities as an important objective. Women could provide a bettereducated, voluntary labour force to provide culture for the masses, as well as dispensing charity and relief, and there was a consistently high response from women with intellectual training to undertake social work. All the Sturge sisters became involved in the Quaker Mission to the Poor set up in 1865, which was one of the first to accept that 'social' influences were as important as religious ones in trying to redeem the poor. This was the legacy of the educational breakthrough of the 1860s, and the ideal of Liberal Culture. But such idealism had blinded the many, as well as liberating the few. It is Josephine Butler again who comments:

> Ladies ... will 'go in' for female education, but reject all else; or they will practically sanction some part of the movement which meets their taste or is not condemned as 'unwomanly' whilst carelessly refusing even to look into the meaning or merits of any other part.[28]

The strength of sexual stereotypes remained unchanged, women were still even the intellectual inferior of men and all female activities were second best to the ideal of 'the angel in the house busy with her brood of children ready to turn the commercial world of everyday economic laws into something finer.'[29]

The Arnoldian vision of Liberal Culture had deeply influenced attitudes to women amongst Clifton society. But the 'sweetness and light' which ensued had raised expectations perhaps, rather than led to practical achievements. Bristol women were to play an important part in opposition activities on a national and local level, from the campaign for the repeal of the Contagious Diseases Acts, to female suffrage; and in the later years of the century, to the leadership of the National Council of Women and, on a local level, to trade union organization. In the decade 1865–75 perhaps the first, the campaign against the Contagious Diseases Act, had the greatest social and cultural impact. The campaign had been started by three Nonconformist Bristol women who invited Josephine Butler to take over the leadership. She came to Bristol in 1869, since the Social Science Association was holding its annual congress there that year, specifically to speak against the Acts.[30] But women were banned from attending the debate on the pretext that it was a subject only suitable for discussion between qualified professionals. It was a real triumph for Elizabeth Blackwell, who had qualified as a doctor with enormous difficulty, to insist that the exemption did not apply to her, and she in fact, attended the debate.

The meeting of the Social Science Association in Bristol in 1869 is important for highlighting the discussion and concern taking place on a national and local level in the 1860s and '70s about all aspects of social development and change. Percival's ability to persuade

c

Bristol's élite to listen to his Arnoldian views of the future was partly because he appeared to offer plausible solutions to what appeared to be intractable social problems.[31] The Electoral Reform Act of 1867 and the Elementary Education Act of 1870, amongst other developments, placed a huge question mark over the problem of social evolution. Percival's answer was to urge the educated classes to provide leadership and to nurture co-operation between classes in the belief that only through voluntary effort on all sides could social development proceed. Since the social structure of the city had not been rent too savagely by a rapid introduction of the new economic order, Percival's response coincided with the personal beliefs and hopes of many leading citizens. They set out in the decade 1865-75 to improve themselves and the cultural potential of the urban environment.

An immediate need for action arose soon after Percival came to Clifton. In 1864 the fate of Bristol's Institution and the Library Society in King Street, Bristol's earliest civic institution, hung in the balance. The first was in debt, the second had been evicted from the King Street premises as the result of a campaign conducted by Councillor Charles Tovey to get the books put into the care of the council for the benefit of all citizens. Yet the Library Society still had the funds and support from its members. An obvious answer appeared to be an amalgamation of these two private institutions, since one had a building, and the other, financial support. But many problems arose, since the building was not really suitable for the purpose, and each group wished to retain elements of independence. The result was that the small group responsible for most of the activities at the Institution, aided and abetted by Percival, started a long campaign proposing the creation of a new society, a Museum and Library Society, and the construction of a new building to house it. As the years passed and the Liberal Culture ideal became ever more clearly defined, Bristol's richest citizens responded by raising the money to make this project a reality.

A new building in the Venetian Gothic style, like a tiny imitation of the Doge's Palace, was built at the top of Park Street and opened in 1871.[32] The new Society, though growing so closely from the traditions of the Bristol Institution, had somewhat different ambitions. It was generally recognized now that a voluntary organization, aiming at attracting a cross-section of the community, could never be a means of diffusing the latest scientific and technical knowledge. Its main emphasis therefore was on its cultural side, generating and maintaining enthusiasms and interests over a wide range of subjects; its purpose, to extend the horizons of the ruling class and, as cultivated individuals, to fit them for leadership. Such a combination of social, cultural and political factors was enough to make the Museum and Library Society a key institution in the city. The first officers appointed included an earl as president; two baronets, the Dean of Bristol, a canon, a Queen's Counsel and a Fellow of the Royal Society as vice-presidents; and a long list of names from leading families (Conservative and Liberal, Anglican and Nonconformist, old wealth and new) as well as clergy of all denominations, doctors, lawyers, and the headmaster of Clifton College.

Just how seriously this new venture was taken can be illustrated by the fact that leading citizens not only belonged to the Society; they were active in running it. The Frys and Wills families both contributed officers and funds; in 1871 Lewis Fry was a joint Hon. Secretary, and Joseph Storrs Fry, the joint Hon. Treasurer. It thus became the social and cultural centre of the city and was able to achieve a far more decisive impact than its predecessor, the Bristol Institution. Among the many clubs and societies who used the premises regularly were the Bristol Naturalists Society, the Bristol Microscopical Society, the Bristol and Clifton Debating Society, the Bristol Pharmaceutical Society, the Bristol and Gloucestershire Archaeological Association, and the Clifton Antiquarian Club. Other musical, literary and debating societies used the Society building for special meetings. Such activity marked a veritable explosion in the growth rate of the organized use of leisure time.

The pursuit of music, particularly, was becoming enormously popular. Until the late 1860s, however, Bristol had no large hall, apart from the Victoria Rooms built in 1843, which could not house the largest orchestras now on tour. Again a small group of men, drawn from the same group who were to create and finance the Museum and Library Society, formed themselves into a private company for the purpose of building a new hall. The Colston Hall Co. was launched in the mid 1860s and the building was finally opened in 1867. Situated near St Augustine's Parade on the site of the Tudor building which used to house the Colston School, it was conceived in the philanthropic tradition of old, since the directors had no intention of making a profit from their venture. Bristol had no town hall and the Colston Hall was aimed at fulfilling this function, providing an amenity for the use of all citizens. W. H. Wills provided a £3,000 organ for the hall as an indication of his goodwill. The new building contained three halls, one capable of seating 2,500, and two smaller ones, containing 700 and 400 seats respectively. It gave a great boost to the musical life of the city, and in 1873 Bristol held its first music festival.

In all these activities, the citizens of Bristol were only reflecting a trend which was widespread at this time. The British Association, for instance, kept figures of voluntary scientific societies which were formed in large towns, and the peak for the whole nineteenth century was reached in the decade 1871-81.[33] However, it was now obvious that amateurs could no longer do more than take an intelligent interest in the advancement of science. A growing need was felt for advanced institutions of science and technology, able to provide professional training. Bristol, in fact, had one of the first trade schools for vocational training in the early Victorian period, though it was limited to training boys, destined for a life at sea, in the arts of navigation. The school was taken over by the Society of Merchant Venturers, which in the 1860s was increasing its philanthropic role, especially in secondary education. Also moving in the same direction in the 1860s were leading Nonconformist businessmen such as Handel Cossham, who had campaigned in the city for an advanced institution of science and technology. The result was the project put forward in 1874 for the establishment of a School of Science and Literature for the West of England.

This plan was to be transformed by the impact of the 'cultural renaissance' in the city and the leadership of a small group (prominent amongst whom was the Rev. J. Percival) into a plan for a new university. Bristol, in fact, provides the classic case illustrating Veblen's theory of the leisure class in relation to institutions of higher learning. 'It is in learning proper', he writes, 'and more particularly in higher learning that the influence of leisure-class ideals is most patent.'[34] However, the men of the 1870s would never admit to his view of learning as a kind of magic, equivalent to religious rites, aimed at impressing those excluded from the ritual and keeping them subservient. The ideology behind the founding of Bristol

University was the Liberal Culture of Matthew Arnold and the belief, also held by small but active groups at the universities of Oxford and Cambridge in the decade 1865-75, in the urgent need to provide the means of a higher education in provincial cities, in theory at least, available to all. The problem was how to create a university out of a local institution.

The Rev. John Percival gave much thought to this, writing a pamphlet published in 1873 entitled 'The Connection of the Universities and the Great Towns'. His ideas closely echo those of Matthew Arnold. Local institutions, Percival wrote,

> if founded under local influences ... are certain to have almost exclusive reference to the practical wants of the neighbourhood and will consequently attract only special classes of students and produce little or no effect in the way of liberal culture. Thus they will be found to lack the one element which specially distinguishes a University, and which is above all things required in our wealthy trading communities.[35]

The point he is making is very similar to Arnold's comment:

> It would be everything for the great seats of population to be ... made intellectual centres as well as mere places of business; for want of this at present, Liverpool and Leeds are mere overgrown provincial cities whilst Strasbourg and Lyons are European cities.[36]

Concern over the future of university education was widespread in the 1850s and '60s. The two Royal Commissions set up in 1850 to investigate and advise the universities of Oxford and Cambridge of their need to reform were symptoms of this. The work of John Henry Newman provided a redefinition of university education, whilst his encouragement of university colleges in Ireland was one of the earlier practical attempts at university extension. In Bristol, Percival was convinced that more could be done by co-operation between the great towns and the older universities of Oxford and Cambridge. The towns could provide the buildings and finance their upkeep; the older universities could endow professorships from their vast resources; and personnel to take them up, who would live permanently in the city of the new university. Students who then underwent a course of study satisfactorily, could be awarded with a university degree. Percival managed to enlist the support of Benjamin Jowett, Master of Balliol, Oxford, who promised help and financial aid towards transforming the proposed educational institution in Bristol into a university.

A meeting of some significance was held on 11 June 1874. It was held to promote the original scheme of a School of Science and Literature for the West of England, and Jowett and Percival had to persuade the meeting to change its mind. What is more, they had to persuade the affluent to financially support their scheme for a university. The major plank of Jowett's argument was that a university was essential, because what was needed more than anything in a large city like Bristol was the promotion of Liberal Culture.[37] This was needed for the sake of the prestige of the city, as a means of contributing towards a higher civilization in the future, and for the personal benefit of the individuals who came into contact with the university. 'No man', he said, 'will be a first rate physician or engineer who is not something more than either, who has not some taste for art, some feeling of literature or some other interest external to his profession.'

Here was the classic statement of one of the most influential attitudes to the use of leisure time. Jowett had precise views of Liberal Culture; he was also prepared to outline three distinct elements in his attitude to leisure which he considered relevant to the social conditions of the modern city. The first was the recognition of the need for some excitement in the daily lives of individuals. 'Excitement' here is used to refer to the release of passions and enthusiasms which are a psychological necessity for mental health. One of the facts about life in an industrial, urban environment was a constantly increasing level of routinization, affecting every aspect of daily existence, in the educational sphere, at home and work. Elias and Dunning have written that 'in a society in which propensities for the serious and threatening type of excitement have diminished, the compensatory function of play-excitement has increased.'[38]

Jowett, Percival and others believed that in a civilized society, excitement was to be found in the liberal arts. Canon Barnett, in his pamphlet 'The Ideal City', describes their vision:

In our Ideal City, Art will grow out of common life, undisturbed by contrasts of wealth and poverty. The people will have pleasure in their work and leisure to admire what is beautiful.... People will have been educated to find interest in knowledge and beauty. They will have learnt that sufficient excitement is to be found in massing up knowledge of how men think, live and act, and in creating higher and higher forms of beauty.[39]

To give this ideal some kind of reality, however, facilities for higher education had to be made widely available. As Samuel Morley, MP said at the opening ceremony of the college:

This institution will utterly fail of its great object if those who have the management of its affairs do not secure for the working population of Bristol ... the means of information on the right application of which, everyone of us, whatever our position, is deeply interested.[40]

The second element Jowett was to stress was the fact that in the context of the modern industrial city, social contact and cultural activities had to be more organized. This was related to scale, the numbers of people who could be potentially involved, and was also part of the routinization process as well. Jowett specifically states that art, music and literature in the city must be pursued in an organized and regular form to ensure its future, and to enable people to fit cultural activities into their increasingly complex daily timetables. Finally, the third element was Jowett's insistence that the physician, or engineer must also have some strong interest outside his work. It was a recognition of the effects of specialization on the human psyche. The specialist was still viewed with suspicion as being at the opposite end of the pole to the ideal of the Renaissance man. In this situation, it was the duty of the individual to provide an additional dimension to his understanding and outlook during his leisure time.

There was no room here for the modern idea of leisure time as a period of relaxation. But at least Jowett and Percival were asking the two basic questions about the use of leisure. These are first, what are the personal leisure needs of an individual living in the more complex and civilized society of the modern provincial city? And second, what institutions or opportunities exist to fulfil such needs? Their answers however, were moulded more by idealism than insight into human nature. Their model was classical Greece and their faith was in Liberal Culture. But the social and political consequences of their vision, as well as the cultural ideal, was enough to swing the meeting in their favour. The vote was cast overwhelmingly in favour of transforming the proposed institution into a university college. In subsequent years, the strength of this early determination proved enough to maintain support for the college during lean times; and the local business families, especially the Frys and the Wills, provided sums for building and expansion which made possible the development of the college into a respected institution of higher education.

III CULTURAL ACTIVITIES 1875-98

The founding of the University College marked a climax in the 'cultural renaissance' of the decade 1865-75. As if to give the city its seal of approval, the British Association paid a second visit in 1875. Once again the city's upper classes were drawn into a round of lectures and social gatherings, creating a sense of unity amongst themselves and civic achievement. A handwritten diary of a young girl of middle-class background, covering the period of the British Association Congress, has been preserved,[41] and her account of the dinners and soirées, parties and guests, provides an illuminating picture of middle-class social integration, within the city, and with the middle classes of similar status from other cities. If the Anti-Corn Law League had been that 'uniquely powerful instrument in the forging of middle class consciousness',[42] the British Association Congresses helped to keep the whole process going indefinitely throughout the nineteenth century. The British Association was to pay a third visit to the city in 1898 and, during the period between visits, the cultural life of the city was developed from the seeds sown by the 'civic renaissance'.

However, Percival's ideals of an integrated society, sharing a common cultural heritage and common cultural experiences, were to become severely dented in the social context in which they were to operate. He could believe his school was a way of bringing 'sweetness and light' not only to the boys but to the city at large, and he was responsible for founding the Clifton College Mission as a bridge between the boys and the town. But cultural diffusion in a class society did not automatically lead to nurturing ideas of social equality. Sometimes the opposite was the case, since membership of the private Library and Museum Society and the exclusive cultural clubs which used the premises acted as a clear barrier in social and cultural terms. Indeed, it is arguable that their social exclusiveness, as much as zeal for cultural improvement, was the main reason why numerous clubs and societies continued to flourish in the 1880s and 1890s.

Perhaps the best way of illustrating this is to focus on one of the most respected of the societies, the Clifton Antiquarian Club. Its lineage was typical as it was founded, like the Museum and Library Society itself, by a small group of men drawn from the Literary and Philosophical Society. The Literary and Philosophical Society still continued as the 'éminence grise' behind the cultural activities of the middle classes, and in the period 1860–80 membership of this élite group numbered around 300 men. From this society, those with a special interest in local history and antiquarianism decided to form the Clifton Antiquarian Club. To maintain control over the social exclusiveness of the Club, membership was limited to fifty with ten honorary members. If any places became vacant, candidates to fill them were elected at a general meeting by ballot; but first they had to be nominated by two members and approved by the Club committee, and it only needed one adverse vote in ten at the general meeting for the candidate to be excluded.[43]

In the only extant lists of membership of the Literary and Philosophical Society and the Clifton Antiquarian Club which cover the same year, which happens to be 1888, the overlap between the organizations in membership is considerable. Thirty-two of the fifty members of the Clifton Antiquarian Club were also members of the Literary and Philosophical Society. Membership of the main cultural societies in the city was thus obviously a matter of privilege and social status. Ordinary citizens with an interest in local history had to pursue that interest in different, less exclusive institutions, particularly evening classes, now that the Athenaeum and other cultural organizations for the lower orders were declining. But if cultural idealism faltered on class distinction, it did lead, for those within the magic circle, to new experiences and dimensions in their lives.

In the pursuit of a common interest, differences between members of politics and religion for instance, could be totally subordinated. The President of the Antiquarian Club was the Roman Catholic bishop of Clifton, the Hon. and Rev. William Clifford D.D., yet Anglican and Nonconformist clergy also belonged to the club. The Club's obituary of Clifford published at his death in 1893,[44] praised him for the fact that in his association with the Club, the bishop put history before religion. He was not in the least embarrassed entering Anglican parish churches in search of antiquities. The Club conducted its affairs in a mixture of the social with the serious. Meetings were held regularly, papers read and outside lecturers invited to speak, but only after everyone had partaken of a good dinner at the Imperial Hotel, Clifton. Membership was exclusively male and the camaraderie amongst members was an important factor. Yet the antiquarian interest was taken seriously and the proceedings of the society published in journal form.

The popularity of societies such as the Clifton Antiquarian Club owed much to the moral dimension of the cultural crusade of Arnold and his followers. For the middle classes of a provincial city, brought up often within the strict confines of evangelical religious orthodoxy, the pursuit of pleasure for the sake of pleasure had an aura of sin about it which was difficult to dispel. The ideal of a higher civilization and the need to improve oneself through cultural activities though, did much to lessen the inhibitions. Unfortunately, like all ideals let loose on an unsuspecting society, it became deformed and disfigured by those who misunderstood it or used it to serve less idealistic ends. Percival might have been faintly amused by one of the founder members of the Bristol Chess Club who wrote:

> In youth, before the intellectual faculties are fully developed, infantile amusements are the best calculated to invigorate the constitution and prepare the mind for the reception of more lofty attainments; but when we become men, we must put away childish things, and it is then of importance that we should select those amusements and recreations ... at least harmless, if not beneficial.[45]

The conscious echoes of biblical language only serve to highlight what can happen to a moral crusade, when the substance of the ideal which gave it life, is lost. 'Sweetness and light', freedom and democracy, a cultural consensus and social equality, were the life-blood of the idealists; but society in provincial cities was more prosaic and far more responsive to economic and social realities. Social changes in the 1880s and '90s, especially the pressure on the ranks of the middle classes by the substantial rise in white-collar jobs, were to transform attitudes to Liberal Culture. The pursuit of culture became, not a means of spreading 'sweetness and light', but an indication of status. The moral values which had underpinned the earlier crusade simply served to fossilize attitudes to Liberal Culture, literally endowing works of art with a morally beneficial influence, and turning 'music into classics, art into old masters and literature into rare books, possessions symbolic of status.'[46]

It was largely in vain that William Morris, the Pre-Raphaelites and the Impressionists in France led the campaign against such a death wish for the cultural life of the future. They fought to break through these conventional attitudes by trying to demonstrate that 'culture' was not an absolute to be worshipped from afar. It was an indication of artistic sensibility, something living, organic, constantly changing, requiring the active participation of the individual. But such views were too anarchic, even positively politically dangerous, for the cultural élite of a provincial city. Percival's place as headmaster of Clifton had now been taken by the Rev. J. M. Wilson, who did his best on a personal level to continue the activities and ideals of his predecessor. But the boys at his school came under new and far more compelling interests than concern for cultural improvement. The pursuit of sport had taken a veritable grip of public school institutions and the new hero was the sportsman, regardless of his intellectual capabilities. Social barriers and the natural anti-intellectualism of the English middle classes shattered the ideals of the 'civic renaissance'.

IV THE 'MUNICIPALIZATION' OF CULTURAL INSTITUTIONS

The civic cultural institutions however, lived on, and the turn of the century was to see the final stage in their development when they were placed in the care of the municipal council. By that time, of course, the cultural ideal had worn a little thin, and the social realities of economic changes in the city had become ever more apparent. Yet in spite of growing protest about economic inequalities and bad social conditions, there were no voices raised against the municipal council undertaking responsibility for cultural institutions. Perhaps there was apathy, but there was no rejection of the fruits of the 'civic renaissance'. In the period 1895–1905, Bristol was to acquire a museum, new central library and an art gallery for the benefit of all citizens. Yet the working classes had been conspicuously absent from all art exhibitions held for many years at the West of England College of Art. Newspapers commented regularly on this fact.[47] Protest at these new municipal responsibilities though, was probably muted as all these institutions were acquired through private benefactions.

The impulses which drove the small group of rich benefactors to undertake this expense, were varied. Sir Charles Wathen, the Liberal Nonconformist Mayor of the late 1880s, paid off the debts of the Museum and Library Society in 1893, on condition that the council took over the building as a civic museum.[48] He was an old man, in fact he died in 1893, but like his friend and colleague, Joseph Dodge Weston, he had spent a life-time in the cause of extending educational facilities for the public. His concern for this was most poignantly shown by his sudden death whilst actually in the council chamber, during the course of a debate in which he was trying to persuade the council to finance a huge industrial and fine arts exhibition. His gift to the city was made in the belief that the Museum and Library Society stood for all the best cultural traditions in the city, and that by making it municipal property, this would bring its benefits within the reach of all citizens for ever.

Unfortunately however, when the Library and Museum Committee of the Town Council was formed, and took over the running of the institution, no one seemed to have any precise ideas on how the public could really benefit in practice. No one seems to have read any discussions on the subject such as W. S. Jevons's article of 1881 on 'The Use and Abuse of Museums'.[49] In fact, as far as the committee was concerned, its main duty was to maintain the museum on a shoe-string budget and to bring its benefits to the public simply by opening its doors to all. The curator did try to make his collections more intelligible to the public and more useful, by visiting schools with small exhibitions and by giving lectures to evening-class students once a week. But the funds supporting these activities were small, because the Committee had become obsessed with another matter.

Since the museum and library building was now municipal property, its appearance was a direct measure of the status of the city, in the provincial, municipal competition. Thus the major resources of the Committee were spent on decorating the exterior of the building. The Venetian Gothic façade lent itself to embellishment, particularly the row of blank shields over the entrance of the building. These were used for an imaginative display of civic pride with the city coat of arms and the arms of leading citizens placed in carefully considered positions. In municipal affairs, the council had had no former moment of glory to cast a shadow over subsequent activity, as in Birmingham. The slate in Bristol was clean, awaiting the imprint of the ebullient and successful middle classes.

The acquisition of the museum placed to the fore the urgent, but much-shelved problem of a new central library. The library of the Museum and Library Society could not be added to the Bristol central reference library in King Street simply because there was no room. The King Street library had been cramped and inadequate for twenty years and had been unable to augment its collection, though of course, money for that was not available either. The problem was solved by another private benefactor, though this time not a well-established political and social figure. In 1899 the town council received a bequest on the death of a Mr Vincent Stuckey Lean of £50,000 for the purpose of a new central library.

This was somewhat of a surprise because Mr Lean, though very rich (his father having been a founder of Stuckey's Bank), was a quiet man, something of a recluse and comparatively unknown. His name had been entirely omitted from the volume of biographies of contemporary worthies brought out in 1898 in time for the British Association visit, and some hasty research had to be done on his life for the occasion of the Library Association visit to Bristol in 1900.[50] But for his passion for books and book collecting, he would have sunk into anonymity at his death. But he had amassed a collection of over 3,000 volumes, some of them rare and valuable, and he wanted to keep them intact by leaving them as a single collection to the city library. Since the central library was already much too crowded to house such a collection properly, Mr Lean was prompted to supply the wherewithal to build a new central library.

His action caused great repercussions in the town council and the city. Bristol now had a municipal museum and the means for a new central library. But this only made more glaringly apparent to those sensitive about the city's status, the lack of an art gallery in the city, comparable to the institutions in other provincial cities. Sir W. H. Wills, whose family tobacco empire had made them the richest family in the city, decided to come to the rescue. He began by donating £10,000 to the council for the purchase of the Rifle Drill Hall, which was adjacent to the museum and up for sale in 1899, for the purpose of an art gallery. The outline of Bristol's cultural institutions was complete.

But their role as public institutions was unclear, the day-to-day arrangements and future developments left to the responsibility of committees of the town council, which had little to guide them except an acute shortage of funds. The Library Committee was desperate in view of the new bequest, as the penny rate had already proved inadequate. It repeatedly urged the council to adopt the Public Libraries Act of 1902 which allowed a twopenny rate, but demands from other sources were straining the council's resources. Eventually, in 1904, the Museum Committee agreed that if they were very economical they could manage on a $\frac{1}{4}d.$ rate and thus, if the rate was raised to a $1\frac{1}{2}d.$, the Library Committee could have a $1\frac{1}{4}d.$ rate. The town council maintained the art gallery in the first year of its existence with the interest earned on the Stuckey Lean Bequest. From their inception, such institutions of Liberal Culture seemed too great a burden for the city at this time to bear.[51]

In view of their demand on the rates, the question of their role in the city was considered seriously. But the committees responsible for handling the bequests were held fast by contemporary attitudes to the municipal provision of cultural institutions. This was mainly that they should have as magnificent buildings as possible as an indication of the city's status; that they should be permanent; and once established, run as cheaply as possible. The Library Committee for instance, in spite of the urgency of the need for a new central library, let several years slip by, whilst they held a competition for architects to submit their designs.[52] Sixty-one sets of plans had then to be carefully vetted. Finally in 1903 they selected the winner, from a London firm, and building could begin. An indication of their priorities is evident from how the bequest was apportioned:

Buildings	25,000	
Site	4,000	
Furniture and fittings	5,000	
Books	5,000	
Capital invested (to supply income)	6,000	
Contingencies	5,000	
	£50,000	Vincent Stuckey Lean bequest

There were no big grants to replenish the depleted stocks of the central library. The emphasis was on the building and its permanence. On 20 June 1906, seven years after the bequest was made, the brass plaque commemorating the gift of Vincent Stuckey Lean was screwed to the wall in the expensively marbled entrance hall, and Bristol's new central library was opened with due ceremony. It was to be a popular and much used institution since by then, the library system of the city had become an integral part of urban life.

The question of the design and role of the art gallery was not, however, left to a committee of the town council. Contemplating his original bequest and the possibilities of the Rifle Drill Hall, Sir W. H. Wills became dissatisfied with the project. He decided to take over the whole scheme and reconstitute it himself. The building, he intended, was to be more than an art gallery. It was to be an outward and visible sign of the importance of Bristol as shown through her municipal buildings, and it was consciously planned to outshine its counterparts in other cities. The architect was appropriately, a member of the Wills family, a cousin of the benefactor,[53] and the question of cost was ignored in the pursuit of municipal magnificence.

Festooned with classical impedimenta and topped by a group of symbolic statues, with the city coat of arms blazoning forth from a colonnaded façade (and a large plaque on the front commemorating that it was all a gift of Sir W. H. Wills to his fellow citizens), the new art gallery provided the perfect symbol of the power of the ruling élite and civic consciousness at the turn of the century. It is an historic building and the comment of the chairman of the Museum and Art Gallery Committee on its opening is equally significant. He wrote: 'a sense of relief and satisfaction was felt now that Bristol was the happy possessor of a temple of art worthy of her position amongst the cities of the Kingdom.'[54]

The relationship of the art gallery with Bristol's humbler citizens was not given much thought. Nobody considered it was incongruous that the new gallery only owned twelve pictures and had no funds to buy more;[55] that its upkeep consumed funds which might otherwise have gone to the hard-pressed and much used public library system. The use of the building, apart from supplying a splendid setting for the reception for the king and queen, who visited the city in 1908 to open some new docks,[56] was exceedingly limited. It was not a popular institution since the masses did not visit it. It was not an educational institution since its collections at the time were so limited. It was not a patron of the arts as it was never endowed with sufficient funds to act in this way.

It was, in fact, a classic example of the power of the formalized Liberal Culture ideology over the minds of a generation. Civic pride, municipal ostentation and competition with other cities were also important elements. But underneath the glittering façade there was a serious intention. It would be too crude to describe this middle-class effort to endow the municipal council with cultural institutions as the middle-class answer to the socialist state; as symbols of an ideal of life which were the justification of capitalist enterprise. Yet the final evolution of the dominant cultural institutions of the city owed everything to those of the ruling classes whose immense wealth differentiated them so sharply from the masses. For many of Bristol's citizens, who were to make up the majority, the existence of such institutions was probably of little or no concern.

The municipalization of the main cultural institutions came after a big boundary change in 1897 when some of the fastest-growing suburbs were included within the city. It was the beginning of the end of the personal involvement of the ruling élite. As if to provide a glittering finale to this period of power, the British Association chose to visit Bristol for the third time in the century in 1898. For what was probably the last time, all the nobility, gentry, clergy, professional men, wealthy businessmen, aldermen and town councillors (still largely recruited from the upper classes) joined together to reiterate their faith in knowledge and Liberal Culture. Of the three visits of the British Association to Bristol in the nineteenth century, that of

1898 was by far the most lavish. The programme was packed with social and cultural events.[57] A tower was built commemorating the epic voyage of Sebastian Cabot five centuries before to the New World. But also perhaps, commemorating Bristol's new departures in recent economic prosperity and the social achievements of the ruling élite.

4
BRISTOL'S LEADING CITIZENS — A GOVERNING ELITE?

The provision of leisure facilities and cultural diffusion had become the concern of rich and powerful citizens. A small social group, these people formed an élite, able to exercise a high degree of influence on the city's social life and institutions. As town councillors they moulded the municipal response to changing social conditions; as philanthropists and socio-religious workers, they led the 'civilizing' mission to the poor, the great voluntary effort by numerous agencies, to improve the social environment of the city. Who were these people? How did they exercise such power? To what extent did their social backgrounds influence their attitudes to the city? Is it possible to use the term 'élite' in the singular, since a large, well-established city like Bristol would be likely to produce a number of élites based on different economic, social and religious interest groups?

The answers to these questions are not always clear because of the lack of source material. But at least the answer to the last question can be given in the affirmative. In nineteenth-century Bristol, there was a remarkable social development, the formation of an élite, which united the powerful elements in the city's social structure in a way which had never been achieved before. They formed a 'governing élite'. The significance of describing them as such is to differentiate this kind of élitism from that based on 'specialist' concerns or limited groups. Professor Nadel suggests

> the decisive pre-eminence of the governing elite lies not in its elite character as such, but in its fuller corporate organization and the measure of coercive power which it wields in virtue of this organization. It is first and foremost a ruling group and only incidentally an elite.[1]

This distinction is particularly relevant to an understanding of Bristol's governing élite. Sectarian and political disputes of the early part of the century were pushed into the background as leaders of different groups found co-operation amongst themselves, more in their interest than formerly. A good illustration of this development was the gradual elimination of conflict between the powerful Society of Merchant Venturers and the city's Chamber of Commerce, particularly over the dock question. Until the docks were taken over by the town council in 1848, they had been under the control of members of the Society of Merchant Venturers. Opposition to the Society of Merchant Venturers, which led to the takeover, was centred on two organizations, the Bristol Chamber of Commerce and the Free Port Association. These latter organizations were dominated by Nonconformist businessmen and shipowners in contrast to the Society of Merchant Venturers, largely Anglican and Tory.

In the second half of the century the Chamber of Commerce gained a new importance, earning its charter of incorporation in 1874. By this time, conflict between these groups had eased and there was an interchange of personnel between the Society of Merchant Venturers and the Chamber of Commerce. There were now growing levels of integration amongst the upper classes, especially between Anglican and Nonconformist, including even the established 'outsiders', the Quakers.[2] Changing circumstances and common interests were drawing them together. A strong impetus to this movement was the ever-increasing means of exercising power over the community. In the nineteenth century there was a veritable spate of voluntary organizations for every kind of social, political or religious purpose, providing an organizational base for influence; whilst the growing powers of local government brought a new prestige to the town council.

The élite was drawn from the already select few with wealth and status. But what enabled them to form an élite, and to co-operate with each other across religious and political barriers, were clearly defined interests. The burgeoning voluntary associations bred a new sense of responsibility in their leaders, not just for the sectional interest which they represented, but for the city as a whole. The constant demands for funds, for leadership and for concern over the social conditions of the city, placed those of the rich who responded in a special position. They could recognize the value of each other's contribution and be widely recognized in turn. This was the fundamental factor which made them an élite and gave them their influence. In three areas of civic life, in philanthropic work, in the religious life of the city and in service on the town council, the position of the élite was recognized and revered and it was work in these three spheres of activity which most clearly influenced the social attitudes of the élite to the city.

I PHILANTHROPY AND THE ELITE

Philanthropic activity provided the background to the response of 'social citizenship', the clearest ideological response of the élite to the modern city. Philanthropy, of course, was also the age-old response of leading citizens to social problems. In a city like Bristol, this had been well established and maintained over the centuries. The munificence of one of the city's greatest seventeenth-century benefactors, Edward Colston, was freshly impressed on the minds of leading citizens each year, through the activities of the Colston Commemoration Societies, established in the eighteenth century. But events in the nineteenth century, particularly the concept of 'social citizenship', help to reshape the philanthropic tradition in new ways.

One of the more important new influences on philanthropic work was the growing strength of the relationship between philanthropy and local government. In the early nineteenth century, the relationship had been tenuous. Indeed, the funds from the municipal charities had been misappropriated by the mayor and corporation. Corruption was rooted out, however, after the 1835 Municipal Reform Act, when a Whig-dominated committee of Municipal Charities Trustees was appointed to watch over the activities of the Tory town council. The reforming decade of the 1830s in fact, was to have a considerable impact on the philanthropic world, though Bristolians were slow to accept the redefinition of poverty incorporated in the 1834 Poor Law Amendment Act. The City's Corporation of the Poor, established in 1696, met the initial demands of the Act, so that there was little change at first.[3] Bristol's Guardians gave relief to more paupers than any other city of comparable size.

However, from the mid-century, the connection between the highest civic office and philanthropic activity became even more pronounced, particularly the practice of what was, in effect, 'civic' philanthropy. This was the donation of large sums of money, not for the relief of the poor, but for the benefit of the town council and for boosting civic splendour. Alderman Proctor gave his large house on the Downs in Clifton to the Corporation in 1874 as a new Mansion House for the mayor (the previous one having been burnt down in the Bristol Riots of 1831). Joseph Dodge Weston, mayor five times in the 1880s, spent a fortune on civic entertainments, gaining a knighthood for public services. But the peak in this special relationship between philanthropy and political power was reached in 1893. Mr R. H. Symes was co-opted to the office of Mayor without even being a member of the town council. His wealth, county connections and philanthropic zeal gained him general acceptance, and he reinforced this with strenuous charitable effort whilst in his first year of office.[4]

This intertwining of civic office with philanthropic activity helped to strengthen another major influence changing the nature of philanthropic work in the nineteenth century. This was the widening of the scope of philanthropic work from a local to an urban basis. This was in some ways a new departure, in spite of Bristol's long tradition of civic and philanthropic activity. In earlier times, isolated groups, like the Quakers, had been leading philanthropists without becoming involved in civic affairs. However, from the mid-century, as the town council slowly began to take up its responsibilities for the health and welfare of all citizens, philanthropists found themselves responding to the wider context of the city. The identification, for instance, of 'urban' poverty as opposed to the localized poverty of parish, widows and orphans, etc. represented a significant shift in philanthropic thinking.[5]

The range of activities and numbers of different groups involved in charitable pursuits in the city at the mid-century, make generalizations hazardous. The development of a rational approach to philanthropic work and the quest for efficiency, resulted in attempts such as the Charity Organization Society of London,[6] which was imitated in Bristol. Yet the response of philanthropists to the wider context of the 'modern' city had a multitude of implications far beyond that, both for the philanthropists themselves and the activities they engaged in. They were becoming aware of the growing importance of the social and political role of philanthropy in the changed economic and social conditions of a 'modern' city.

In these circumstances the barriers of what had, traditionally, constituted philanthropic work could easily be broken down; and it was in this context that the social attitudes of the governing élite became profoundly influenced by their experience in philanthropic work. Traditionally, philanthropic concern had been directed towards the individual. Whilst this still remained the basic response, from the 1860s a new element became increasingly more apparent. This was concern over the evil influences of the environment on the individual. Such a concern meant that the objectives of philanthropic concern became immeasurably extended. There was a greater readiness to accept responsibility for spiritual, intellectual and emotional destitution, as well as the more immediate problem of material poverty. This can partly be explained by the fact that the whole apparatus of the city's philanthropic organizations was based on a total lack of knowledge of the extent of destitution. For the élite though, such a broadening in their scope of activities gave a meaning to the rather misty concepts of 'social citizenship' and the 'urban community'.

The significance for philanthropists, was that their work was seen now, not only as a means of relieving destitution, but also as a positive method of creating the 'good society'. Traditions of philanthropic work, however, were still strong enough to rule out collective action towards such a broad-based goal. Rather the emphasis remained on individual responses from amongst members of the élite. In this way, members of the élite could become associated with certain projects and thus gain influence in a particular field. Temperance, education, medical work, youth work, environmental improvements, civic amenities, were all dominated by a small group of individuals, who sometimes had more than one major interest. The group remained small and interconnected by religious, social and political ties, and in this way became a 'governing élite'.

The power of the élite rested on their ability to persuade enough people to respond in some way to the social problems they recognized, so that corporately, by the contribution of much individual effort, an overall impact could be made. Their role was to be at the centre of the leading organizations, providing, by example and by advocacy of 'social citizenship', a sense of direction to this otherwise, hardly co-ordinated, philanthropic effort. By heading subscription lists, acting as presidents and chairmen of particular ventures, they managed to give an impression of unity of purpose even if there was no collective concentration on any particular problem. But they were not just figureheads. Direct power could be exercised in the dispensing of large sums of money available from the city's rich endowment of charitable agencies.

The financial resources were extensive. The ancient endowed charities of the city had an income of £50,000 a year when examined by the Endowed Charities Commission in 1873. In the course of the century, the Society of Merchant Venturers began to use its not inconsiderable resources in philanthropy and educational work. The Colston Societies, with the Colston Commemoration Societies, the Anchor, Grateful and Dolphin, each annually raised subscriptions often exceeding £1,000. There was a whole network of smaller charities beyond these, both ancient and modern, and therefore income to spend. The Bishop's Committee of 1884 estimated that a sum of £200,000 was expended in the city each year, though unorganized almsgiving accounted, in their estimation, for £50,000 out of the total.[7] Not all of it obviously passed through the hands of the governing élite. But the Municipal Charity Trustees, the Master of the Society of Merchant Venturers, the Mayor and Sheriff, the Presidents of the Colston Societies between them handled the major proportion of it. In the philanthropic field they were certainly supreme. Such resources convinced them of both the efficacy of the voluntary principle in responding to social conditions, and the importance of their own role.

II RELIGION AND THE GOVERNING ELITE

'Social citizenship' was the moral basis of the power of the élite in their philanthropic role. But the moral influence of members of the élite lay beyond their philanthropic work. It was based on religion. The Bristol élite, like its counterparts in Birmingham, Liverpool and elsewhere, considered its final justification and the source of its influence to be religion. The importance of Nonconformist religious institutions and ministers in the formation of Chamberlain's Civic Gospel of the late 1860s and '70s has been clearly demonstrated.[8] The importance of religion to Bristol's governing élite, was just as profound.

On a very basic level, all denominations would have agreed that the challenge of their time was to bring Religion, Cleanliness and Temperance to the urban masses. On a broader front perhaps, was a desire to improve standards of public behaviour, though not all were united behind the Lord's Day Observance Society.[9] But whatever degree of Puritanism was displayed by different denominations, one point of great importance emerges from their common responses. This was the creation of a religious sub-culture. Those who belonged to this sub-culture were to promote a pattern of social life in a modern urban environment which was by far the most selfconscious attempt to shape the future social evolution of the city. Since the élite belonged to this sub-culture, it was to have a considerable impact on the development of social institutions in the city and the organized response to leisure.

The development of a common, religious sub-culture in the city was a feature of the late nineteenth century.[10] The key word here is 'common', as all denominations influenced patterns of social behaviour and social response from their inception. But the remarkable fact about the religious sub-culture in Bristol in the period 1860–1914 was a gradual drawing together of the divergent social patterns of different denominations into a common pattern, in which differentiation between sects became blurred. One journalist writing on the religious life of the city in 1908 singles this out as the most important change he had witnessed. He wrote,

> There has been a lowering of denominational barriers. The distinction may remain but differences are far less accentuated than formerly and points of agreement are so important that the fullest and friendliest cooperation has grown up among members of what are often known as 'the Evangelical Free Churches'.[11]

He might also have included the evangelical elements of the Church of England.[12] The basis of this co-operation was the common experience they all shared. All the main denominations had to face two major challenges as the city grew in size. These were the shift from the centre of the city of formerly influential congregations and the social segregation of the classes in the new suburbs; and what they left behind, the densely populated, central areas of the city where the poor remained, godless and unconverted.

As Dr Kent points out, it may be regarded as axiomatic that the strength of religious institutions depends not on the number of people who are existentially committed to a particular theological outlook but on the social roles which are available to the institutions as such.[13] The double challenge of suburban living and the urban poor gave the churches and chapels a social role, in a period of change, such as they had rarely enjoyed before. To seize this chance, however, needed funds and religious denominations were voluntary organizations. Thus the influence of lay members, particularly wealthy lay members, grew in direct proportion to the effort made to meet these challenges. Since Bristol had a well-established evangelical tradition, both amongst the Church of England members and the Nonconformists, a considerable effort was made. Those lay members who were closely identified with this development and who contributed time and resources, were thus able to gain an influence and prestige which put them amongst the governing élite. Perhaps the most outstanding fact was that there was no sectarian discrimination in Bristol. The governing élite was drawn from the Church of England, the Quakers, Congregationalists, Baptists, Wesleyans, even Roman Catholics, so long as the individuals concerned contributed in some way towards meeting the double challenge.

This level of co-operation was due partly to the fact that all the larger denominations now had leading lay figures of considerable wealth and economic power. It also lay in two developments relating to the history of the religious life of the city which made it unique. The first was that throughout the nineteenth century there was a reasonably equal balance between Anglicans and Nonconformists. The figures in the 1851 census are 44·5 per cent Church of England, 55·5 per cent Nonconformists. Thus neither were outstandingly dominant. The second fact is that according to the three main statistical surveys of religious affiliation taken in Bristol (in 1841 by the Bristol Statistical Society; in the 1851 Census; and in 1881 by the local newspaper, the *Western Daily Press*), church or chapel attendance remained remarkably constant over the forty-year period.[14]

Roughly a third of the population attended a church or chapel. This was, indeed, a notable record in comparison with other large towns. According to C. S. Miall's calculations, taken from individual, unofficial surveys of religious strength in various large cities in 1881, church and chapel attendance was appreciably higher in Bristol than in towns of a comparable size. Bristol had a figure of 40 per cent in 1881; in Sheffield it was 23 per cent; in Bradford 27·1 per cent; and Nottingham 24·2 per cent. As for a comparison with Bristol's much larger rival port on the west coast, Liverpool, the latter city could only muster a figure of 19·9 per cent.[15] The religious sub-culture thus obviously enjoyed a very considerable influence in Bristol.

The outward and visible sign of the social impact of religious sects and their wealthy lay élites, was a spate of building of new churches and chapels which gives a considerable impression of vigour and progress. As Professor Chadwick has commented. 'Between 1860 and 1890, perhaps between 1840 and 1900, all denominations possessed a sense that they took part in a great movement of religion.'[16] The Church of England in the city, after the blow of losing the bishopric in 1836, rebuilt its confidence with a major effort to match the growth of the city by extending the number of parishes. Between 1823 and 1903, forty-one new parish churches were built in Bristol which, with mission chapels, provided about 36,000 sittings.[17] Efforts were particularly concentrated around the two Church extension schemes, the first in 1868, which was launched by Bishop Ellicott of Bristol and Gloucester, and received strong support from the Rev. John Percival and others; the second in 1898, after the restoration of the see to the city in 1897 and the appointment of the Rt Rev. George Forrest Browne D.D. as the first incumbent.

The most outstanding feature of the 1898 Church Extension Scheme was that high amongst the list of subscribers were Sir Edward P. Wills and the Rt Hon. Lewis Fry, who were Nonconformists. Nonconformists indeed, had figured prominently in the subscription lists to the restoration and extension of Bristol Cathedral.[18] The contribution of Nonconformists to this appears even more remarkable in view of the fact that all the main denominations were making heavy financial demands on their supporters for building purposes. It is a clear indication that the élite felt that their common interest in the religious sub-culture was more important than their denominational difference. The 'civic' aura of the Church Extension Scheme of 1898 was heightened by the fact that the people invited to the meeting to launch it were chosen as representatives of the most influential social groups in the city. The Lord Mayor and Sheriff were there, and there were representatives of the Society of Merchant Venturers; of the local gentry; of leading businessmen and professional people; the criterion for their selection being their wealth and influence, not their religious affiliation.

The social base of interdenominational co-operation under the leadership of the élite, lay undoubtedly in the growth of exclusive social suburbs, where the leading congregations of the major sects were to be found. Clifton, Cotham and Redland were the exclusive areas. The Church of England was well represented with five churches in Clifton alone, and the Congregationalists, Baptists, Unitarians and Wesleyan Methodists, all had important chapels in these suburbs.[19] The Congregationalist Highbury Chapel in Cotham, built in 1843 and numbering many ex-members of the old Bristol Tabernacle (including a major proportion of the Wills family) amongst its congregation, became so influential, it was known locally, as the Nonconformist Cathedral of the West. The Congregationalists also had a large and influential congregation at Redland Park, Redland. The Baptists and Wesleyans both ran theological Colleges in the western suburbs, and the Wesleyan National Congress was held in Bristol in 1867 and 1877.

The Baptists, though much of their support was found in other parts of the city, did have one very influential congregation at the Tyndale Chapel at Redland, built in 1868. Tyndale Baptist Chapel only had a congregation of about 200 members, but a high proportion of them were involved in social and philanthropic work in the city. Many of these had formerly been associated with Broadmead Baptist Chapel, but the close-knit, socially cohesive group at the Redland Chapel were able to pursue socio-religious work with a single-mindedness which brought greater influence. For instance, Charles Townsend's father had been a deacon at Broadmead Baptist Chapel all his life. But it was the son, deacon at Tyndale, who was elected President of the Baptist Association, who was Honorary Secretary of the Bristol City Mission for many years, who entered politics in the Liberal cause, becoming a town councillor from 1872 to 1892 when he was elected MP for North Bristol. With men like this in its congregation, Tyndale Baptist Chapel had an influence far exceeding its numbers. The same could be said of the Quaker and Unitarian groups in the city, who had some of the most wealthy and influential citizens amongst their ranks.

The existence of the religious sub-culture was crucial to the influence of the élite. But the strength of different religious sects only provided the potential. The catalyst necessary to bring together leading laymen of different denominations, to give some unity to the religious sub-culture, was a sense of social purpose. This was supplied, and supplied in abundance, by dedicated members of the clergy, particularly those in charge of congregations in the middle-class suburbs.[20]

For a brief while many of the religious, social and political questions of the day were considered to be within the province of the clergy. They could support political parties, they could thunder at their congregations from the pulpit about their social role, they could undertake campaigns for the provision of social amenities by the town council. Their influence, particularly the influence of men like the Revs Glover and U. R. Thomas, was very great since their congregations contained many of the town councillors and leading philanthropists in the city. For the clergy and ministers of churches and chapels in the poorer, non-fashionable areas of the city, the going was tougher. Yet they were in no doubt that they manned the outposts of civilization amongst the populace, and they undertook much social, philanthropic and political work.

Already by the 1860s and '70s, these developments had brought significant changes. As new men were brought in to staff the churches and chapels being built with increasing rapidity in the third quarter of the century, they brought with them the new approach to social and religious work. Their response was partly, obviously, the outcome of their individual outlook, but it was also related to their experience of working in the context of a 'modern' urban environment. Not all of them were concerned with congregations. The Rev. J. Percival and the Rev. J. M. Caldicott both worked in education, each facing the challenge of building up or revitalizing a school. The schools they were concerned with, Clifton College and the Bristol Grammar School, were élitist organizations; the first as a public boarding school, obviously more so than the latter. Both men, however, were anxious that their institutions should serve, not just a small social group, but the city at large; and again the concept of 'urban community', and the emphasis they gave in their teaching to 'social service' of rich and privileged to the poor and downtrodden, provided a means whereby their institutions could have a wider impact.

The growing strength of the religious sub-culture, provided the élite with an influence beyond the range of specific religious and educational institutions. Not much is known historically about the mechanics of social change, particularly at the grass roots, provincial, suburban level. But sociologists have outlined the problems facing those in large cities, particularly of socially ambitious individuals.[21] There are problems of personal contact, of establishing norms of behaviour, the compulsion to differentiate. The churches and chapels, particularly in the middle-class suburbs, provided a possible solution to all of these. Rich and wealthy members of the congregation had social glamour; whilst the philanthropic and socio-religious activities provided a means to a public reputation, and a measure of social differentiation beyond dispute, since a gulf existed between philanthropist and beneficiary. The keynote in social relationships was deference: deference particularly to the élite. The position of the élite was reinforced by social emulation, in the hope that in their turn, those of the middle classes not belonging to the élite could, themselves, command a measure of deference.

Not all the religious denominations were devoted to this élitist tradition. Some sects, notably the smaller ones, engaged in straightforward evangelical activities, in time-honoured tradition. This evangelical religious activity often had little to do with the governing élite. The sects primarily engaged upon it, the Free Methodists, Bible Christians, Methodist New Connexion, Christian Brethren and the Salvation Army, drew their support mostly from much further down the social scale. They made their impact by mass evangelical meetings and conversion spectaculars in the Moody & Sankey tradition, with some success. In the census figures of 1881 the Salvation Army claimed 15·4 per cent of the church-going population in the city. In this way, these smaller sects contributed largely to the strength of the religious sub-culture, without any direct connection with the governing élite.[22] It remained true however, that the very existence of the religious sub-culture contributed, indirectly, to the influence of the élite.

III BRISTOL'S TOWN COUNCIL

The centre of the arena for the daily exercise of the élite's power though, was the town council. The proceedings of the town council in Bristol provide great insight into the city's governing élite. The machinations of the outgoing oligarchy after the 1835 Act had ensured that nothing so vulgar as municipal elections by ratepayers should disturb the political composition or atmosphere of Bristol's town council. As regards the former, the boundaries of electoral wards were drawn up by a barrister who favoured the Tory cause. The representation of the wards, limited by property qualifications made compulsory for prospective councillors, and regulated by the number of burgesses in each ward and the rateable value of their property, reinforced Tory power. Clifton, a Tory stronghold, joined to the city by the boundary extension of 1835, enjoyed by far and away the largest representation per population on the council.

TABLE 4.1 Representation in a sample of Bristol wards, 1860

Ward	Inhabitants	Representatives
Clifton	17,500	9
St Augustine	14,300	6
Bedminster	20,000	3
St Philip & Jacob	25,000	3
St Paul	15,000	3

As regards the atmosphere of town council's proceedings, they much resembled those of an influential gentlemen's club. The old council house was small, with a dark, ornately carved council chamber. The actual numbers of councillors and aldermen was relatively small, being 64 altogether, 48 councillors, 16 aldermen. As for the aldermanic bench, the outgoing oligarchy of 1835 voted in a totally Tory bench and, since election to the bench rested with themselves, the situation was perpetuated without even a single exception until 1893.

The result of all this was to ensure that the town council remained attractive to the city's governing élite. Thus the major transformation of that élite, by the injection of the Liberal, Nonconformist business interest, was clearly revealed by the membership and activities of the

TABLE 4.2
Political parties of Bristol's councillors and aldermen
1880–1910

	1880	1890	1900	1910
Liberal councillors	22	20	24	29
Liberal aldermen	0	0	4	12
Conservative councillors	26	26	28	31
Conservative aldermen	16	16	17	10
Labour councillors	0	2	4	6
Labour aldermen	0	0	0	1
Independent	0	0	0	3
Unknown	0	0	7	0
	64	64	84	92

council. Unlike the multifarious philanthropic and religious institutions, the town council illustrates more precisely the nature of the élite. Obviously, not all members of the élite belonged to the council and not all councillors were members of the élite. But for those of the élite already heavily committed to support the philanthropic, social and religious institutions in the city, the town council had obvious attractions. The growing dimensions of municipal responsibility, could provide an effective extension to their influence.

On the whole, Bristol's town council was parsimonious and extremely conservative in its view of its role. There were not two opposing schools of thought within the council of 'economy' versus 'expansion' such as were found elsewhere.[23] The leaven injected by the Liberal Nonconformists to disturb the *status quo*, was their understanding of the concept of 'social citizenship' which they wanted to see extended within the sphere of the town council's activities. Yet it was to be as a complement to the existing philanthropic and social work, not a substitute for it, or even the spearhead of 'social citizenship' within the city. All that was wanted was to awaken the council to a new understanding of its responsibilities. If the council accepted the idea of an 'urban community', then its actions would be more directly related to the welfare of citizens.

The extension of its powers, particularly in sanitation, public health and education would then be carried out, not according to the minimum laid down by statutory laws, but according to the needs of the community. The meagre income from the rates would be

TABLE 4.3
Occupation of Bristol's councillors and aldermen
1880–1910[25]

	1880	1890	1900	1910
Gentlemen	2	2	3	6
Professionals	8	7	18	19
Merchants and industrialists	28	27	23	20
Shop and tradesmen	12	20	27	34
Labourers	0	0	3	6
Others	16	9	10	7
	64	64	84	92

supplemented by private individuals, to ensure the resources for such a development. 'Social citizenship' could not be further away from 'socialist citizenship', gaining in the 1880s, its first successes in Bradford under the leadership of the Independent Labour Party.[24] 'Social citizenship' was the cause of the Liberal Nonconformists in Bristol, themselves unable to make any headway until the 1880s. The overwhelming power held by the Tories, in view of their complete control of the aldermanic bench, kept the going rough. The first dent in their overall majority was not made until well into the Edwardian period.

However, one of the main features of the town council between 1835 and the boundary extension of 1898, had been the dominance of merchants and industrialists amongst the councillors. In the 1880s they reached their peak of influence and, since most of the Liberal Nonconformist councillors were themselves from the merchant and industrialist group, they began to succeed in persuading their colleagues to accept the challenge of 'social citizenship'.

The dominance of the merchant and industrialist group had been built up largely by a small number of well-known Bristol families, who undertook service on the town council as a supplement to their social, religious and philanthropic roles in the city. Most of this group tended to be Tory and Anglican. But some Liberal Nonconformists also belonged to this tradition. Leading families of this group were the Hare family, who supplied six councillors in the period 1835–97; the Castle and Lucas families, who supplied five councillors; the Bush, Ricketts, Terrell and Wills families, who supplied four;

Tripp, Fry, George, King, Miles, Nash, Vining and Wait, three members.[26]

If all these people had been elected at the same time (which they were not, since their elections, and period of service, stretched from 1835 to 1897) they would have held every seat on the council and half the aldermanic bench as well. This illustrates the level of continuity of personnel on the town council, though, and the influence of a small group of families. There was one family, the Conservative Poole Kings, who provided continuity of service from pre-1835 Municipal Reform Act days until well into the twentieth century. Richard Poole King, member of the old pre-1835 council and then the new, was then followed by his younger brother, W. T. Poole King, who was a councillor himself for over twenty years. Finally, R. J. Poole King's son-in-law was Alderman F. F. Fox, first appointed to the bench in 1865 and still there in 1898 – a past Master of the Society of Merchant Venturers and former High Sheriff of the city.

This state of affairs contributed greatly to a softening of the conflict between the two main political groupings, Liberal and Tory. For a place on the most important municipal committees, membership of the élite and a reputation for social and philanthropic work was more important than party politics. For twenty out of the twenty-seven years between 1870 and 1897, four men shared between them the office of Mayor. Although the Tories had a constant majority, two were Liberal and two Conservatives. All were wealthy, all received knighthoods for their public services. The two Tories were Sir Robert H. Symes and Sir George W. Edwards; the Liberals, Sir Joseph Dodge Weston and Sir Charles Wathen. Biographical details of their lives clearly show the interrelatedness of philanthropic, religious and municipal activities and how their contribution in these areas, helped to place these men amongst the élite.[27] Details from two of them, one Conservative and one Liberal, will suffice.

Sir George W. Edwards was an Anglican and a Tory. He was Mayor 1877, 1878, 1879 and 1887 (Jubilee Year) when he received his knighthood. He was born in 1818, had business interests in tobacco, was a town councillor, then alderman in 1874; Master of the Society of Merchant Venturers 1880; President of the Parent Colston Society, 1868; President of the Grateful Society, 1879; President of the Gloucestershire Society, 1883; President of the Dolphin Society, 1886; Chairman of the Bristol Bishopric Committee;

Treasurer of the Bristol Church Extension Commission; Chairman of the Bristol Central Conservative Association and Bristol South Conservative Association; Treasurer of the Bristol Music Festival Society; President of the Bristol Madrigal Society.

Sir Joseph Dodge Weston, on the other hand, was a Nonconformist and Liberal. But the pattern of his public life was remarkably similar. Born 1822, he was a highly successful businessman, starting from his father's hardware store, then making a fortune in iron and steel, coal and heavy engineering industries. In 1865 he was elected to the Board of Charity Trustees; 1868 he became town councillor; 1870, President of the Anchor Society; 1871, made JP; 1879, President of the Grateful Society; Mayor 1880, 1881, 1882, 1883 and 1884; brought dock debate to a successful conclusion 1884, with purchase of Avonmouth; Chairman Bristol Liberal Federation; Liberal MP; main interests, industrial exhibitions, philanthropic and social work, Bristol Royal Infirmary and the new Children's Hospital, supported free libraries, parks and museums whilst on the town council; died 1895.

With its atmosphere of a gentlemen's club, and a family network amongst members, Bristol's town council appeared to have changed remarkably little over the period 1835 to 1897.[28] But appearances of continuity were deceptive because there is no doubt, that there was a significant change during the late 1860s and early '70s. It was at this time that a small group of Liberal Nonconformist town councillors first appeared on the council. This group, recruited from the well-established Nonconformist religious and philanthropic families, were dedicated to changing the council's views on 'social citizenship'. They were to provide a new level of leadership on the town council which gradually, over the next two decades, was to transform municipal affairs.[29] A measure of their calibre was the fact that of the seven town councillors in the period 1870–97 who were to become MPs six of them were Liberal Nonconformists, most belonging to this new group, first elected in the late 1860s and early '70s.

Lewis Fry became a town councillor in 1866; Joseph Dodge Weston in 1868; Mark Whitwill, on his third try in 1870. W. H. Wills got elected in 1870, and Charles Townsend, 1872, to name the inner nucleus of this new group. Their entry into the town council was, for some of them, the first major step of their public careers, since they were still relatively young when elected. Lewis Fry was 34 (he was 38 when made first chairman of the School Board). Charles

Townsend was 40 when elected, and served on the council continuously until he was 60 (he was 42 when made first President of the Chamber of Commerce after its incorporation in 1874). Mark Whitwill and Weston were slightly older, 44 and 46 respectively, when elected, since they had both had successful business careers first. Their influence on the town council, small at first, grew gradually, as the personnel of the council changed over the next two decades. New councillors still represented the same interests as before, and the key families still usually managed to provide a member. But between 1860 and 1880 there was a complete turnover of membership, an infusion of fresh, if not very different, blood.[30]

The triumph of the small, Liberal Nonconformist group of the late 1860s and early '70s was to inject a new enthusiasm into the town council's proceedings. Their ability to do this sprang from a different appreciation of their role as councillors, compounded largely from their experience in socio-religious work and philanthropy on the one hand, and politics and industrial relations on the other. The former had, by the 1870s, opened their eyes to the problems of the social environment of the city. Lewis Fry, Mark Whitwill, W. H. Wills and Charles Townsend, had all been involved in developing the cultural and educational institutions in the city; the Bristol Museum and Library Society, the Athenaeum, the University College, and they were also deeply involved in missionary work amongst the poor.

Veterans to a man of Sunday School teaching, their activities spilled over to the Bristol City Mission, the Quaker Mission, the YMCA, and the Temperance movement, to name a few of the more important activities flourishing in the late 1860s and early '70s. It was a combination which put this group firmly on the side of the 'civilizing mission' in socio-religious work in the last quarter of the century. In this position, they were determined to use their power and influence on the town council to bring municipal resources to their aid, and were thus ready to respond in a different way from the majority of the council on the interpretation of Acts of social policy and the implementation of permissive legislation. Their status as members of the governing élite gave them influence: influence that they were ready to use to condition the social response of the municipal council to changes in the urban environment.

IV CASE STUDIES OF THE ELITE

Yet for all their desire to change and improve the city these men represented, not the beginning of a new departure, so much as the final flowering of old social traditions. The power of Bristol's élite in the late nineteenth century rested on the organizational base which leading citizens had built, bit by bit, in the course of their philanthropic, religious and social work. To illustrate this are the case histories of the two families who had perhaps, the greatest social and cultural impact on 'modern' Bristol, the Fry family and the Wills family. A brief outline of their major contributions to the city can provide a fitting conclusion to this survey of the 'governing élite'.

In the early Victorian period both the Fry and the Wills families lived in the city of Bristol close to their small factory or shop.[31] The Frys belonged to the Quaker group who had taken over an ancient friary in Broadmead for their meeting place, and the Wills were leading Congregationalists at the Bristol Tabernacle. In the 1830s the Frys moved from their home in Union Street to Clifton, and in that year the subsequently famous name of W. D. & H. O. Wills was used for the first time. Both the family fortunes were to be made in the late Victorian period to the extent that, by the 1870s and '80s, they were amongst the richest families in the city and reached new peaks of affluence in the Edwardian period. With increasing affluence came increasing social and political power.

To take the Fry family first, and to limit the details to the four brothers, sons of J. S. Fry: Joseph Storrs, born 1826; Edward, born 1827; Albert, born 1830; and Lewis, born 1832; the number of activities in which they were involved is quite astonishing. Joseph Storrs was the leading influence behind the family business, and it was thus fairly natural that he should be concerned with the Bristol Chamber of Commerce. But he also found time for much socio-religious work, mainly connected with the Bristol Friends' Meeting House. He taught at the Quaker Sunday School and the Quaker Adult School (becoming the President of the Adult School movement in the city); he supported the social work at the Quaker Mission, local hospitals and medical charities; he spent much time working for young people and boys' organizations, becoming President of the Bristol YMCA in 1877; he was also involved in cultural activities, being Hon. Treasurer of the Bristol Museum and Library Society in 1871; and he had many local social and cultural interests.

Edward left Bristol for London where he became a distinguished barrister and QC and gained a knighthood. In his youth in Bristol however, he had been involved in the socio-religious work of the Quakers in the city and had also been one of the staunch supporters of the Bristol Institution, giving his services as lecturer free. Albert was an engineer; he was also keenly interested in educational and socio-religious work. He was on the original committee formed to consider the plan for a university college in 1873, and from 1882–1903 he was the hard-working chairman of the university council.

The youngest brother, Lewis, was a solicitor. He became a town councillor and an MP and therefore naturally became involved in numerous social and cultural activities in the course of his public life. He was President of the local Law Society and a leading member of the local Liberal Club. His socio-religious work, like his brothers', centred on the Quaker institutions, Sunday School, Mission, organizations for youth, and medical charities. In the cultural field, however, his overriding interest was in education. He was the first chairman of Bristol's School Board, Governor of Clifton College, Pro-Chancellor of the University College, and President of the Clifton High School for Girls. He had cast his vote on the side of education and Liberal Culture from the earliest manifestations of the 'cultural renaissance' of the city, being deeply involved in the creation of the Bristol Museum and Library Society in 1871, serving as one of the first Hon. Secretaries. On the town council, his main concern was with the diffusion of the ideals of Liberal Culture throughout the community up to and beyond the limits allowed by legislation for public health and education. He and his close friend and Liberal fellow councillor, Mark Whitwill, were constant advocates of public parks, swimming baths, sporting facilities and public libraries. He was first elected as MP for Bristol in 1878, and for the next quarter century was one of the middle-class MPs who were gaining ascendancy in numbers in the House of Commons, in the period following the second Reform Act.[32]

The record of the Wills family in public life was just as outstanding. Many members of the family had been active in the religious and cultural life of the city since at least the early Victorian period. The socio-religious activities centred on the Bristol Tabernacle, which ran a Sunday School and a Mutual Improvement Society for young men which was to be the embryo of the YMCA in the city. The Wills family were deeply involved in this, and in the Bristol Athenaeum, the cultural and educational institution for the modest middle classes. They were also concerned in the Bristol Institution and the Bristol Museum and Library Society. Their major impact on the social and cultural scene, however, came with their increasing fortunes in the 1870s and '80s.

Gifts to the city of an organ in the Colston Hall of 1867; a convalescent home, gifts to the university, the donation of an art gallery for the city, money for public libraries, are only some of the items of Wills's philanthropy. The major philanthropist of the family, Sir W. H. Wills, was described by the local press at the time of the opening of the art gallery in 1906, as 'a local Mr. Carnegie'.[33] There had, however, been a significant shift in the course of the late Victorian period in the Wills family relationship with the city of Bristol. The family had acquired, at first, houses in Clifton or outer suburbs like Stoke Bishop, but by the turn of the century the most affluent had all moved out into the counties. From direct, personal involvement in the creation and day-to-day running of socio-religious and cultural activities in the city, there had been a move towards philanthropy through large donations. After all, especially since the formation of the Imperial Tobacco Company at the turn of the century, the personal fortunes of the four leading members of the Wills family was well over £1,000,000 each.

But they were not alone in this trend. The Frys too became involved in spectacular donations to favoured institutions; in both the Frys and Wills case, an excellent example being the university college. Another example was the much publicized fund-raising in the city for a convalescent home to mark the Queen's Diamond Jubilee in 1897, when the major donations came from the Wills, the Frys and the Robinsons, the last being the Nonconformist family with the paper and stationery firm of E. S. & A. Robinson. But in many respects this display of ostentation was far removed from the major family traditions of social service of both the Frys and the Wills, for most of the nineteenth century. The historian of the Wills tobacco firm, Dr Alford, comments on the family that, with the possible exception of Sir W. H. Wills, flamboyance and ostentation were not to their taste. Most of the Wills family over successive generations were profoundly influenced by their Nonconformist outlook both in social relationships and personal behaviour. 'Sobriety and distaste for personal extravagance', he writes, 'which sometimes appeared as petty meanness, are their most apparent personal characteristics.'[34]

In some respects the same could be said of the Fry family. Joseph Storrs Fry, for instance, who remained a bachelor, did not change his style of living as his fortune multiplied. He lived in the same house in Clifton, with a modest household of domestic help and a single carriage. The political outlook of Lewis Fry and W. H. Wills (who became a Liberal MP for Coventry in 1880) developed from a sense of responsibility for those less fortunate than themselves which, as Alford points out, 'was the mainspring of their political radicalism'.[35] It was this which gave them such close contacts with the political organizations of working men in the 1870s. But both the changing nature of political radicalism and the increasing distance between the wealth of the Frys and Wills and the rest of the community by the end of the century, had profoundly altered their social relationships. What had been radicalism and social concern in the 1870s, became much more obviously paternalistic, possibly the result of the fact that both families now employed thousands of workers in their business concerns.

This shift was of fundamental importance to the concept of 'social citizenship', the basis of the élite's response to the modern city. Paternalism replaced co-operation between social groups. The élite could make large donations to civic institutions without any widespread indication of demand from the populace. The city was their city. The city's status, their status. God was on their side. The kind of thinking this could lead to is clearly illustrated by the will of Joseph Storrs Fry, socio-religious worker and paternalistic employer.

> He left small legacies to an enormous number of people in humble circumstances in Bristol whom he must have known in connection with his religious and social work, and legacies – all carefully considered – to everyone employed in whatever capacity, in the works (the Fry firm).[36]

The moral certainty displayed by Fry could only have been built on the substance of power and influence he had enjoyed as a member of the élite in the late Victorian period. It was a 'golden age' for the few who belonged to it, who were ready to combine their own personal success with the successful, social development of their city.

5
MUNICIPAL FACILITIES FOR LEISURE AND PLEASURE

In the course of the second half of the nineteenth century Bristol's town council, along with other similar local government bodies in all substantial towns, found itself providing amenities for citizens which were not primarily utilitarian in the strictest sense of the word. These developments took time to become established, yet the large towns set the pattern which stimulated and encouraged others to follow. The history of the provision of municipal facilities for leisure and pleasure in Bristol were thus most directly influenced by what was happening elsewhere. This chapter will therefore seek to place their development on a comparative basis with other large cities, as well as to explore the growth of these facilities in their local context.[1]

There was a close relationship between the worst known conditions and the response of municipal councils towards improving the physical and social environment. In the early Victorian period, Manchester led the way in the provision of public parks, though Birkenhead, with the horrid warning of Liverpool just across the water, tried to start its own development around a park. Salford had one of the first public lending libraries. Chamberlain's 'Civic Gospel' in Birmingham was launched when, after years of neglect, Birmingham had achieved the unenviable record of the largest number of deaths of any city from diseases transmitted or encouraged by dirt and pollution.

As local bodies acquired ever greater powers, and administrative units were enlarged to encompass whole cities, responsibility for the welfare and recreation of citizens did begin to appear more relevant. Such a change was reinforced by two of the major themes in civic life in the post-1870 era. The first was directly concerned with the developments taking place in public health and education. In both these areas, enormous strides were taken in the period 1868-75 to collect together all previous legislation and to lay down minimum standards clearly, to make these standards compulsory and also uniformly administered by a further reorganization of local government machinery. But the fact was, that improving levels of public health and education was an open-ended process. There was no upper limit, in theory, to what was possible, except knowledge, imagination and resources. In this way, these activities could provide a practical nucleus for further development, such development in its turn providing a test of the degree of change in outlook of the municipal council which implemented it.

This was to contribute greatly to the second theme running through municipal life particularly from the 1870s. Demands for changing attitudes in local affairs bred a civic selfconsciousness, leading to a competitive spirit between municipalities. 'Municipal pride', as a historical factor is difficult to assess. There is no doubt that certain national bodies such as the British Association helped to nurture it; in the British Association's case, by only accepting invitations to hold its annual congresses from cities which had shown concern over the social and cultural environment. But probably as important in the provision of leisure facilities as the competitiveness that this engendered, was the definition of what kind of social institutions constituted an acceptable response. One of the curious facts about the municipal provisions for leisure and pleasure was how little their development owed, in most instances, to popular demand. This was most obvious in the contribution made by town councils towards an urban civilization which was seen largely in terms of the concept of Liberal Culture. This could be measured by acquiring three kinds of cultural institutions, a library, an art gallery and a museum, usually equipped with a lecture theatre. City council after city council struggled to acquire these three institutions.

In some respects, such 'municipal pride' was a hindrance to an imaginative response to the potential the city councils now had, of improving the social environment. But it was influential in reinforcing the ideals of 'social citizenship' and the 'urban community', since the acquisition of these institutions usually depended on the gift of a private benefactor. The introduction of these ideals amongst town council debates could also lead, in time, to a widening of the council's interpretations of its duties in other spheres such as public health and education. This process was gradual, but once responsibility for the welfare of the urban community had been introduced, it was quite logical that a concern to prevent disease could be directed towards a concern to keep people healthy; and similarly a concern to provide the rudiments of an elementary education could develop a concern about the uses that education was put to in adult life. Thus municipal power, municipal pride, the concept of 'social citizenship' and the practical dimensions of local government activity in public health and education provided the framework within which municipalities developed facilities for leisure and pleasure. Fortunately for the majority of the citizens, institutions have a habit of developing outside the framework within which they were nurtured and gaining an independent momentum of their own. The history of the leisure facilities provided by Bristol's town council bears witness to this.

Bristol's record, however, in the provision of parks and open spaces, swimming baths, recreation grounds and gymnasia, public libraries, and all the paraphernalia of the Liberal Cultural ideal, the museum, art gallery and new central library, is neither outstanding nor particularly important in itself. Much more significant was that these developments, multiplied in other cities, presented the most optimistic outlook for the future. The choice before municipal councils at this period was either to carry out the letter of the law, which in the sphere of public health for instance, merely meant observing minimum standards of sewage disposal, water supply, housing regulations, street cleaning, and the removal of nuisances; or to respond to a wider concept of social needs by providing parks, open spaces and swimming baths for the health, recreation and pleasure of citizens. The latter option was to provide a basis for the development of ideas on how to control, in future, the process of urbanization so that it was a socially beneficial rather than destructive force. Control over the physical process of urban growth grew round the nucleus of housing by-laws. This was the core of experience which was to lead eventually to the passing of the first Town Planning Act in 1909. Meanwhile, in the years leading up to this the municipal provision of recreational facilities made an important contribution towards educating both councils and citizens towards accepting the need for such legislation.

Concern about the urban environment, however, had as long a history as nineteenth-century urbanization itself. The housing of the working classes, the pollution of the atmosphere, the congestion of inner central areas, the destruction of the surrounding countryside, the social problems of poverty and crime, highlighted by their concentration in cities, were all developments which drew a response from a wide variety of people. But the response of municipal councils in terms of future planning and control could only be limited. Central areas could be redeveloped to remove congestion and to create a 'civic' centre as in Birmingham.[2] Pressures of density and lack of space could be relieved by suburban development, encouraged by municipal improvements in roads and public transport. Yet there was nothing to stop suburban growth multiplying the same sort of problems formerly confined to the central areas; and there was no regulation of the cycle of growth and decay which followed the ever constant push of the suburban frontier outwards. Urban blight seemed an inevitable corollary of urban growth. Municipal councils had no resources to deal with the problem, but under the impetus of the concept of 'social citizenship' they could try and persuade local landowners on the suburban frontier to supply land, either cheaply or as an outright gift, to be preserved as parkland, a future oasis in a desert of brick.

In this way, the municipal council began to have a certain influence over the physical and social environment of the suburb. Municipal facilities for recreation and leisure, including branch libraries as well as parks and swimming baths, came to be considered as part of the basic social equipment of urban life. They became an essential part of what was considered to be 'civilization', the practical, cultural dimension of what could be provided through 'social citizenship'. Some social reformers, such as Canon and Mrs S. A. Barnett, even went so far as to work out in minute detail the kind of civilization which could be achieved by 'social citizenship'. In their numerous publications, the Barnetts quite often related their whole social philosophy of cultural unity, rich and poor learning to consider one another and working for some common end, to the provision of municipal facilities for recreation and pleasure. Municipal parks could make all suburbs equally pleasant to live in so that the different classes would live in close proximity to each other. Then

> simpler living and higher thinking would bring rich and poor nearer together; ... Libraries, Art Galleries, good music, Univer-

sity teaching, must be as near to a West End as to an East End suburb. There can be no real unity so long as the people in different parts of a city are prevented from admiring the same things, from taking the same pride in their fathers' great deeds, and from sharing the glory of possessing the same great literature.[3]

Not everyone was prepared to follow the Barnetts in all respects. By the turn of the century, however, a remarkable number of rich men had given generously to their cities in pursuit of this ideal; and one or two multimillionaires, such as Andrew Carnegie, had gained a world-wide reputation for their munificence to many different towns. One of Carnegie's larger contributions was of £500,000 in 1904, to Dunfermline (population 30,000), his native city, for civic improvement. This project was to provide a direct link between the municipal provisions for leisure promoted by 'social citizenship' and the evolution of town planning in the future, since both of the people asked to draw up plans on how the bequest should be spent were to be influential in the town planning movement.

T. H. Mawson, the landscape architect, became a lecturer at the first School of Civic Design in Liverpool;[4] Patrick Geddes, a planning propagandist, developed an original approach to planning which proved enormously influential. Geddes's Report of 1904 entitled *A Study in City Development: Park, Gardens, and Culture-Institutes. A Report to the Carnegie Dunfermline Trust* was far more than a plan for physical improvements.[5] In it was outlined in practical detail, how urban life could be transformed and the cultural life of citizens enriched by the provision of municipal amenities, open space, culture institutes, places for meeting and talking, etc. Geddes also emphasized the organic nature of urban growth and therefore the constant need for change and renewal to maintain a healthy environment. Geddes's plan for Dunfermline was not accepted. But his Report was read by many of the young town planners who were gaining increasing influence in the Edwardian period.

I THE DEVELOPMENT OF PUBLIC LIBRARIES

One of the most outstanding contributions to the cultural life of the city was the development of a public library system in nearly all towns and cities through the means provided by permissive legislation, especially the first two library acts of 1850 and 1855. The 1850 Act authorized local authorities in large towns to institute free public libraries; the 1855 Act extended the number of towns which could adopt this measure by lowering the population limit to those of 5,000 inhabitants. The 1855 Act also produced the basic factor affecting the development of the whole system; local authorities were entitled to levy a one-penny rate for the maintenance of public libraries. The penny rate remained statutory from 1855 to the Libraries Act of 1919.[6] To try and find capital for a new branch library and yet maintain existing libraries at an acceptable level, all on a penny rate, was a matter which exercised the finest judgment. It largely explains why the public library movement only really gathered momentum in the last two decades of the nineteenth century when boundary extensions were more frequent, contributing to an increase in income from rates.

Because of such limited financial resources throughout the period 1870–1914, the public library movement had to rely heavily on the support of benefactors. The most outstanding contribution was made by Andrew Carnegie, who set up a trust fund to supply the capital for branch libraries and library development on a national scale. Most large towns managed to find a local benefactor. William Brown of Liverpool was one of the first with a gift of over £40,000 for a new central library for that city, established in 1860. Forty years later Bristol was to gain her new central library as the gift of Vincent Stuckey Lean, a retired banker. A branch library was provided by her local Mr Carnegie, Sir W. H. Wills. The key questions which arise from this are why did the library movement attract this support, and how did its financial situation affect its development?

The first question is closely related to the social ideals of the advocates of a public library system, who were able to convince potential benefactors of their worth. High on any list of those who were influential in this matter were William Ewart, MP for Liverpool in the 1830s and '40s;[7] Edward Edwards, formerly assistant at the British Museum and subsequently the first librarian in charge of the largest library established under the 1850 Act, which was in Manchester;[8] and Thomas Greenwood, who became the public propagandist for public libraries, publishing his monograph *Public Libraries, their Organisation, Uses and Management* in 1886, which subsequently went, almost annually, into new editions. The crucial fifty years spanned by these men from the early 1830s to the 1880s mark the creation, consolidation and promotion of the social ideals of the library movement.

However, whilst the form, purpose and administration of town libraries were being worked out, a new more potent factor was entering onto the scene. This was the development of social concern about the literacy of the urban masses and the lack of 'civilizing' influences on their lives. Politicians and employers, social reformers and educationalists, were all deeply concerned about this problem, with increasing intensity in the last quarter of the century. Gladstone, in the tradition of his namesake William Ewart, was a strong advocate of public libraries and quite clear in his mind what was at issue: 'These libraries, these gymnasia, these museums, this system of public education, they are all instruments with which a war is carried on. War against what? War against ignorance, war against brutality.'[9] Public libraries were pioneering institutions in the fight against ignorance.

But especially from the 1870s, they could no longer be considered to be in the vanguard of the attack. Their role was somewhat changed. Improvements in education were bringing the achievements of universal literacy closer. The challenge now was not ignorance, but 'barbarism'. The uses of literacy was the crucial issue which would make or break the civilization of the future. The social ideals of the public library movement had to be defined in the context of this change. As popular institutions, libraries had to serve popular needs. But in the face of the growing commercial provision of literature for the masses, appealing to basic unrefined emotions, what stand should the public libraries take?

The nature of the threat was spelt out by social reformers concerned with the 'civilizing' process such as Canon Barnett, who quotes the words of a Dr Garnett written in 1902:

> Free libraries were principally established to meet a different condition of things from that which prevails at present. . . . There is at present more half-knowledge than dense ignorance . . . the system of general public instruction ensures at least a minimum of knowledge, though not of taste. Thus, continuance in what

may be termed a semi-civilized condition is not only bad for [the working classes] but presents a danger to the class immediately above them – the danger that, to attract an uninstructed multitude, the standard of literature may be gradually debased. This is a real and serious danger.[10]

Public libraries, once beacons of light in the darkness of ignorance, now were to be transformed to 'citadels of culture', bastions against an incoming tide of mediocrity.

The social ideals behind the library movement thus became, as the movement progressed, ever more complex and the ambivalence of their position remained. They were institutions of Liberal Culture providing a service to be enjoyed by all citizens equally; they were popular institutions responding to demands, even if those demands were for recreation and pleasure. They were also positive social institutions dedicated to the 'civilizing' process, with a useful social purpose in raising standards of taste and behaviour.[11] A leader in the *Western Daily Press*, 11 May 1874, reads:

> No one would object to such an institution [i.e. public library] on the ground that it is not a benefit to the public. The only arguments that we have ever heard urged against free libraries are that they cost the rate-payers something and that if books and newspapers are to be had for nothing, nobody will buy any. Both arguments are utterly fallacious. Where there is ignorance, there is crime; where there is crime, there is cost. An agency that diminishes ignorance, diminishes public outlay and there is not an intelligent ratepayer to be found, we should think, who will say that he would rather pay a penny in the pound to support criminals than he would pay a halfpenny in the pound to support a free library.

They could even, indeed, be considered to be charitable institutions. The Act was adopted in Bristol as a philanthropic gesture of the rich ratepayers bestowing social benefits on the poor. The Library Committee, set up to plan the project, did not dream at first of supplying the city with a public library system. For roughly the first decade after the adoption of the Act, effort was concentrated on opening small branch libraries and reading rooms in poor areas.

Bristol had not adopted the Act back in the 1850s, despite the efforts of an enthusiastic Nonconformist town councillor, Charles Tovey, to interest the council; and in spite of the fact that Bristol had already what was possibly the oldest municipal library in the country, founded by some merchants in 1613. That library had been saved in the eighteenth century by a private library society and was incorporated into the private Museum and Library Society of 1871. Tovey tried to point out that this was municipal property, meant for all citizens, in a monograph he wrote on the subject in 1853. But all his efforts met with apathy.[12] The change that was needed to interest the council in public libraries was the growing importance attached to them as beneficial social institutions, purveyors of wholesome recreation and cultural enlightenment to the poor. By 1874 many leading citizens were in the grip of the 'cultural renaissance'; the meetings for the promotion of a university college were held in that year; and in 1875 the British Association paid its second visit to the city. An element of civic selfconsciousness boosted the public library campaign.

The development of free public libraries in Bristol illustrates several facets of the changing attitude of municipal concern for the recreation and pleasure of citizens. The first was the extreme reluctance of the council to undertake such a role. The Library Committee not only levied a halfpenny rate instead of the penny rate to which it was entitled; but also its first decisions were extremely cautious in the hope of mollifying the opposition. The promotion of public libraries on the council in fact, was largely the work of the small group of Liberal Nonconformist councillors who had entered the council in the late 1860s and '70s. The key leader in the campaign for the adoption of the Act had been Joseph Dodge Weston, and the Library Committee formed to administer the Act included Weston, W. H. Wills, Lewis Fry, Mark Whitwill, Charles Wathen and Charles Townsend, the entire nucleus of that small group. Since they were all also involved in socio-religious and philanthropic work, they could thus all naturally respond to the idea of providing libraries as an extension of philanthropic activity; the only difference being that the financial support should come from rate-paying citizens for the benefit of all.

The first library opened under the Act was in Fry's and Whitwill's ward of St Philip. There was no need to provide a building since the old St Philips Literary Institution, legacy of the 'improving' activities of earlier days, was available. It was opened in July 1876 with a stock of 5,400 books, 4,400 of which were in the lending department, at a total cost of about £2,000.[13] Since the question of finance was always crucial to the library movement, it was fortunate that branch libraries were by far the cheapest of the social amenities demanded from the town council. In view of this, branch libraries were opened in other poor areas; St James in 1877, and Bedminster, 1878. The ratepayers had received their initiation in contributing towards social improvements instead of social necessities.

The experience was to lead to a fresh response to have great repercussions on the public library movement. If, so the ratepayers and residents of the middle-class suburb of Redland argued, in a memorial to the town council in 1881, libraries were a social asset in one area, why not in their suburb too? Public libraries need not be philanthropic institutions but part of the essential equipment of urban life. The town council responded by supplying Redland with a branch library considerably larger and more expensive than any other branch library yet provided. It cost £8,000 for site and building alone, and was stocked with 10,000 books.

At the opening ceremony of the Redland library, 4 June 1885, Joseph Dodge Weston, in his capacity as chairman, made a speech in which he outlined the development of the public library system in the city so far. He pointed out that 'the committee have been animated by the feeling that at the present time, more than formerly, something like this institution and the other free libraries have become an absolute necessity.' Libraries had proved their educational value. 'The books issued ... had not been of one particular class; they related to science, law, politics, commerce, history and last but not least, love (laughter and applause).' Redland library was equipped with 'works on theology, poetry, general literature, physical science, the applied sciences and works of a technical character'. Thus libraries were not only for the poor, they could also serve the needs of 'the clergy, professional men, students, mechanics and those who had just left school'.[14] Weston's emphasis on the range of potential library-users and subject-matter available was still necessary, in spite of the adoption of a library by Redland's middle-class residents. The city librarian, John Taylor, sent constant reports to the local press on such matters to alleviate suspicion and prejudice. He produced one such list as the following, to illustrate to a lady correspondent that public libraries were not only for juveniles.

Selected list of books and number of times borrowed from Redland Library year ending 1886[15]

	times		times
Ruskin's *Ethics of the Dust*	12	German Dictionary	10
Macauley's *England*	40	Michael Field's *Culluvhoe*	25
Freeman's *Norman Conquest*	13	Wood's *Natural History*	24
McCarthy's *History*	24	G. Cumming's *Lady's Cruise*	34
Sidney's *Arcadia*	4	Liddon's *Bampton Lectures*	24
Jameson's *Sacred and Legitimate Art*	20	James's *English Literature*	15
		Alford's *Greek Testament*	3
Spencer's *Biology*	12	Ganot's *Physics* (3 copies)	57
Geikie's *Textbook of Geology*	13		
Flammarim *Astronomie Populaire*	6		

From the opening of the Redland Library, the development of public libraries in the city was largely a question of finance. Little could be done until boundary extensions increased income from the rates. Yet libraries increasingly met a popular response. Thomas Greenwood provides three tables on the use of libraries in Bristol, the number who borrowed and visited for the year ending 1889, the category of books most in demand in 1889, and the occupational status of library-users from figures for one sample month in 1891.

TABLE 5.1
Use of Bristol's libraries for the year ending 31 December 1889[16]

Libraries	Books read on the premises	Issued on loan	Users of Magazine & Newsroom	Borrowers' Tablets issued	Cash taken
Central	21,235	41,633	210,300	670	£63.19. 3
St Philips	83,587	59,123	306,000	881	65. 9. 6
North District	48,187	74,085	202,700	1,049	76.15. 5
Bedminster	32,826	57,770	256,225	539	40. 1. 0
Redland	14,578	129,369	416,400	1,760	145.10. 3
Hotwells	17,832	54,438	160,650	524	59.10.11½
Totals	218,185	416,418	1,552,275	5,423	£451. 6. 4½

TABLE 5.2 Classes of books issued for home reading[17]

Libraries	Theology	Poetry, Drama, etc.	Juvenile Literature	Fiction	Science, Arts, etc.	General Literature	History, Biography, Travels, etc.	Totals
Central	769	3,020	7,947	24,709	2,115	1,135	1,938	41,633
St Philips	629	3,570	15,642	32,641	2,316	1,753	2,572	59,123
North District	1,039	6,376	13,102	47,550	1,889	1,008	3,121	74,085
Bedminster	433	8,314	9,518	36,659	850	358	1,638	57,770
Redland	1,750	7,038	20,278	84,161	4,915	2,406	8,821	129,369
Hotwells	506	3,321	13,728	30,961	1,853	1,161	2,908	54,438
Totals	5,126	31,639	80,215	256,681	13,938	7,821	20,998	416,418

Thomas Greenwood had proved his point that the library system was widely used in Bristol. E. Norris Matthews, city librarian from 1893–1918, struggled to achieve the most possible under the penny rate. As the ex-librarian of the Bristol Museum and Library Society, he was to preside over the transference of the library stock as the Museum became municipal property. He was also cheered by the gift of a new central library from the amateur book collector, Vincent Stuckey Lean, who wished the town council to maintain his private collection in perpetuity. Yet the branch library system grew quite slowly. Reading rooms only were financially possible at Eastville and Stapleton; St George's gained a library as a gift from Sir W. H. Wills; Shirehampton, as a gift from Carnegie; Fishponds and Avonmouth had libraries built by the council. The achievement of the public library movement from the 1870s to 1914 was in many ways quite remarkable in Bristol and in all major cities. But the constant problem of meagre financial resources meant that the movement, for all its vigour, only achieved stunted growth. Shortage of capital for buildings and book stock, low pay and a lack of training for librarians, only slowly being counteracted by the efforts of the Library

TABLE 5.3 Report (from 4th edn) of occupational status of library-users for the four weeks ending 28 April 1891 in Bristol libraries[18]

Occupation	No. of Borrowers	No. of Visitors
Apprentices	554	576
Artisans	2,354	2,792
Assistants	3,567	1,108
Clerks	2,553	1,055
Employers	778	399
Errand Boys	253	604
Labourers	210	692
No Occupation, Males	621	1,017
No Occupation, Females	10,476	504
Professional People	1,183	
Schoolboys	6,904	
Students	1,273	
Total	30,726	

Association, dealt it severe body blows. Without private benefaction it might never have lived, since the resources available to town councils were quite inadequate.

II MUNICIPAL PROVISIONS FOR RECREATION AND SPORT

If libraries were a financial strain however, swimming baths and public parks were even more so, as they were far more expensive. But to offset this, they did have an immediate practical function obvious to all citizens as measures to improve standards of public health. Yet the public health movement was very much a product of the mid- and late Victorian period. Parks and open spaces in towns and cities had a much longer history as part of the English urban tradition, preserved by the comparatively low densities of urban population until the nineteenth century. In early seventeenth-century Exeter, the town council had purchased the Northernhay as a park 'for the private recreation of ye Maior, Aldermen and Comon Councell';[19] whilst in the early eighteenth century an amateur botanist and historian, Dr Deering, chose Nottingham to live in, since, with its orchards, river meadows and large gardens, 'were a naturalist in quest of an exquisite spot to build a town or city upon, could he meet with one better to answer his wishes?'[20] A strict line between town and country was drawn, if at all, only in London, though even there the existence of royal parks and the formal gardens of the eighteenth-century developers obscured the issue.[21]

The creation of a totally 'urban' environment was a phenomenon of the nineteenth century and, for most cities, the late nineteenth century. The anti-urbanism of some middle-class suburbs and the Garden City movement were both important responses to this fact.[22] But they were the means of escape for only a few, rich enough to pay for, or provide, an idealized rural setting. For the majority of those living in large cities, relief from noise, dirt, dust and congestion could only come from the organized preservation of parks and open spaces, as close to the most densely built-up areas as possible. This was the challenge which town councils gradually came to face, particularly in the last quarter of the century. The history of how and why municipalities showed concern over facilities for the health, recreation and pleasure of citizens is as complex as the reasons which drew municipalities into supporting the public library movement. Elements of compulsion were provided by the public health movement.

However, some wider dimensions had been introduced even in the earliest nineteenth-century responses to the problem. In 1833 a Select Committee on Public Walks had reported on the threat to the recreation of citizens of high density development. A further element was provided by the vogue of the early nineteenth century for botanical gardens. In Bristol a zoological and botanical garden was set up privately in Clifton in 1833. In Liverpool a botanical garden enterprise had been established much earlier, in 1802. This botanical garden was taken over by the town council in 1841 to become Liverpool's first nineteenth-century park, and the council subsequently managed to secure the services of Joseph Paxton for the layout and organization of glass houses and specimens.[23] Some burgesses of Liverpool though, were prepared to look beyond the demands of botany, and had shown a lively appreciation of the need for parks and open spaces, especially for the recreation of the lower orders, as early as 1816. They sent a memorial to the town council urging the purchase of land for this purpose and the provision of a 'Floating Bath' in the centre of the city.[24] Such optimistic beginnings however, were completely crushed by the continuously rapid expansion of the city and the soaring level of urban land values. The only force to make municipal councils more than uneasy about the loss of open spaces was the public health movement.

It owed much, in the early Victorian period, to a medical error. It was believed that the dreaded 'zymotic' diseases which proved such a health hazard in large cities were transmitted through pollution in the air. Open spaces were considered to be the only preventive check since they could provide, in one journalist's phrase, 'reservoirs of wholesome air which are sometimes even termed a city's "lungs", a vital aid to the purification of the blood of everyone of the citizens.'[25] As the Blue Books of the early 1840s piled up the evidence of the appalling sanitary conditions in large cities, municipal councils in some of the larger ones could be shocked into action. Manchester acquired three major parks in 1845, paid for by public subscription, plus an exchequer grant. Liverpool on the other hand, did not respond similarly. As a witness said to the Select Committee in 1844,

'the value of land is so great in the vicinity of Liverpool and the Council have had so many demands upon it that they do not feel justified in incurring such an expense.' Some land was bought in 1848, but was not laid out as parkland until 1865 when an Improvement Act was passed and Liverpool, too, gained three major parks.

The problem of cost remained crucial throughout the nineteenth century. A branch library could be stocked and opened for about £2,000 to £3,000 at a minimal level, but a park required a capital expenditure which was much more likely to be in the region of £30,000 to £40,000. Few councils had the resources to cover such investment. In fact, only in the late 1880s and 1890s did it become at all usual for local authorities to foot the bill for the provision of a park, as only then were their incomes sufficiently increased to pay the interest on a treasury loan. One of the most remarkable facts about the provision of public parks and open spaces in large towns is that their cost was largely borne by individuals or private enterprise schemes. The role of the local benefactor on the physical environment of the city had never been greater.

The reasons why so many towns found benefactors to give land and money for the recreation and pleasure of citizens were varied, the arguments of the public health movement being only one factor. Local conditions and the individuals concerned were usually decisive in determining how any one town responded to the situation. In Cardiff before 1835, when the town was still quite small (10,000 in 1841), the local council of the town was dominated by the Lord of the Castle, the Marquis of Bute.[26] The town people were allowed to use the castle grounds, Castle Green and the area now known as Cardiff Arms Park, which was probably the town's common land. During the period of rapid expansion in the next thirty years, these rights were withdrawn from the public; Cardiff Arms Park becoming a sports ground closed to the public in 1875.

However the Bute family remained concerned about the welfare of citizens, providing a small botanical garden for public use at their own expense. They then, in 1887, politely forced three other local landlords to join them in contributing to a gift of 121 acres for a huge park at Roath. By the end of the century the Marquis was ready to part with the central Cathays Park on the condition that the area should be used for municipal and public buildings to be set in a 'park' environment. The building of a new town hall, assize court, municipal offices, technical schools and university college, all amongst the lawns and trees of Cathay Park, made Cardiff a shining example of the 'City Beautiful' movement in Britain.[27] Birkenhead, founded hopefully on the same ideal with a park in its central area, had no Marquis of Bute to control the use of land; and the provision of park acres per population dwindled from the very good figure, for nineteenth-century towns, of 159 people per acre in 1861 to 404 people per acre in 1891.

Control by local landlords was thus of vital importance in some towns. Birmingham benefited greatly from Adderley Park opened in 1846, and Calthorpe Park opened in 1851, which were leased to the council by their owners, C. B. Adderley (later Lord Norton) and Lord Calthorpe.[28] Yet other towns managed to hold onto their common land, such as Plymouth, where the Hoe had been a place of public recreation from time immemorial. Some of the northern towns preserved common land outside the town, Crankeyshaw Common near Rochdale being a case in point. An alderman on the Rochdale Council, Alderman Duckworth, was the principal benefactor, contributing £800 in 1877 to the cost. Bradford raised money for its early parks by public subscription. Having acquired Lister Park in 1870 in this fashion, thirty years or so later a benefactor stepped forward, the Baron Masham, with a gift of £47,000 to build a public hall in the park in memory of Dr Edmund Cartwright, inventor of the power loom.[29]

Such a development was an indication of the fact that gradually public parks had become far more deeply identified as a measure of 'social citizenship' and local benefactors were encouraged by the strengthening of municipal pride. In the absence of alternative financial resources to provide for these amenities, these factors had to be given the strongest support possible. In this context, the royal family did sterling service for the public park movement. Some cities, reluctant to take on the responsibility of a park, did so in the jubilee year of 1887, Bristol being a case in point, gratefully accepting land from a local landowner, Sir Greville Smythe.[30]

Such a step marked a degree of change in social attitudes on the part of the town council which was quite remarkable. It was the culmination of growing pressures for change which developed from the public health responsibilities of the town council as a sanitary authority. The extent of the change was evident in the provision of swimming baths as well as public parks, which had initially been a measure to encourage the working classes to be clean. When the Baths and Washhouses Act was passed in 1846, few major towns had an adequate and constant water supply, and no washing facilities were provided in any homes, apart from those of the rich. Even so, not all towns adopted the Act, and Manchester's town council, so prompt in responding to the need for more open spaces, did not establish a Baths and Washhouses Committee until 1876. Bristol's council had been scared into adopting the Act and providing a baths and washhouse at Broad Weir in the wake of the cholera epidemic of 1849, but although the water supply for the poorer areas of the city remained totally inadequate, the cholera scare of 1866 was too mild to get a response.[31] A second baths and washhouse was not provided until 1870.

In this second project however, a new element was introduced. The 1870 baths at Mayor's Paddock were equipped with a first- and second-class swimming bath.[32] The provision of such facilities was no break with the utilitarian public health purpose of such institutions. Citizens, though mainly small boys, had been used to bathing as a method of getting clean, using local facilities where available. In Nottingham they swam in the Trent; in Bristol it was the much used Floating Harbour, source of the local water supply and repository for the neighbourhood's sewage. However, in the 1870s, events began to outstrip the strictly public health attitudes of the Baths and Washhouses Committee. The sport of swimming began to be taken seriously.[33] Local swimming clubs were formed and competitions held between them.[34] Meanwhile the improvement of the city's water supply was marked, and thus the utilitarian need of baths and washhouses correspondingly less. Houses still had no bathrooms, but laundry work could be done at home. Bristol's Baths and Washhouses Committee, in common with those in other councils, had to make a decision about the direction in which they should proceed and they had to take the full council along with them in that decision.

What happened, was that swimming baths for the sport of swimming were considered to be a proper object for the municipal contribution to the recreation of citizens. It was an expensive decision to take. Even the 1870 utilitarian public health institution at Mayor's Paddock had cost over £14,000, roughly a fifth of the total annual income of the council. The man who persuaded Bristol's council to adopt the new approach was Mark Whitwill, a member of the Baths and Washhouses Committee and the Sanitary Authority, so he was well placed to base the case for further expansion on public health arguments. But he made no attempt to do so. Instead, he issued a challenge to the council that caring for the health of the community meant caring for the physical health of the individual. This meant not only helping all citizens to be clean, but also providing facilities for physical exercise and recreation. There was some Conservative opposition because of the prospect of further heavy expenditure, but such was the eloquence of the Liberals that the opposition was overruled. Indeed, the town council became swept away with a tremendous burst of enthusiasm for this new conception of their duties, and plans were immediately put in hand for a swimming bath to be built according to this new approach.

The project was the Jacob's Wells Swimming Bath of 1884, and the enthusiasm for it was reflected by the fact that no expense was spared on the building.[35] The first plans were so lavish that a few modifications, in the cause of economy, were made. But the mood of the council was not for economy, and the building remains as a living witness of the momentous change in attitude of the council towards its social responsibilities. The highly decorated façade of the building, with the liberal use of stone and the municipal coat of arms carved in stone and surrounded by a pediment, was a monument to municipal pride, evidence that the council's response was more than a philanthropic gesture, it was a fulfilment of the ideal of 'social citizenship'. Gradually all large towns came to accept this new approach to the municipal provision of swimming baths. Even Manchester joined the league in 1906 when the Victoria Baths were built at the cost of £59,000, an extravagance the council was to rue. Soon cities of the second rank in size gained public swimming baths, such as Cheltenham in 1887 as part of the Jubilee celebrations; Exeter in 1893, and Southampton in 1892. A final point of significance is that such facilities were not confined to the working-class areas. In Bristol, when two private baths, the Victoria Baths, Clifton, and the Royal Baths, Kingsdown, came onto the market in 1897, the Committee decided to buy them, 'being of the opinion that if the baths were closed, demands might be made on the inhabitants of the localities in which they are.' Swimming baths for the sport of swimming had become accepted as necessary social equipment for the recreation of citizens of all suburbs.

That such facilities should be provided by the municipal council from the rates was a breakthrough indeed. But the way had, to some extent, been prepared by the activities of committees responsible for parks and open spaces. It was one thing to acquire some land as a city's 'lung', but unless it was already a natural beauty spot, there was the considerable problem of how to administer it for the maximum benefit of the citizens. In most parks two lines of development were followed. One was based on the tradition of the botanical garden. The park was used as a naturalists' museum containing rare botanical specimens carefully marked, the whole park often landscaped professionally by a landscape gardener.[36] The second was to use the land for physical recreation with the provision of facilities for numerous sports. In this way municipal councils had already found themselves providing facilities for the physical recreation of citizens. In fact, demand for such facilities, particularly the demand for football and cricket pitches, gave a considerable boost to the campaign for public parks. Mark Whitwill and Lewis Fry, for instance, campaigned constantly for a park for the eastern suburbs of the city from 1877–87. The land finally procured by the council for this purpose had been used all this time, informally, for football games. When it became a park, Eastville Park, the Bristol Rovers, one of Bristol's more successful professional teams of the 1890s, claimed to recruit their best players from the boys who played in the park.

Bristol's main sports ground was the Downs, preserved in 1862 by a special Act of Parliament by the Society of Merchant Venturers and the town council. The Downs had been saved from the speculative builder as an area of outstanding natural beauty. The wide open spaces proved excellent for all forms of team games. Fresh municipal responsibilities however, were to contribute directly to the facilities provided in parks and open spaces. The unemployed had always been a concern of the Lord Mayor, and circulars concerning work promotion schemes had been sent to municipalities since the 1890s. In 1905 the unemployed Workman's Act authorized local authorities to set up, on an official basis, schemes for providing work. After road building, improving the parks seemed a worthy and beneficial objective for this increased burden on the rates. In Bristol's three main parks, open-air swimming baths were built, a boating lake provided in Eastville, and bowling greens and tennis courts in the others. An outstanding example of the intensive use of land for physical recreation was provided by the ninety-acre Platt Fields park in Manchester. It contained 46 tennis courts, 2 bowling greens, 9 cricket pitches, 13 football pitches, a boating lake and a paddling pool. For those too old, infirm, or just unwilling to take strenuous exercise, music was provided in the summer evenings from the bandstands to be found in many parks.

III CONTRIBUTION OF MUNICIPAL EXPERIENCE TO A GREATER DEMAND FOR TOWN PLANNING

This all conjures up a pleasant image of the wider possibilities and experiences now open to those destined to live in large cities. An effort of imagination had been responsible for these developments as few town councils in the mid-century years had considered it their duty to try to improve the social environment of their city. But for all the effort made, the reality fell far short of an ideal which was based on touching the lives of all citizens. Open spaces near the most densely populated areas either did not exist or were far too expensive for municipal councils to purchase, should a benefactor fail to come forward. The majority of Bristol's 387,000 inhabitants had only the sporting facilities of three parks to meet their needs. Sports facilities for all who wanted them was an impossibility.

There were several ways out of this dilemma which were pursued with varying degrees of vigour by municipal councils. The first was to try and find small pockets of land in central areas, even burial grounds, which could make a little open space available in the immediate vicinity of densely built-up areas. There was a strong public health motive in the early days to promote such facilities, as over-full burial grounds in large cities were established as notorious health hazards. In fact, in some towns the control of this problem was the stimulus which brought councils to recognize their responsibility for open spaces, as the history of the Parks & Cemeteries Committee of Bradford suggests. Great importance came to be attached to these small areas of open space as those concerned with the problem of the physical environment of cities became aware of the impossibility of establishing large parks where they were needed most. Canon Barnett wrote in his pamphlet 'The Ideal City' that it was the duty of the municipal council to provide public parks so that they made 'the heart of the city as pleasant for residents as a suburb.'

Patrick Geddes, in his method of urban renewal which he termed 'conservative surgery', placed great emphasis on the need for small spaces in the densely populated areas, where children could play and mothers met briefly in the course of their daily rounds.[37] A succession of fortuitous circumstances however, rather than conscious planning, brought the attention of Bristol's town council to the preservation of small open spaces. Brandon Hill had been ancient common land, belonging since earliest times to the people; and the eighteenth-century developers had left enclosed open spaces such as Queen's Square as part of their urban design. In the nineteenth century, space was only rescued haphazardly. The Rev. Wilson of Clifton College saved the small space of wasteland in St Agnes Parish, and the council laid it out as a park. Similarly, small gardens at Cotham and Mina Road were saved. More controversially, the Haymarket, site of fairs and local revelries, was eventually taken over by the council after a long struggle caused by complaints about public behaviour during the visits of the fairs. These were all important gains for the preservation of open space in the city, but the overall vision of Barnett or Geddes was certainly not taken as a plan for action. The council was prepared to take over small areas when they were offered, but not pursue a policy of acquiring or creating small spaces where they were needed most.

The record of Bristol's town council in the provision of larger open spaces was similar. Existing parks were taken over as the boundaries extended, but there were no new major developments. Other councils sought new ways out of the dilemma of deteriorating proportions of open space to population (as far as resources permitted), the largest cities taking the lead. Liverpool, for instance, compensated for the lack of space within the city's boundaries by purchasing country estates, sometimes with mansion included, in the neighbouring countryside. Three estates were bought before the First World War, Calderstones Park, the Harthill Estate and Bowring Park.[38] This way out of the dilemma depended largely on improvements in transport for citizens, which did not occur on any great scale until the inter-war period; and such estates were hardly suitable for increasing the sports facilities for which there was a growing demand. This brought municipal councils back to considering, as the city boundaries pushed inexorably outwards, the use of space within the boundaries. What was needed was control over suburban development so that some open spaces could be preserved. In this way, municipal recognition of the need for public parks came to be added to the growing support for the town planning movement.

The town planning movement was most directly concerned with the major problem of the social environment, housing. However, facilities for leisure and pleasure became incorporated into visions of the future. J. S. Nettlefold, member of Birmingham's municipal council and first chairman of the council's first housing committee in 1901, wrote:

> Millions of English town children have no playground within practical reach except the streets. The young men find it extremely difficult to obtain suitable cricket and football fields.... Each year makes it harder for men to get allotments on which they can not only get rational enjoyment, but also materially increase the family food supply. The women have no place to go out to where they can enjoy an odd hour, and often find no better choice than the front door step, or the nearest public house. We cannot, by legislation, make people healthy and happy, but we can give our town dwellers fewer temptations to irrational excitement, and more opportunities for beneficial enjoyment than they have at present. We can, if we will, let light and air into our towns; we can, if we will, make the most and not the least of the sunshine.[39]

Nothing achieved by Bristol's town council alone would have warranted the same kind of optimism and foresight. Yet the public parks movement, in which Bristol had played its part, had opened the way to a new vision of the future. It provided an image of the ideal which was carried to its ultimate development in the industrial village of Bournville, ringed with parks and generously supplied with open spaces and a village green. It was the contribution of private benefactors, steeped in ideals of 'social citizenship'.

However, in some ways, and on a much humbler level, ordinary citizens in large cities were gaining more space. This had little to do with 'social citizenship' and everything to do with regulations on housing, street widths and traffic circulation. Nettlefold was hostile to street playgrounds and in favour of parks, open spaces, grass, trees and flowers. But regulations did mean wider streets, away from main thoroughfares and subject only to light traffic, which could serve as relatively safe playgrounds for children and meeting-places for adults. This was a direct result of municipal intervention in regulating the lay-out of cities, which was little regarded at the time and has been subsequently ignored. Yet it was a real improvement in environmental conditions. Private benefactors of parks and open spaces gained all the publicity. But the public measures of by-law regulations were quietly transforming the immediate environment of many citizens.

The role of the municipal councils in promoting the health and welfare of citizens was thus at a turning point in the years up to the First World War. As municipalities became caught up in the town planning movement and the problems of housing, the old ideals of 'social citizenship' began to fade. The ideal of the future was very much the garden suburb, though the provision of parks and open spaces in this context had none of the social and moral overtones of the public park movement of the nineteenth century. Without such overtones, the impetus towards providing municipal facilities for recreation and pleasure became arrested. It had relied too heavily on private benefactors and the philanthropic spirit, and a concept of the 'best' influences of civilization as defined by a small educated minority. Without these to carry the vision forward, future development had to await the formulation of a new sense of direction, more broadly based on the aspirations and demands of the people.

Meanwhile, what was left was the legacy from the past. By 1914 the development of municipal facilities for the education, recreation and pleasure of citizens had been made into a composite whole, which reformers and planners understood as 'urban civilization'. They knew now what it was, and it gave them hope for the future. T. C. Horsfall, a leading propagandist for town planning and President of the Manchester Citizens' Association expressed this when he said:

The town of the future – I trust the near future – must, by

means of its schools, its museums, and galleries, its playgrounds, parks and gymnasia, its baths, its wide, tree-planted streets and the belt of unspoilt country which must surround it, bring all inhabitants in some degree under the *best* influences of all regions and all stages of civilization, the influences of which, but not the best influences, contribute, and have contributed, to make our towns what they are.[40]

6
THE 'CIVILIZING MISSION' TO THE POOR

Paralleling the attempts made by the municipal council to improve the social environment were numerous voluntary organizations with the same objective. These voluntary organizations nearly all had one feature in common: they relied heavily on the support of religious bodies; and they had one common objective: they hoped to eliminate those hostile elements to be found in an urban environment which prevented the urban poor from leading Christian lives. In the late Victorian period there was, thus, a widespread attempt by socio-religious institutions to provide wholesome influences on the lives of the poor, on adults and children alike. It was a very remarkable attempt because those engaged upon it were pioneering investigations of just what were the 'hostile' elements to be found in large cities, and what was the extent of social needs of the urban poor, over and above the problems of poverty and destitution. In the search, these socio-religious organizations found themselves engaged on a 'civilizing' mission to the poor, directed largely towards improving the facilities and activities available for leisure.

Not all religious denominations became caught up in this movement. By the 1860s, there was already a noticeable difference developing in evangelical and missionary work between different sects. On the one hand, the old fashioned missionary, exhortation method was given a new lease of life through mass evangelical meetings such as those of the Americans, Moody and Sankey, and this tradition remained the mainstay of the response of the smaller evangelical Free Churches to the problem of the unconverted urban poor. The old established and larger Nonconformist sects however, together with some of the more socially concerned elements in the Church of England, had already had their fill of evangelizing by this method.

THE 'CIVILIZING MISSION' TO THE POOR

The Congregationalists and Baptists had founded the Bristol City Mission in 1826, and the Wesleyans the Inner City Visiting Mission in 1828. The Anglicans had made their evangelical effort through the Diocesan Visiting Society, and the Unitarians had a Domestic Mission in 1839. Their success had been very limited. They were therefore much more willing to consider the influence of social conditions which had so obviously militated against all their efforts.

This willingness was further reinforced by a growing sense of responsibility amongst leading members of these religious groups who, as town councillors and philanthropists, were being made aware of the rapid growth and social changes taking place in the city. Their knowledge of these changes was small. Suburban segregation tended to minimize contact between different social groups. But ignorance at least freed the imagination from the horror of the overwhelming facts of poverty and enabled experimentation to take place on many different levels. The ideas developed were not often entirely new. The nucleus for institutional growth had already been established. Sunday schools, elementary schools, Bible classes and adult education, ragged schools and reformatories, visiting societies and philanthropic work and, above all, the Temperance movement, had pioneered fresh responses to social conditions from the late eighteenth and early nineteenth centuries. What was new in the development from the 1860s, was the growing emphasis given to the need positively to attract people to organizations and institutions by offering them something more tangible than salvation in the next life; and the growing desire to foster communities and community spirit in both the poor areas and the rapidly growing new areas of the city.

This latter concern for community unleashed new ideas on the desirability of developing social facilities in each district as an essential part in building up a local community. Further, the provision of facilities and the organization of activities provided a means of contact between rich and poor which contributed, in a more personal way than merely municipal facilities, to nurturing a wider concept of community, one that extended to the city itself. These ideas were the formative influences which led to a broadening in the scope of philanthropic and religious work. The process was slow and uneven. In the 1860s, evidence of the change was slight, largely confined to specific movements like the Temperance movement and the YMCA which, in different ways, were both aiming at transforming social behaviour. Even in these movements the understanding of social conditions in cities and recognition of the need to counteract them were slow to develop.

The Temperance movement was helped by the fact that the attack on drink brought the evangelical vision of heaven and hell firmly down to earth. Heaven was the realization of a private dream of a secure home, family life, sobriety, religion and happiness; Hell, the public disgrace of drink, the public house, vice, dissipation and despair. The shift from the Salvationist Life Hereafter, to Life Here and Now, did much to concentrate temperance workers' minds on the problem of urban living. The significance of this move was to become more apparent as the Temperance movement was taken up by greater numbers of religious sects and socio-religious workers in the city. The effect was felt both administratively, in the way the movement became organized, and in temperance workers' understanding of the 'social evils' they were up against.[1] As far as the former went, it was realized that a single, central organization for Temperance in the city was useless in view of the size of the city and the extent of the problem. If you want to reach people, then you have to go and meet them, in their own localities, on their own street corners. The Band of Hope Union was introduced into the city in the 1850s and district branches set up, so that by 1871 there were 31 Bands in the city; by 1881, 43; and by 1891, 55.

Yet this type of organization brought in its train further problems. Setting up a Band was a matter of conviction and an adequate supply of socio-religious workers and resources. Its continued existence, however, required support. With district organization, that meant building up local support. The usual long-term method used by evangelical religious sects had been to reach out for the children and set up Sunday Schools. The temperance workers followed this pattern and set up Junior Bands of Hope. But for the temperance worker, this investment was too slow and there was no guarantee that even the most model Junior Band of Hope member would be able to withstand, on reaching adulthood, the lures and pleasures of the Demon Drink. Social life, after all, in most poorer districts centred on the public house which, apart from its alcoholic attractions, acted as a headquarters for all kinds of social and political activities.

Temperance workers had to face this challenge by creating teetotal institutions which could fulfil these functions and then expend their energies on making these institutions more attractive than the pub. It was obviously an expensive and difficult task and nothing spectacular was done in Bristol until the Quakers, always the pioneers in Bristol's Temperance movement, set up a coffee house, the British Workman Coffee House, in 1874.[2] Since no one could pretend that coffee had the same attraction as alcohol, a number of activities were organized at the coffee house, clubs formed, lectures held, billiard tables acquired, and any other piece of equipment for recreation and entertainment thought suitable by the managing committee.

Not all temperance workers were either able or willing to follow the example of the Quakers. Some Bands or Temperance groups, particularly those run by the smaller evangelical Free Churches, still concentrated on an evangelical approach; mass meetings, salvation and signing of the pledge. Yet, even these groups had to find somewhere close at hand where they could act out their rituals. In the mid-century years Bristol began to acquire a number of small, district Temperance Halls, where such meetings could take place, and on the evenings when there were to be no exhortations to sign the pledge, it seemed natural and sensible to provide some kind of entertainment to sustain the resolution of the converted. Penny readings, spelling bees, lectures and small musical entertainments came to be organized with increasing frequency in the winter seasons of the 1860s.

Since these activities met with an overwhelming response, it soon became obvious that the temperance workers in their desire to deliberately change social behaviour, had tumbled on social needs, hitherto unexplored. The need for entertainment and recreation even amongst the very poor, and the need for each locality to have a hall or meeting-place which could be used for social, cultural and political activity, a matter of considerable importance in an era of direct communication. This pattern pioneered by the temperance workers, of a group of reformers setting out to meet a social evil as they saw it and in the process uncovering a social need, was to be repeated again and again in the course of the socio-religious work of the late nineteenth century. The temperance workers were the pioneers, but in many ways they were the most limited. After all, if you start from the premise that you are fighting Drink, there is a limit to the range and type of activities which appear relevant.

I THE 'CIVILIZING MISSION' AND THE YMCA IN THE MID-CENTURY YEARS

There was one institution, however, the Bristol branch of the YMCA, which did have cultural pretensions from its inception, and was an important, formative influence on socio-religious work, bridging as it did, the gap between the cultural and religious life of the city. Belief in the importance of reaching and training a group of young men had at its core the idea that such a group, formed from amongst the lower orders, could become social and religious leaders. As C. B. P. Bosenquet wrote in 1868,

> Young Men's Societies in the last 20 years had done much good ... [they] gave their members opportunities for self-improvement, and they, in their turn, taught in Sunday Schools and engaged in lay work such as night and ragged schools and penny banks.[3]

The Bristol branch of the YMCA was formed by the amalgamation of two such Bible classes and Mutual Improvement societies for young men, run by Nonconformist chapels. The problems for the promoters of the YMCA, however, were two-fold. They had to be sure of the kind of training they wished to offer their recruits, and they had to attract members. This was to lead to an inherent tension in the organization. Because of this, the history of the YMCA in its early years in the city (it was established in 1853) provides an insight into the forces shaping both the views of the socio-religious workers on their role in the cultural life of the city, and the kind of response that attended their efforts. Since these forces have implications for the whole development of the civilizing mission to the poor, it is worth looking at the early history of the YMCA more closely.

Perhaps one of the most typical features of the YMCA was that it was not meant for the very poor. The original association, formed in London in 1844, had been a development of the activities of the Metropolitan Early Closing Association and was aimed at the leisure hours of clerks and shop assistants. Those responsible for forming the Bristol branch had similar affiliations. Leading Nonconformists, particularly the Wills family and leading laymen of the Congregationalist Bristol Tabernacle, had been concerned with the Early

Closing Association in the city. These people had also been active in the organization of the Bristol Athenaeum, the poorer man's Literary and Philosophical Club, part of the Nonconformist contribution to the cultural life of the city. With the YMCA, however, there were several significant shifts in emphasis. First and foremost, the YMCA was Nonconformist, whereas the Athenaeum had had a semblance of being a non-sectarian institution. Second, the YMCA was a crusading, active body aimed at persuading people to change their views, become members, etc., whilst the Athenaeum had merely been a facility available to those who chose to belong to it. Third, the YMCA was to bring churches and chapels into the sphere of the cultural life of the city through its educational work and its concern for elevating every aspect of the lives of its members.

It was a very positive approach, part, perhaps, of the Nonconformist bid to control the social development of the future. As Robert Leonard said at the opening ceremony of the Bristol branch in 1853, 'As knowledge advances in the youthful mind, the mere acquisition of it creates an appetite for further attainments and this craving should be met by all who feel interested in the well-being of our social system.'[4] The young men of the YMCA would promote Nonconformist religion; epitomize the Nonconformist way of life, habits, manners, attitudes; act as a leaven amongst their contemporaries to produce a society which respected Nonconformist values.

This perhaps sounds little different from the message of the evangelical missions of the Free Churches. But the vision of the founders of the YMCA was of cultural development within this religious framework. The future role of the young men of the association was not only to lead, but also to transform, first themselves, and then, through activities organized by themselves, numbers of people hitherto unreached. The YMCA was organized initially in 1853 more like a Literary and Philosophical Institute with a strong emphasis on educational facilities in spite of the fact that it had grown from two mutual improvement Bible classes run by chapels.

It was virtually a Nonconformist liberal arts college with a circulating library of over six hundred volumes on Christian, scientific, philosophical and historical literature and regular classes on subjects as diverse as French, Hebrew, Greek, drawing, mathematics, English grammar and vocal music. Later, classes on Latin, arithmetic, photography and writing were added. Supplementary to this there was a larger general group designed to attract all members, which started as a conversation class on literary and scientific subjects and became an influential literary society, formed to affect mutual improvement by 'essays, analyses of literary works, formal discussions, general conversations, occasional recitations'. Zeal for cultural diffusion under the aegis of Nonconformist control spilled over from the activities for the young men to an attempt to reach the general public straight away. A series of public lectures was held annually during the 1850s and '60s.

On a national level this was part, no doubt, of the growth of Nonconformist power and influence, shown most clearly in the rise of the Liberal party. The local fortunes of the Bristol YMCA owed its continued support and development to the remarkable loyalty of the group of men responsible for its foundation. Certain leading Bristol families, particularly the Wills, Frys, Leonards and Oatleys gave much money and personal service to the Association for a period spanning the first half-century of its existence and beyond. It was a sustained effort and the personification of devoted service for the cause was provided by the secretary of the Association, James Inskip, followed by his son, who between them served the Association from 1869–1909 and 1909–53. Since these were the families being integrated through this period into Bristol's social and cultural élite, the fortunes of the YMCA take on a new significance.

In many ways the 1850s was a honeymoon period. The idea was new, the experience gained both at the Bristol Athenaeum and the different denominational Bible classes, close and relevant, and views on suitable activities could be liberal. By 1855 the library had even been made available to ladies for a charge of six shillings a year, though there were already 600 male subscribers; whilst the public lectures were usually very well attended. This was not so remarkable, since the choice of subjects for the lectures was mainly free from heavy religious bias. The primary aim appears to have been to educate, elevate and refine the listeners, which must have been a welcome relief from evangelical moral homilies. A typical example was the occasion of a lecture on 'Beauty' given by a lecturer from London to a packed working-class audience at the Broadmead Rooms. On the platform sat not only the founder members of the Association, but also clergy and ministers, both Anglican and Nonconformist, an indication that here at least, cultural diffusion need not be a sectarian battleground. A list of YMCA public lectures of 1854 with the place of origin of the lecturers, is as follows:

Lectures: YM Institute		Lectures: Broadmead Rooms	
Subject	Lecturer from	Subject	Lecturer from
Robert Boyle	Frome	Beauty	London
Sir Walter Raleigh and his times	Devizes	Vindication of Uncle Tom's Cabin	London
Evening on the Continent	Bristol	J. Milton, Man, Statesman, Poet	Bristol
Work of fiction	Bristol	Evening with Cowper	Bristol
Visit to Waldenses	Bristol	Balance of Creation	Manchester
Public Spirit	Bristol	Individualism	Islington
Life and Writings of H. Kirk White	Newport	The Crusaders	London
Life in England 100 years ago	Bath	The age we live in and its demands on the	
A week at Geneva	Bristol	Church of Christ	Birmingham

In the 1860s, this period unhappily drew to a close. By then it had become apparent that cultural diffusion under religious control could not proceed whilst the urban working classes in ever growing numbers, with the increase in the city's size, were becoming indifferent to religion. The confidence of the YMCA committee wavered. Perhaps after all, the most important thing was to win new converts for the chapels, now feeling the pinch of outward social migration. The YMCA's support had been based largely on the inner city chapels. The energies of the young men were directed to the work of salvation and in place of reading philosophical works, they would be found in the streets or their places of work busy handing out the 80,000 tracts that the YMCA received from the philanthropist George Müller and the Dublin Weekly Tract Society.

Hardly surprisingly, membership began to fall. The annual public lectures still continued however, though the subjects were either religious or moral and, with one exception, were all delivered by clergymen. In 1867 the Colston Hall (of which the Wills family again were part benefactors, with others) was opened and the lectures could thus be heard by much larger audiences. People still came, and a typical lecture of this period was one on the subject of the 'Sins, Dangers and Temptations peculiar to Youth', which drew a capacity

The first list of lectures given at the Colston Hall was as follows:

Subject	Lecturer	Lecturer from
Fire and Water	Rev. W. Arnot	Edinburgh
Mendicity	Rev. J. B. Owen	Chelsea
Nature of Life	Dr Edwin Lankester	London
Tongues in Trees	Rev. A. Raleigh	London
John Bunyan	Rev. N. Haycroft	Leicester
Our Bards	Rev. J. Gutteridge	Preston
Minor Morals	Rev. R. MacMaster	Bristol
The First Crusade	Rev. J. D. Brocklehurst	London
The Philosopher's Stone	Rev. J. P. Chown	Bradford

audience (hundreds were turned away) and must have gained in added impact when the hall keeper turned off the gas lights by mistake so that the only light was the oil lamp of the speaker in the dark, packed hall.

On the whole, though, the 1860s was a period of low ebb in the fortunes of the YMCA. There was enough momentum left in the organization in 1861 for a full-time salaried officer to be appointed to run the Association, yet in 1862, a loss of £20 was made on the public lectures. The major supporters of the YMCA did not lose their resolve however, and in 1863, when no. 4 St James Square was offered to the Association as a permanent site for the bargain price of £500, the President, W. D. Wills, and George Thomas both contributed £200, and Messrs Leonard and Budgett £50 each to make the purchase possible. In spite of this, YMCA policy seemed to lack the certain sense of direction it had displayed in the early years.

II SOCIO-RELIGIOUS WORK IN THE 1860s

In this it was not unique, but a sensitive indicator of the uncertainty amongst socio-religious workers in that decade. The 1851 census had revealed the size of the problem of the unconverted urban masses. Some sects redoubled their evangelical mass-meeting activities in an attempt to reach out to them. Others, with much experience in social and religious work, were not so sure. The Quakers, particularly, largely responsible for the introduction of the Temperance movement into the city, were concerned. Long years of work in the temperance cause had shown that it was one thing to sign the pledge in the emotion-drenched atmosphere of a mass rally, quite another to stick to it, days, weeks, years afterwards, through good times and bad.

In the light of this understanding, the Quakers began to move forward, not because they had a new theoretical approach to hand, but because the logic of their experiences pointed in a certain direction and they were bold enough to take it. The Quakers were to be the pioneers in Bristol of the broadening of the scope of socio-religious work, to be developed in the late Victorian period to a fine art, the art of 'caring for the whole man'. Central to this concept was the idea that the churches and chapels should take a positive responsibility for the urban family, not just on Sundays, but on every day of the week. The working day was divided up into sleeping time, working time and leisure time. The first two were obviously outside the influence of voluntary bodies, but the third, the leisure time of the individual, was ripe for development. Workers could be brought closer to an understanding of Christian principles if they were encouraged to seek pleasures in ways which were harmless and beneficial not only to themselves, but also to their families and thus ultimately, to society as a whole.

For the Quakers in the early 1860s, such a conception of their role was at first, very far from their thoughts. The Quakers were one of the most Puritanical sects in their views on social behaviour and amusements. Such activities as dancing or theatre-going were considered to be nothing less than succumbing to the machinations of the Devil. Yet they were always willing to be unconventional or face the charge of eccentricity in the pursuit of doing good. They were also ready to respond to specific needs when they became apparent. In 1849 there was a cholera epidemic and the Quakers organized a committee to offer relief to victims, known as the 'Rice committee' since its main function was to organize donations of rice amongst the needy.

This committee set a precedent which was used when another, totally different, specific need was recognized. In 1861, at the Annual General Meeting of the YMCA chaired by the Earl of Shaftesbury, the Quaker, Arthur Naish, brought the attention of the meeting to the plight of the 'navvies' brought in to construct the Bristol and South Wales Union Railway. The 'navvies' were stationed at Baptist

Mills, and their conditions of work and lack of any kind of social amenity, even the stabilizing influences of home and family, led to cases of drunkenness and dissipation, which was a challenge to the socio-religious workers. The Quakers decided to respond by forming a 'navvies' committee to organize temperance work, evangelical meetings and personal contacts to encourage self-improvement and self-respect. When the 'navvies' moved on, it was obvious to the Quakers that work of this kind was just as needed in the poorer districts of Bristol on a more permanent basis, and in 1863 they rented a house at Narrow Plain and encouraged young men to attend their meetings. After two years it was decided to move to a permanent base for these activities, by working from the building owned by the Quakers in New St in St Judes. This building had been used in 1696 as a workhouse for indigent Quaker weavers and the nineteenth-century Quakers, inspired by this tradition, prepared to continue to provide social relief from here.[5]

The question was, what sort of relief was suitable? When the first committee met in 1865 they were fairly cautious and decided merely to expand their Sunday School work in a new area, and step up their temperance and evangelical work. The names of those on this committee were S. Capper (pioneer with Robert Charleton of temperance in Bristol), J. S. Fry, W. Sturge, F. Cotterell, R. Ashman, E. Fardon, Cephas Butler, T. Hunt, H. Gregory, J. Barclay, Miss Saville, A. E. Bobbett and J. Grace, some of whom were members of the social and cultural élite of the city. Their early days at the Quaker mission were a crucial formative influence on their social thinking, and in many ways it was a baptism of fire.

The initial impact of working in this poor district of the city was somewhat overwhelming. An emotional description of what it could be like has been left by one of the most successful missionaries at the Bristol City Mission, C. R. Parsons. He was writing about fifteen years after the founding of the Quaker mission in the early 1880s, but his experiences, which he vividly describes, were likely to have been similar to those of the Quaker committee attempting evangelical work.

> A city missionary's life [he wrote] is a difficult and arduous one: it needs much grace and much close walking with God for there is much to hinder his own personal growth in truth and

holiness. To be brought into contact with so much strife, and wretchedness and vice – to see much poverty and misery he cannot relieve; to hear on all hands loud complaints against Providence and hard sayings against God; to stand in the midst of contagion and disease, to see the profound indifference of vast masses of the people to their present and future well-being; to witness harrowing scenes of terrible death beds, more or less depresses the soul and exhausts the whole man.[6]

The Quaker committee of 1865 brought face to face with this reality, began to argue about how they should proceed.

There were several crises since the minority who wished to continue only along the well-tried evangelical lines, had strong support from the Quaker community not directly concerned with the mission. The arguments in favour of extending the scope of their activities won the day. The committee started conservatively enough with a soup kitchen, wood-chopping schemes so that the poor children could earn a supper, and a ragged school for boys. Hoping to combat conditions by constructive thinking, they decided to pay the fees of poor boys required by the School Board for attendance at their schools. Similar constructive action was employed for different groups. Mothers were a prime target. The Quakers attended them when they were sick, and then encouraged them to come to the regular weekly mothers' meetings. At these, and at general tract meetings, mothers and audiences were given little homilies on how to save (a Savings Bank was opened), how to create comfortable and happy homes, how to get on in the world (largely a matter of being sober and regular in the performance of duties), and above all, they were given the tract 'which inculcates the doctrine that soap and water are excellent compounds and there is some virtue in keeping a clean house and tidy children'.[7]

They did not escape criticism on the score of these activities from other Friends. But in the second Annual Report, the Committee gave back its answer.

> In order for our friends to form a just estimate of the work done, they must remember the degradation of many of those we have to deal with; the cry of 'Ten o'clock at night and no fight yet' is

a fair index of the morals and manners of many inhabitants of the district.

The controlling committee of the Mission had begun to understand the social conditions of the urban poor, and they were ready to pit their ideas and resources against the evils that they found. In the next five years, the Mission became the centre for a whole range of activities which were mostly to be carried on, on a regular basis, for the next twenty or thirty years. Many of these activities were designed for the leisure time of the urban poor since these could be justified as 'caring for the whole man'; they also provided the context within which other missionary activities had a chance of succeeding.

The Quaker Mission Committee had begun in the early days to recognize two problems. The first and most important was the difficulty of reaching people and persuading them to come to Quaker meetings. The second, more obvious to those experienced in temperance work, was to provide alternatives to drink and to meet the demands for recreation and entertainment. The Committee decided to try and kill two birds with one stone, and instituted 'a series of entertainments for Wednesday evenings, consisting of popular lectures, penny readings, etc.', which they justified on the grounds that such activities were useful 'in providing blameless amusements blended with instruction for the people as well as in bringing under our influence some who might probably otherwise never visit the hall'. In this activity the Quakers were not pioneering a new development. Penny readings were a national institution, a method of cultural diffusion mingled with entertainment, and they had become well established in the 1860s in Bristol.[8]

III PENNY READINGS AND THE BEGINNINGS OF MASS CULTURAL ENTERTAINMENT

The Quakers, however, were taking the practice of penny readings right into the heart of the poorer areas of the city. The importance of this was considerable, as it completed the network of winter entertainment committees responsible for penny readings, which now operated all over the city, run by Nonconformist and Anglican alike. What many well-intentioned socio-religious workers intended in this activity was probably to influence the social behaviour of their audiences. But this entertainment and the experience gained in organizing such functions in each locality was to generate a response which was later used in the organization of social, political and educational societies by different social groups. One historian of adult education has emphasized the social importance of the entertainments of the 1860s as the breeding-ground for developments within and beyond socio-religious work.[9] It was a formative period for all who were involved, since penny readings and spelling bees were the first organized attempts to reach the general public at large.

On the whole, most winter amusement committees consisted mainly of local clergymen or ministers and their wives, though the organization of entertainments was not exclusively a socio-religious activity. Groups of working men were also anxious to form committees. The problem for the latter was one of inadequate facilities. Apart from one or two local temperance halls, there was little provision for local meeting-places outside inns or public houses. The answer appeared to be the acquisition of a parish room which, while probably under the control of the local clergy, would be hired out as much as possible to earn adequate maintenance funds. By 1870 there was considerable agitation in the cause of acquiring parish rooms. The pleas of the temperance workers and the clergy for funds were, this time, strongly backed up by working men.

The correspondence columns of the *Western Daily Press* became full of letters from working men demanding such facilities. For example, the men of St Michael's parish claimed they wanted a room where they could spend their leisure hours in the evenings and where they could hold public meetings on politics and religion, lectures and other entertainments. With an eye on their main chance of gaining a philanthropic response, they added that such a room would give them an alternative to the pub.[10] In Totterdown the emphasis was placed on the need for a reading room, and somewhere to hold penny readings.[11] It was likely though, that the men of St Michael's parish and Totterdown were not the urban poor. They were probably members of the artisan class, and their demands for facilities illustrates a new selfconsciousness about the use of leisure. In a decade when trade unions were fighting for recognition and legality, there was a desire to break away from the traditional leisure patterns, largely centred on the pub. But a start could only be made if an alternative meeting-place was available. The Rev. T. W. Harvey, who sympathized deeply with this desire, and was to expend his energies at the Clifton College Mission in the 1880s for this purpose, wrote about parish rooms: 'It is doubtful whether it is sufficiently understood how little unity or how little social life there can be among artisan classes without meeting places of this kind.' The local parish room, sometimes provided with newspapers and magazines, became a primitive kind of teetotal community centre.

Their main use initially, however, was for entertainment, and in this area penny readings were an important item. Since even the Quakers were organizing such activities in the second half of the 1860s, their content can give a strong indication of attitudes towards leisure and what was considered harmless and beneficial. The ideal was probably family entertainment, modelled on the moments when the family gathered together in the evenings and recited poems and played the piano to amuse and entertain each other. The same kind of formula was used at penny readings. Their programmes were printed in the local press, and a typical one of 12 February 1870 (by which time such activities had been brought to a fine art) was as follows:

> Programme: Rev. J. H. Bright recitation 'The story of a daughter's love'; song, Mr. Norgate; song, Rev. F. C. Skey 'Hearts of Oak' (encored) and 'The Mermaid'; reading Rev. D. Wright 'Prisoners of Chillon' Byron; song, Mrs. Skey 'My mother bids me bind my hair' (encored) and 'Home, sweet home'; song, Mr. Higgs 'Goodbye Sweetheart goodbye'; reading Rev. F. C. Skey 'May Queen' Tennyson; song Mrs. Byrne 'The beating of my own heart' (encored) and 'The Postboy'; song, Mrs. Brackenbury 'I cannot mind my wheel, mother'; song from trio Messrs. Higgs, Forest and Underdown 'The Bee'.

The emotional impact of such a programme was strongly related to an ideal of home and family life, and a cultural dimension to the proceedings was given by the recitation of poems by Tennyson and Byron. The popularity of penny readings in the 1860s was unquestioned and the newspapers record that frequently people had to be turned away at the door since the halls were already full. Since admission only cost one penny, this entertainment could reach well down amongst the poor, and its popularity certainly indicates a demand for entertainment which was waiting to be exploited.

The Quakers, combining penny readings with their social work, had found indeed, a new formula for socio-religious activities. They were not long alone in the field. In 1865 the Unitarians had added a Workman's Hall to the institutions established since 1846 by Mary Carpenter at St James Back.[12] The evolution of activities here provides an interesting insight into socio-religious work. Miss Carpenter had started with a ragged school, but her experience in the early days of the Lewin's Mead Mission in the 1830s encouraged her to develop along practical lines. Children were taught simple vocational skills at the school and encouraged to attend regularly by being offered a meal there. The school became known as a 'Day Industrial Feeding School', and Miss Carpenter tried to provide for a follow-through of her work by establishing a Children's Employment Agency. She also founded a boys' home where those not in some form of domestic service could live. The developments of the 1860s however, provided a fresh opening. A number of educational and social activities were organized from the Workman's Hall. Penny readings and entertainments were held on Saturday nights, and the cultural dimension was further encouraged when a library was added to the Hall and educational classes were held in subjects including natural philosophy, drawing and music.

This kind of socio-religious work though, made new demands on those engaged upon it. A ragged school could be kept going with the help of a paid assistant; entertainments and educational classes required the skills of educated people. There was a new demand for lay involvement in social work of the more educated members of religious denominations, and this demand, coming in the 1860s, happened to coincide both with the establishment of the most influential congregations of most denominations in the socially superior suburbs, and the 'cultural renaissance' of the city shown in the development of its dominant cultural institutions. There was thus a religious and cultural impetus towards encouraging people to undertake socio-religious work and there was a response, slow at first, but gathering in momentum during the decade of the 1870s.

IV THE RESPONSE OF SOCIO-RELIGIOUS WORKERS TO URBAN GROWTH

The leading Nonconformist sects and the Anglicans were early in the field in this fresh development of social work. The new Bishop of Bristol and Gloucester, the Rev. C. J. Ellicott, appointed in 1863, had been turning his attention to Bristol and the problem of urban development with its threat to the breakdown of the parochial system. In 1868 a Church Extension Scheme was started and whilst funds for establishing new parish churches were accumulating, immediate action was taken to ameliorate the situation by pairing six wealthy churches with six in poor areas. With the funds went the stimulus to create closer social relationships through socio-religious work, and St Mary's, Stoke Bishop, Emmanuel, All Saints and St Paul's in Clifton, St Nathaniel's in Cotham and St Mary's in Tyndall Park, were the leading congregations in this new development.[13] Their attention was directed towards the newly settled areas since in the Anglican churches in the older, poorer parishes such as Redcliff and Temple, the endowments of former generations enabled the traditional patterns of philanthropic work to continue unchanged.

For the Nonconformists however, operating without the parochial system, mission work meant probably a greater degree of personal involvement for the parent congregation and the concentration of energies on one or two projects. The Congregationalists and the Baptists with all their experience at the Bristol City Mission, showed themselves most responsive, after the Quakers, to the changes of the 1860s. The influence of the Congregationalist Bristol Tabernacle had begun to decline as the Highbury Chapel, built in 1843, began to count the leading Bristol Congregationalists amongst its members. The tradition of Bible classes and social work set up at the Tabernacle was carried on by the Highbury congregation at Kingsdown and Broad Plain. However, the most outstanding contribution of the Congregationalists to the new mission type work was made by the Rev. U. R. Thomas when he became the first minister of the new middle class chapel, Redland Park, in 1862. Thomas was only twenty-two when he was appointed and he put much youthful enthusiasm into organizing his congregation immediately in a series of missions, clubs and socio-religious activities with considerable success. A similar response was shown by the Baptists. Their main chapel had been Broadmead, but the wealthy members of the congregation moved out of the city. Tyndale Park Chapel, built for their convenience, was never large, total membership being around two hundred. But, established in 1868, only three years later in 1871, the congregation were running an extended 'modern type' mission in Hotwells.

In the decade since the Quakers had tentatively begun their work, there had been a remarkable change. Then, they had been alone in their new approach to social conditions of the urban poor. Now, in the Report of 1875, the Quaker Mission Committee report that attendance at some of their functions such as the Mothers' Meetings was beginning to fall away as 'there are more meetings of this kind in the neighbourhood.' Then, they had had the feeling that they were tilling virgin soil as they packed their first mission meetings (before the move to New St) into the two tiny, dirty rooms of 12 Narrow Plain and their temperance homilies had met with riotous response, lights being smashed, tables and chairs overturned, and the people in ugly, hostile mood. Now in 1874, they had opened the British Workman Coffee Tavern, celebrating the event by a Tea Meeting. Mr Mark Whitwill had addressed a huge crowd from an upstairs window, and 2,000 people filed through the building afterwards. In the early days after its opening it was in constant use by working men. The change was dramatic and gratifying.

There was no doubt that their socio-religious work had struck a deep chord of response, particularly their work for temperance, entertainment and education. The cultural alternative to the pub, the Temperance Coffee Tavern or parish room provided a new basis for growth and development. For once, socio-religious workers found themselves in tune with the mood of significant numbers of working men, concerned with gaining recognition and respect for their own organizations. Trade union activity had not been strong in the city and the formation of a Trades Council in 1873 was hardly a breakthrough since it was not a strong and well-supported body.[14] But the cause of entertainment, education and/or temperance gained a significant response in these years.

Curiously though, Bristol did not seem to share in the development of that social institution designed to meet working men's leisure needs, the working man's club. The working men's club movement was established in 1862 with the formation of the Club and Institute Union in 1862 under the guidance of the Rev. Henry Solly in

London. Some kind of club was developed in the early 1870s, centred on the 'Hall of Freedom' in Broadmead built by the Owenites in the 1840s, which gained as many as 1,000 members.[15] But by 1880 this club became extinct. Probably poverty and the lack of buildings hampered the movement, and Bristol socio-religious workers did not take up the idea, since their energies were going into their new-type missions.

However, the introduction of a political element in club activities did provide a fresh stimulus. The Conservatives, on the initiative of Mr John Lysaght, opened a club in Old Market Street in 1880. The aim was to gain Conservative allegiance of working men by providing for their leisure facilities. At the opening, most of the Conservative town councillors were on the platform; pictures of the Queen, Royal Family and Conservative statesmen were round the walls and the watchword was 'loyalty'. Members had to promise 'To fear God, to honour the Queen and to be stern in defending the liberties of the people'.[16] In the decade 1865-75 however, the demand for education and entertainment enabled the propaganda element to fade somewhat into the background.

This can be illustrated by the example of Mr William H. Riley, a member of the Labour movement, who came to Bristol in 1875 to organize and educate the workers.[17] The pattern of activities he instituted closely resemble those provided by the socio-religious workers, and his early efforts came to grief when there was a schism amongst his helpers over the issue of Drink. Riley wanted the members of his organization to be teetotal as a measure of their respectability and the seriousness of their intention, in attempts to improve themselves and their situation in the world.

Riley had been involved in the International Working Men's Association and had, for a while, edited the *International Herald*. He was thus both closely in touch with the Labour movement in London and highly idealistic about the future. Those of his helpers who agreed with him on the teetotal issue formed a new organization, a Social Improvement Institute at 6 Brunswick Square. Here they held education classes, discussion classes, and entertainments in a pattern very similar to those activities organized in the new-type mission and parish rooms. However, going it alone, Riley was soon in financial difficulties, and in eighteen months the Institute was forced to close because of lack of resources. In these circumstances it can be seen that the provisions made by the socio-religious workers were meeting articulate cultural and social aspirations of the lower and working classes, and the element of entertainment provided on a local basis had done what no amount of effort in adult education had ever quite achieved before – it had gained a mass, popular response to socio-religious work.

This was heady stuff for the socio-religious workers or those concerned with the role of the church in society. Reminiscing about these days thirty years later, the Rev. J. M. Wilson (second headmaster of Clifton College) said:

> We had clear social ideals for the Church, too varied and perhaps too crude and unformed for me now to dwell on. But not a few of us had a sort of passion for applying to life greater intelligence and a far higher Christian social aspiration; we had an almost boyish belief that the Kingdom of God might be brought very near.

His predecessor, the Rev. John Percival, had been in the vanguard of this group. His work for the cultural renaissance in the city, his belief in the need to aspire to a higher civilization and his concern for the widest possible diffusion of educational facilities for all social groups, gave him a unique vantage-point from which to view this development in socio-religious work. Here was a chance for the educated to extend a helping hand to those less fortunate than themselves, to raise them up, but at the same time and by so doing, to make direct contact between the classes. This could lead to an interchange of ideas and the forging of a cultural unity which was a top priority in the attempt to achieve a higher civilization. In 1869, in line with the work being undertaken at the YMCA and the Quaker, Unitarian and other missions, Percival founded an Association for the Promotion of Evening Classes.

With his new insight into the potential of this social and cultural diffusion, he directly engaged the services as secretary of the Association, of Mr J. W. H. Wall, who was also secretary of the Bristol and District Co-operative Society. It was an attempt at combining cultural diffusion with social co-operation. The Association was not designed to reach down to the urban poor, but to respond to the needs of the respectable working classes; in Percival's own description: 'the clerks,

shopmen, artisans and other young men in business'.[18] The Bristol Co-operative Society was at that time too poor to supply its own education committee with adequate funds, so that Percival's initiative was welcomed. There was a common interest since the co-operative movement was always anxious to extend its membership. Classes were directed both towards intellectual stimulation (for cultural refinement) and straightforward vocational training. The subjects taught were Latin, French, arithmetic, algebra, geometry, higher mathematics, practical mechanics, geometrical and freehand drawing, English grammar and composition, book-keeping and writing, animal physiology, and singing. Appreciating the importance of local facilities in an expanding city, classes were set up at six different centres around Bristol; at the Athenaeum; Corn Street; The Institution, Park Street; Bedminster; Baptist Mills; Cotham and Redland.

Was this the start of a great new experiment? Were the upper classes extending a helping hand to co-operators and the organized Labour movement? Something very like that may have been in Percival's mind, but the Association proved quite inadequate at living up to the ideal. Many classes were thinly attended, and in those which did attract attendance the differences in educational standards amongst students created enormous problems for the teachers. Even the vocational training classes were not filled, probably because the hours of work even of the respectable young working man, put such facilities beyond his reach. The Early Closing Association in the city did not have much success until the 1890s. It all fell far short of fulfilling Percival's vision and Christian social idealism. In 1870 the School Board was set up and Percival became a member, but his educational aspirations were deflected towards another scheme, the scheme for the promotion of a university college in the city for the benefit of rich and poor alike.

Yet the experience of the missions and this new socio-religious work was directing Percival's attention to further possibilities. The Anglican Church Extension Scheme of 1868 had outlined the need for new parish churches in developing areas. Why should not Clifton College adopt one of these new parishes and attempt mission work there on the new lines? It would be an educational exercise for the boys and might go much further than the links of the Evening Class Association with the Co-operative Movement or even the University

College, to bring about mutual understanding between classes and to stimulate common aspirations for a higher civilization. The successes of the socio-religious workers in reaching the urban poor with their provisions for entertainment and recreation, were an indication of how one might proceed.

With a response like that, the Church could exercise an influence over the whole parish, acting as a centre for all that was good and wholesome in social life. The Rev. T. W. Harvey, to be the most effective perpetrator of Percival's dream in Bristol in the 1880s, wrote about their intentions as follows:

> It was part of our ideal that the Church should provide and be a centre of social life for all the parish, not for its congregations only; that all that is innocent and refreshing – in reading rooms and games, in music and the drama, in gymnastics and drill, in clubs and other associations – should find its headquarters in [church] buildings.[19]

The challenge of an increasingly secular society should be met, not with the head-on collision of straightforward evangelical work, but by diffusing moral tone and Christian values to all developments in urban social life. As Harvey put it:

> The Church of England has something more to do than call men to repentance, essential as that work is. She has to teach, to edify, to build up the Christian character. She has a message to the intellect as well as to the heart, to the body as well as the soul, for both have been redeemed by Christ.[20]

This was change through permeation. It was also a commitment of Church resources to the task of improving the social, physical and intellectual environment of the urban poor. The leading Nonconformists in the city were no less committed. Mission work was continued and expanded. However, the spearhead institution designed to diffuse Nonconformist social ideals remained the YMCA. Here, leading members of different Nonconformist sects co-operated to uncover and meet social needs. For instance, in the 1870s the Bristol branch of the YMCA pioneered in providing hostel accommodation for young men away from home. Both the Anglican parochial mission and the Nonconformist efforts to appeal to young men had one thing in common, they had to attract support. This meant in practice, in view of the experience of the 1860s, that they had to provide facilities for recreation and entertainment. What had been a harmless method of keeping people out of the pub and perhaps making contact with them, became the central plank of the next wave of development. Improving the social, physical and intellectual environment of the under-privileged meant concentrating on the leisure time of the workers; those few precious hours not taken up by work, sleep or daily chores.

The obvious potential demand for entertainment in the 1860s had not been lost on other groups besides the socio-religious workers. On a voluntary basis, working men were now forming their own organizations, clubs and societies, whilst on a commercial basis there was an increasing volume of entrepreneurship to tap the market potential. Music halls, commercial entertainment and sport all developed rapidly from this period. The socio-religious workers were thus up against stiff competition. By the end of the 1870s, the penny reading had become something of a joke. As the *Western Daily Press* commented in 1881, 'Spelling Bees, Penny Readings and various other methods of entertaining and instructing the public, have had their day ... the novelty having to some extent worn off ...' What the socio-religious workers set themselves was the task of being the first to respond to new developments and to initiate new institutions in the areas of special interest that had already been mapped out – in their work for young people, for educational diffusion and for community development, particularly in the new parishes. The two most creative and successful ventures in the 1880s in Bristol were the YMCA and the Clifton College Mission in the new parish of St Agnes.

V NEW DEVELOPMENTS AT THE YMCA

The turning point for the YMCA in the city was 1879. In the 1870s the evangelical policies of the previous decade had continued the decline in membership, and the Association committee began to be prepared to make the necessity of attracting support a top priority. A new development came to their rescue, which was to solve all their problems, then and in the foreseeable future. It was, in a word, sport. The evolution of organized sport at the public schools unleashed one of the greatest forces considered to be on the side of the angels in the late nineteenth century. Charles Kingsley had recognized the moral benefits which accrue from healthy physical recreation, especially for the young, and as the theme was developed, in socio-religious organizations in every part of the country, it became dubbed derisively by journalists as 'Muscular Christianity'. There is no doubt that the theoretical basis for relating organized sport and Christianity was somewhat shaky. It could obviously be argued that physical exercise was vital for those brought up in the unnatural conditions of an urban environment and destined to spend much of their life in sedentary occupations, and that a healthy body and a sense of well-being were legitimate objectives for any Christian. Further, sport absorbed energies and thought which idleness might otherwise lead astray to evil outlets, and finally team games and innocent competition were ideal methods of social training in codes of desirable social conduct.

But whether the arguments about the moral value of physical recreation were convincing or not, the support generated by organized sport certainly was. In 1862 the YMCA in Bristol had started tentatively with a short-lived cricket team. Then there were some organized activities in swimming. In 1879 the committee showed its readiness to pioneer in new developments, and built a gymnasium. It was opened by the inevitable figure on this kind of occasion, Mr Mark Whitwill, and its success was immediately stunning. The membership numbers grew by 385 in that year, 286 of whom had joined solely for the privilege of using the gym. From this moment on, the Association went from strength to strength, sure now in its direction to meet the leisure demands of aspiring young men.

In 1883 the major decision was taken to open district branches round Bristol, membership now having reached 1,083, of whom 633 were full members. The first six branches were duly opened at Kingswood, Fishponds, Totterdown, Hotwells, Bedminster and Easton. Each branch ran their own sports teams, football and hockey, harriers and cycling now as well as cricket and swimming. Although support for sport remained the major impetus to increasing membership, the Association's central committee never lost sight of its original aims of self-improvement and extending the horizons and experience of the young men who joined the Association. Evening classes were kept up and extended to include fresh developments such as vocational training in shorthand and typing, and a St John's Ambulance class.

Cultural dimensions were provided by music and drama with, particularly, the YMCA choir and orchestra going from strength to strength. Gradually as leisure time lengthened and young men even began to gain annual holidays, the YMCA was ready to respond to this new demand. In the 1890s the YMCA was organizing holidays at home and abroad. At home, accommodation was provided cheaply in YMCA hostels at seaside resorts (the Brighton hostel, for instance, cost 4*s.* a day, though the Hazelwood Seaside Home at Rye cost only 3*s.* 1½*d.* a day). Abroad, in one year, 1898 for example, there were thirty different tours and cruises organized; such as a weekly tour, destination Lucerne, at the cost of 5 gns inclusive, to a fortnight-long cruise in the Norwegian fiords for 9 gns. In spite of this extension and diffusion of activities and enterprises, the organization of the Bristol YMCA remained largely in the hands of the same people, and a socio-religious atmosphere with a strict code of social behaviour permeated all activities. The evangelical tendencies of the Nonconformists were still there behind the scenes, and sometimes in front of them.

When a new central hall was needed in the early 1880s, fundraising had been conducted on the old evangelical lines. A missionary visit of Moody and Sankey was used for the purpose, Mr Moody being a strong supporter of the now world-wide YMCA movement. Samuel Morley, the liberal Nonconformist MP for Bristol, offered £500 if friends of the Association raised £2,000, a target which was achieved with the help of Mr Moody. The new hall, when built, could seat 1,250 people, and was used for religious services on Sundays. Indeed the weekly Bible class remained obligatory for all full members of the Association, though those who joined to use the sporting facilities only, did not have to attend. Finally in the old socio-religious, Sunday school tradition, a youth department was formed to feed the parent association and its district branches with new members. Just how close the YMCA remained to its past, in spite of its ever developing range of activities, was shown clearly in the Jubilee celebrations of 1903. £2,000 was spent on a varied and successful series of celebrations and the annual conference of the British YMCA was held in Bristol.

What was being celebrated however, was more than just fifty years of existence of the Bristol YMCA. It also marked the achievement of the small group of men who had promoted the idea of the YMCA back in the mid years of the nineteenth century and remained with it, at the helm, through failure and success. The President of the Bristol YMCA in 1903 who welcomed Sir George Williams, the original founder, to the city, was none other than Joseph Storrs Fry. Sir Thomas Leonard, whose family had been concerned with the Bristol YMCA since its foundation, was Chairman of the Jubilee Committee. James Inskip was still Honorary Secretary of the Association, a position he shared with Henry Daniel, another founder member. S. D. Wills was the Treasurer. Arnold Thomas of Highbury Congregational Church, Lewis Fry and Miss Fry welcomed delegates at the main reception. Music was provided by George Riseley, the cathedral organist, and the Royal Orpheus Glee Society. Since the position of, particularly, the Frys and Wills families was now firmly at the top of the city's social and cultural élite, the YMCA's celebrations were a sparkling affair. Among the self-congratulations, the old guard could feel that in spite of their own social rise, they had always been consistently faithful to their view of their social responsibilities and through their many organizations, but especially the YMCA, had made a substantial contribution to the social and cultural life of less fortunately placed citizens.

The achievements of the YMCA in the period 1853–1903 were obvious; in membership, organization and activities. But it was not clear, and nobody was interested in making it clear, how that success was related to the objectives of socio-religious work. The YMCA was, after all, hardly an answer to social problems, nor did it develop the greatest new techniques in evangelizing and saving souls. What the experience of the Association had shown was that organization for young men found a welcome response, especially when related to sport and recreational facilities which were not widely available elsewhere. It was perhaps fortunate for the 'old guard' that many of them, J. Inskip, S. D. Wills, J. S. Fry and H. Daniel, were to die in the course of the next decade before their faith in their own role and their understanding of what constituted socio-religious work was undermined by recent developments. Now a new set of social attitudes was being created in the light of Booth and Rowntree's revelations on the extent of poverty and the facts about the physical deterioration of the nation shown by the rejection of volunteers and recruits on grounds of unfitness, for the Boer War. Such facts shattered for ever the concept of 'caring for the whole man' by providing leisure facilities. The ideal of social and cultural co-operation was to disappear with the rise of the labour movement and socialist doctrines, and the polarization of the interests of the classes which was to ensue. Despite the success of the YMCA, the gulf between the social and cultural élite of the city and young people had never been greater than in the Edwardian period.

VI THE SOCIAL EXPERIMENT OF CLIFTON COLLEGE MISSION

But a great deal of energy, philanthropic spirit and resources were devoted to the organization of socio-religious activities before the limitations of such work became apparent, especially from the 1880s. The other showpiece venture which, apart from the YMCA was to stimulate so much activity from the 1880s was the Clifton College Mission. Whereas the YMCA had concentrated on young people, focusing the attention of socio-religious workers in an entirely new way on meeting the needs of youth, the Clifton College Mission was aimed at the whole community, men, women and children. Further, whilst the YMCA could number its membership in the city at well over the one thousand mark, Clifton College Mission at the peak of its membership (which came, incidentally, in 1909) numbered only 320 men and boys, 112 girls. The importance of the Mission was thus not its numerical strength, but the embodiment it gave to an ideological approach to socio-religious work, developed around the starting point of the leisure time of the individual.

The evolution of this ideology was not limited to this particular experiment in Bristol. It was happening simultaneously elsewhere, particularly in the events at Oxford and Cambridge in the early 1880s, which were to result in the formation of Toynbee Hall in 1883 in the East End of London under the wardenship of Canon S. A. Barnett. Headmaster Thring of Uppingham had pursued the idea of a public school mission and one was set up in connection with his school from 1864, first in Regent's Park and then the East End. Although Canon Barnett was to become a prolific writer on his version of social reform and the aims and ambitions of Toynbee Hall,[21] in the early 1880s all these ideas were still in the melting pot, so that the Clifton College Mission was guided by the outlook and experience of those involved in that mission.

Percival's ideals of cultural diffusion and social co-operation between classes had generated more enthusiasm than success in the educational ventures he had taken up, and his early experience with the Mission was even more of a failure. A poor young curate, the Rev. H. D. Rawnsley, had been sent to one of the roughest parts of the parish of St Barnabas in 1879, where he was expected to form contacts and build up clubs and institutions. He did his best. He went out into the streets and collected teenage boys with whom he played football on Saturday afternoons and took for walks on Sunday, to keep them out of mischief. But they were rough, rowdy and undisciplined, and attempts to organize them into a club met with consistent failure. The Rev. H. D. Rawnsley departed before the end of the year.[22] The ideal of bridging the gap between the Two Nations by setting up institutions where public school boys and town boys could meet, even the possibility that this would lead to some kind of cultural unity, began to appear to be an Arnoldian pipe dream for those seduced by concepts of Liberal Culture. However, the next stage in the fortunes of the Mission was to coincide with several favourable circumstances which promised to wring success out of failure.

The first had to do with the city itself and the special area that had been designated as suitable territory for the Clifton College Mission. In the mid 1870s it had been in the process of development from an area of squatters and cottagers into an industrial and residential area.[23] By 1880 this process was nearing completion and the increase in population density of the parish of St Barnabas led the Church Extension Committee to adopt the idea of subdivision and the creation of a new parish of St Agnes. The Clifton College Mission was thus to be responsible for a whole new parish, uncluttered by the framework of any previous parochial organization. Further, the raw materials with whom the Mission had to deal, the people of the new parish of St Agnes, were changing with the economic and social developments taking place there. Now, instead of tracts of

1 J. Storrs Fry 1826-1913. Head of the Fry Cocoa and Chocolate firm.

2 Mark Whitwill 1826-1903. Ship-owner and Shipbroker.

3 H. O. Wills 1828-1911. Head of the Wills Tobacco Company.

4 Lewis Fry 1832-1921. Solicitor and Member of Parliament.

Leading examples of Bristol's Liberal Nonconformist élite, all concerned with voluntary socioreligious, philanthropic and educational work.

5 Bristol Art Gallery, the epitome of the capitalist ideal of 'social citizenship'. The giant inscription, centre front of façade, reads: 'The Gift of Sir William Henry Wills Bart., to his Fellow Citizens 1904.'

6 Art Gallery interior, the 'temple' of art.

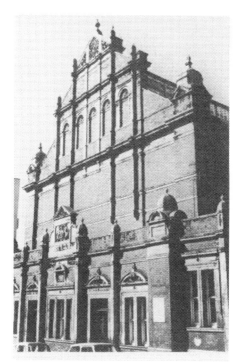

7 The architecture of 'municipal pride', Jacobs Wells' Swimming Bath 1884.

8 Expensive stone facing for city coat of arms over doorway.

9 Central Library, Bristol, built with the Stuckey Lean Bequest.

10 The height and spaciousness lend dignity to the interior of the Reference Section, Central Library.

11 The cultural centre of the middle classes, Bristol Museum and Library 1871, a miniature Doge's Palace, photographed soon after completion.

12 The entertainment centre for the masses. The People's Palace 1892, one of the Livermore chain of provincial music halls, a replica of one already built in Dundee.

13 Street entertainment made respectable. A crowd gathering to watch a cycle rally August 1886, Queen's Avenue, Clifton.

14 Street entertainment of an 'improving' kind. The Industrial and Fine Arts Exhibition 1893; temporary building erected at cost of £11,000 on space created by arching of River Frome, Colston Avenue.

15 The Bristol YMCA, by S. Loxton.

16 The bridge to 'cultural unity', Clifton College Mission to St Agnes, Men's and Boys' Club.

17 Self-governing independence, St Agnes Working Men's Club Committee. The Rev. T. W. Harvey is included, however, seated in the middle row, third from left.

wasteland and the hovels of the squatters, there were rows of neat houses in grid-iron street pattern.

It was a little claustrophobic since the density was quite high, but the Rev. J. M. Wilson, the second head of the College and most intimately connected with the fortunes of the Mission, managed to procure a small piece of waste ground still left undeveloped, which he had transferred to the town council for the purpose of a small park. As for the people themselves, they were poor, but their very ability to move into the new terrace houses was an indication that they did not belong to the poorest strata. Given the incidence of the poverty cycle, St Agnes must have been one of the better staging posts on the way up. Thus the social and environmental circumstances which faced the Mission in the early 1880s was substantially different from even the conditions of five or six years before. In the early 1880s, St Agnes was a new development area.

The second circumstance which tipped the balance in favour of the Mission was much more general. It had to do with changing attitudes towards socio-religious work. Behind all these new developments was a changing conception of what constituted a religious life. This change had been pioneered by the Nonconformists, who had always been prepared in the nineteenth century to experiment with new ways of tackling social problems, thus extending the range and scope of socio-religious work. Yet such activities had nearly always been combined with rigid codes of personal behaviour which did not stop at outward appearances but concentrated as well on the inner resources of the individual; the seeking of motivation for action, searching for personal salvation, concern over the state of one's own soul. The ultimate of a pious person was a soul at peace, and even Mary Carpenter, who used her more than usual endowment of energy to promote the social welfare of the poor, was always questioning her own motives in her diaries and letters.[24] The Winkworth sisters, who were to do so much for women's education in Bristol, had a long correspondence with F. D. Maurice in the mid-century years. But education was hardly mentioned. The main subject was one of the sister's problems in accepting the religious doctrines of her faith and achieving peace of mind and a clear conscience.[25]

Gradually, however, there was a shift in emphasis between the two aspects of a religiously guided life – personal piety and good works – in favour of the latter. The Nonconformist chapels in the new middle-class suburbs gave a considerable impetus to this, especially the work of such men as the Rev. U. R. Thomas at the Congregational Redland Park Chapel, with his commitment from the start to social work, involving all his congregation in social activities. It was at this chapel, in 1886, that the Rev. J. M. Wilson preached a sermon pinpointing this change in the emphasis of what constituted a religious life (incidentally also illustrating the levels of co-operation between different denominations that such a shift made possible). Wilson asked the question of the congregation, 'Are we better men than our fathers?', and then answered 'No', continuing:

> There was no one like my father: it is not merely filial piety and reverence for age that makes men say so – it corresponds to a real difference ... to be an eminent Christian meant a life of much retirement, much introspection and conscious spiritual experiences. The type has perhaps somewhat changed. Our generation desires less selfconsciousness, more work for others.... This change in the ideal of individual life is the key to the progress of church life.

Reflecting the ideology which was behind the Clifton College Mission, Wilson outlined how the rich may help the poor through socio-religious institutions:

> And the range of interest is very wide. It is not only in directly religious teaching but in the not less necessary work of preparing the soil for the seed to grow; in work for education, temperance and recreation; in art, in gardening, in home industries and economies, in all that makes home and family life more attractive and safe.[26]

'Preparing the soil for the seed to grow' was an exceedingly wide objective for any church, chapel or mission to undertake, given the limitations of voluntary work and small financial resources. There were the obvious dangers that by attempting too much, such resources would be too thinly spread to have any impact whatsoever. But here, as far as the Clifton College Mission was concerned, was the last, and possibly the most important, of the circumstances in its favour in the early 1880s. This was the appointment of the Rev. T. W.

Harvey as the warden of the Mission and the parish priest of St Agnes. The Rev. Harvey was found to have great ability, both to organize and nurture social institutions, and at the same time, to maintain sufficient support and the interest of the rich. The secret of his personal success lay in his ability to bridge the gap between the poor parish and the supporters of the Mission without losing the confidence or trust of either.

What enabled him to do it was not only his personal qualities but also the flexibility of his brief, 'preparing the soil for the seed to grow', and the tradition of cultural diffusion and social co-operation which had been bequeathed as a legacy to the Mission by its founder, the Rev. J. Percival. This left Harvey free to communicate with his parishioners, less inhibited by class pretensions or the need to concentrate on socio-religious propaganda. Harvey came to Bristol in 1880 at the age of thirty-one. He came from a poor background; he had been educated at Grantham Grammar School and Cambridge, where his natural sympathies for the working classes were reinforced by theological studies under Westcott; and he had taken up Christian Socialist views. In the 1870s he had taken part in the socio-religious activities, providing recreation, education and amusement,[27] which had been the successful formula since the '60s, and he was very ready to accept and pursue the Percival/Wilson approach to mission work.

It was an important tradition to inherit, because it gave him a somewhat different starting point to the Missions of the Nonconformists. The Quakers, Congregationalists and Baptists were all just as committed to cultural diffusion, by the 1880s, in their various missions. But they had reached that point via their evangelical work, temperance work, work for education and young people, and the provision of recreation and entertainment. Thanks to Percival, Harvey's inheritance had been all these things, but, above all, education and social co-operation. There was thus a big difference between Harvey and the Nonconformist missions as to what they understood by cultural diffusion, a difference which can best be illustrated by a brief comparison and contrast between the Rev. U. R. Thomas of Redland Park Congregational Chapel and the Rev. T. W. Harvey. Thomas was prepared to run a settlement type mission at the Quarry, a shanty town on the edge of the downs, in a manner very similar to the Clifton College Mission at St Agnes. His aim was the encouragement of home and family life through providing temperance entertainments and better recreational activities. He was even convinced that cultural activities, especially music, should be supported for its own sake. But the people of the Quarry were always on the receiving end of his, and his congregation's, ministrations.

Harvey, whilst pursuing many similar activities, had a different objective. He wanted to make it possible for the people of St Agnes to achieve an independent cultural existence. As D. J. Carter points out in his recent thesis,

> It is significant that whereas Thomas was an idealistic liberal who saw himself as a conveyor of culture (as with his flower gardens), Harvey saw himself as a sort of midwife to an independent culture; he merely provided some of the conditions in which it could flourish.[28]

In this, Harvey was much more in tune with the developments taking place under Canon Barnett at Toynbee Hall. Both were trying to build up a civic structure which would offer new opportunities and experience to the people of poor parishes; a civic civilization which would touch the lives of everyone.[29]

Clifton College Mission of course, was a much humbler institution than Toynbee Hall. It was a school mission, not a university settlement, and it was hidden away in Bristol, not strategically placed in the East End of London in the full glare of press publicity, feeding 'the sense of sin' so acutely felt at this time by middle-class social reformers.[30] Yet the Clifton College Mission buildings were impressive, too, in their own way, and a visit to St Agnes became a regular item for visitors to the city. What early visitors to the Mission would have seen in 1883 was the Working Men's Club. Harvey was so intent on building a community centre rather than a congregation, the Working Men's Club was opened three years before the church was consecrated. No expense was spared on the Club buildings. There were reading rooms and a library, a large room for meetings, a billiard saloon, and refreshment rooms. The organization of activities there, was immediately put into the hands of a committee of working men, unregulated by Harvey.

After the Club, two more extensions were quickly made to the Mission buildings. The first was a parish room. Again, in the hope that the Mission buildings would be the centre of all social life in the parish, regardless of religious affiliation, the parish room was built and equipped far more like an opulent private drawing-room than a public hall. It was large enough to seat 200 comfortably, and it had 'a large open fireplace, stained glass windows, excellent pictures, a rich carpet and handsome chairs'.[31] It was an interesting example of the cultural ideal of home as the centre of cultural existence, though in one sense it was contradictory. It was designed to attract people out of their own homes to the detriment of the other part of the cultural ideal, family life.

However, the logic of social co-operation provided some answer to this. Mutual improvement and social co-operation could only take place, after all, if groups met together. The homeliness of the parish room would help such efforts to succeed by making participants feel as if they belonged. The second extension to the Mission buildings was a gymnasium. Harvey fully appreciated the lesson so recently demonstrated by the Bristol YMCA, that sport and physical exercise were the most effective means yet found of attracting young men and boys to socio-religious institutions. The Clifton College Mission gym was of truly magnificent proportions, fully equipped for all forms of gymnastics and drill, whilst in the cellars beneath there were showers and washing facilities. The Mission was to organize football and cricket teams (who played on some local farmer's field still left close by), and a cycling club.

The Rev. J. M. Wilson was very grateful at the obvious success of the Mission and his initial hostility to Harvey, the non-public school man whom he would not have appointed, had there been another candidate for the post, melted away. Harvey reinforced his position, personally, by subsequently marrying the Rev. Wilson's sister. Such social harmony masked many of the problems of running the Mission and the somewhat different directions that their experiences were taking Wilson and Harvey. Wilson stuck to the idea of a non-religious civic structure, hopefully centring social life under the indirect influence of the Church. The park he acquired for the parish has been mentioned, and Wilson used his influence to persuade the School Board to set up an elementary school in the area.[32] He gave his support to activities at this school, particularly the evening classes held for older children. In 1885 he provided the means of instruction in violin playing at the school, which had now become an evening class centre under the joint control of the School Board and the voluntary Evening Class and Recreation Society. Wilson did not press for a free public library. A library and reading room were already provided at the Mission buildings.

If Wilson's bent was more towards the creation of a civic infrastructure of cultural institutions, Harvey was directly involved in social co-operation. He was convinced of two things. First, the need to communicate directly with working men. Second, the necessity of combating the evils of urban life: drink, bad housing, low pay, long hours and inefficient poor relief, alongside, and with the support of, the working people themselves. The method he chose to start towards these objectives was to run a Mutual Improvement Society which was to flourish as long as Harvey was at the Mission. Since it was held at the Working Men's Club, it was no matter of preaching to the converted. Debates on political, social and moral subjects were held each week. Harvey's biographer gives a description of what took place.

> Here some sixty men gathered of all sorts, and if Harvey could get an infidel to start a discussion, he was supremely happy. There was a rule that the class should close at 4 p.m. and a bell was provided for the secretary's use to notify when the magic hour had arrived, but Harvey, when properly off, brushed aside such regulations – 'It's no use, Mr. Secretary, we can't leave this subject' – and would turn round once more to pursue his argument.[33]

Gradually Harvey's commitment brought him closer to the Labour movement. In 1883 the Trades Council had invited the Rev. J. Percival back to Bristol to give them their annual address. Percival had spoken enthusiastically on his usual lines of cultural diffusion and social co-operation and had urged the Bristol Co-operative Society to increase its educational efforts. It seemed natural that such developments, if followed, should take place at St Agnes and when the Co-operative Education Committee, led by Vaughan Nash, took up the cause of education in 1886, it operated under Harvey's chairmanship. As H. P. Smith, the historian of adult education writes: 'St. Agnes was for a whole generation a nursery of activities which bring us very close to the W.E.A.'[34] Harvey though, did not limit himself to educational activities; he identified himself with the daily experiences of his parishioners. When a natural disaster struck the parish in the mid 1880s, as the River Frome burst its banks and flooded many of the houses in the neighbourhood, Harvey was the first on the scene and acted as the organizer of rescue work.

He was also prepared to face man-made problems. From the mid 1880s onwards until his retirement from the Mission in 1900, Harvey was often called upon to act as an arbitrator in industrial disputes. Whilst not part of the Labour movement, he was widely respected by employers and workmen and at the same time he never lost the support of Wilson and Clifton College. This might partly be explained by some of the contacts the College had with the Socialist movement in the city. The Bristol Socialist Society was founded in 1884 and its Vice-President in 1885 was John Gregory, the poet-shoemaker at Clifton College who was also very active on the Trades Council.[35] Perhaps the most personal influence linking the College with the Labour movement was H. H. Gore.

Gore was an old Cliftonian, inspired by Percival to dedicate his life to the improvement of working-class life. He was an Anglo-Catholic, eccentric in his personal appearance, since he always wore flowing robes and sandals, although he earned his living as a solicitor. He chose, however, to live in a slum court and to devote his free time to socio-religious work and the Socialist and Labour movements. His Christian Socialism enabled Clifton College to continue channelling to him considerable support, whilst his socialist convictions got him an invitation to speak at a meeting held by the Trades Council in 1889 urging the Bristol dockers to come out in support of the Londoners. When the Bristol dockers finally came out, they won after only three days.[36] Harvey played no part in this dispute, but his social situation was, in many ways, similar to that of Gore. Perhaps it is a comment on the idealism of Percival and Wilson that this remained possible. It is certainly a comment on this type of socio-religious work that when Harvey retired in 1900, few of his staunch supporters in the Mutual Improvement Society were regular attenders at the church, yet the Bristol Trades Council presented him with an illuminated address, in grateful recognition of his many services to the Labour movement.

'Preparing the soil for the seed to grow' had not had the result that was expected. Commitment to religious affiliations remained a minority activity, though the overall evangelical achievement of all denominations and sects in the inner areas of the city was not inconsiderable. Bristol remained near the top of the league of large cities in terms of church- or chapel-going population. But Clifton College Mission had never been an evangelical mission. Harvey never asked the people he met in conjunction with his clubs and societies if they went to church or not. Yet if evangelical activity had been played down, it was certainly hoped that the Mission would provide a meeting-ground for the College boys and town boys, a bridge between the Two Nations.

Percival, and later Wilson, had believed that public school boys, by supporting and visiting the Mission, would learn about life in a town parish and would find common interests with town boys by sharing in activities. Only cruel experience over the years that followed was to show that this supposition was, in fact, incorrect. One of the few constant activities involving the boys and the members of the Mission was the annual rugby football match between the school and the Mission boys (who were taught to play rugby football especially for this match); and Wilson had the grace to admit in 1900 that: 'Practically games and boys clubs and summer camps are the only elements of life really in common between public school boys and a town parish.'[37] A common culture was a myth. The Mission was then a failure in terms of saving souls and in terms of providing a bridge between the Two Nations. Gradually other major criticisms of this type of socio-religious approach began to mount up.

It was fine to organize sporting activities to attract young men and boys, but such facilities could be luring away young people from the evening classes and technical instruction which they should be attending in their leisure time in their own interests. The dedication of the Mission buildings to the social life of the parish rather than to the Church began to be questioned when the congregation failed to grow. Should the Church be responsible for recreation? Should all these social activities occupy the entire time and energy of a parish priest? Above all, the enthusiasm for the Mission in the early days had provided the funds for the buildings to be erected and fitted out on a lavish scale, but the cost of maintenance, year in, year out, became a heavy drain on available resources. Such doubts did not prevent funds being raised to build the last extensions onto the Mission buildings in 1908. In this new wing were special facilities for women and girls, who up to that time, had not played an important part in Mission activities. Mrs Harvey had organized one or two activities for them in the 1890s, but the social and cultural atmosphere of the Mission was a masculine affair.[38] The urgency and importance of the weekly meetings of the Mutual Improvement Society were not to be diluted by intrusions of the fairer sex.

In spite of these criticisms, the success of this venture was, after all, the final justification for all the effort, energy and resources that had been expended on the parish. Wilson was ready, in the year of Harvey's retirement, to accept the fact that they had failed in many of their initial objectives. But both of them were prepared to defend their activities on the grounds that cultural diffusion and social co-operation had taken place in St Agnes, albeit not in the way they had originally envisaged it. Their conviction requires some explanation, since it must rest on more than the setting up of another Mutual Improvement Society.

In a sense it did, since the St Agnes Mutual Improvement Society belonged to a tradition which lifted it out of the run of the normal. It was the last and most successful institution set up in the tradition of Christian Socialism and adult education which had been given a new impetus in the city by Benjamin Jowett of Balliol and the Rev. John Percival with the founding of the University College. Then Jowett had considered that the most important part of university education was that it should be freely available, and that university facilities should be placed within the reach of working people, especially the artisan class. In a speech in Bristol in 1874, Jowett said: 'They could not bring this class to the universities, and therefore they must take the universities to them.'[39]

The failure of the Bristol University College to reach these people had stimulated Percival to seek for other means of promoting adult education. His links with the Co-operative movement were designed towards this end. But it was Harvey at the Clifton College Mission who had the time and resources to put flesh on the educational ideal. The importance of this went far beyond what is understood by adult education in a modern context. Then, it was not only a matter of self-improvement, it could also be a liberating social influence on all those who came into contact with it. The demand for leadership in the 1880s and '90s in the Labour and Co-operative movement was supplied by men who had had their early training in just such a Bible Class or Mutual Improvement Society as the one in St Agnes.

H. P. Smith, who was born and brought up in St Agnes (and given the middle name of Percival as a mark of respect for the reforming headmaster) emphasizes two points about the kind of adult education provided at the Clifton College Mission which he thinks were important.

The first is that even for working men with no religious faith, a biblical culture was common ground among them. As the classics were used as liberating agencies in the education of the middle classes, the Hebrew tradition, in its Christianized form, was the cultural media for the artisans and the working classes. The value of this tradition was particularly important in relation to the second point. This was the fact that this form of adult education depended enormously on a close relationship between teacher and taught. The initiative for activity was from the student, and the Hebraic tradition of unpaid teachers, working for gain during the day, free in the evenings to discuss and dispute, was particularly apt. H. P. Smith writes: 'By and large the power of initiative among adult students was the determining element in the advance. Its touchstone was a vision of voluntary teachers at work in an atmosphere of plebian idealism.'[40] The crucial factor which lifted the St Agnes Mutual Improvement Society out of the norm, was the freedom Harvey gave to all members from the start. In such an atmosphere, true communication was possible, social co-operation and educational advance.

7
SOCIO-RELIGIOUS PROVISIONS FOR LEISURE 1890-1914

The YMCA and Clifton College Mission were, in Bristol in the 1880s, two major institutions which were responding to the new conditions of urban life as they saw them. Both concentrating on the leisure time of individuals: one organized on a district basis and aimed at a specific group, the other a parochial organization aimed at the local community, they offered fresh cultural dimensions to those who came into contact with them. In other cities, similar developments in socio-religious work were taking place, and settlements, home missions and youth work were established by universities, public schools and religious denominations. Such a development, touching at many points on social attitudes and an understanding of the urban environment, sparked off many different responses.

In the Church of England, the teaching of F. D. Maurice, particularly, stimulated individuals influenced by his views to interpretations of Christian Socialism which went well beyond what was acceptable to the Church as a whole.[1] Personal commitment to socialism and feelings of outrage at the appalling social conditions endured by many of the urban poor were bound to lead to economic and political views which would question the economic and social structure of society as it then stood. Stuart Headlam and the members of the Guild of St Matthew, founded in London in 1884, had reached that extreme, but they were always a tiny minority amongst the rank and file of Church of England clergy and not one of them was able to retain a living in a wealthy, urban, middle-class suburb for any length of time.[2]

Such a response was, in the main, far too intellectual and uncomfortable for congregations, themselves in the process of consolidating their own social position. In this situation philanthropic work provided a more congenial outlet for social concern, especially since social concern for the poor was a mark of religious piety. In the early 1880s the Bishop of Bristol and Gloucester set up his committee to enquire into the condition of the poor, which reported in 1884. It surveyed the philanthropic scene in Bristol with some complacency, except in the new developments relating to the recreation of the poor. Here, the committee found that in Bristol, 'there is not amongst all its benevolent associations, any which has in view the Recreation of the People, except a branch of the Kyrle Society, which appears to be very slightly supported.'[3] The Working Men's Club and Institute Union, the Open Spaces and Recreation Committee, the People's Entertainment Society and the Kyrle Society, which were all flourishing in London, were held up as worthy examples to imitate. They were all good causes and promoting them was a much more congenial path to take than the thorny route mapped out by the extremists amongst the Christian Socialists.

As for the Nonconformists, events were taking them along similar paths, though economic and political questions were, as they had been traditionally, still of secondary importance compared with evangelism. Perhaps General Booth of the Salvation Army could be seen as an extreme of the Nonconformist approach. Viewing the trends in socio-religious work, he was moved to write, with a certain savagery, in *Darkest England and the Way Out*, that Christ came to save the world, not to civilize it.[4] Social measures in his organization were directed towards the outcasts and the poorest in the community, not so that they would be 'improved', but so that by saving their bodies, their souls, too, may be saved. The elaborate system of social relief he outlines in *Darkest England* takes into account the latest findings of Charles Booth on the extent of poverty, particularly the 'submerged tenth' somehow existing on incomes below subsistence level.

The Salvation Army in practice, was now one of the most effective of the smaller evangelical sects. This owed probably less to Booth's social planning for the future than to his brilliant administrative qualities and flair for propaganda. The combination of social relief with evangelism was certainly eye-catching, as were the Salvation Army hostels built like fortresses. The emphasis he placed on saving souls and moral regeneration, however, were the traditional ones which provided the mainstay of the activities of the smaller evangelical sects, such as the Free Methodists, the Primitive Methodists, Bible Christians and the Christian Brethren. Yet, if these provided the evangelical extreme of Nonconformity, then the larger and older established denominations, the Congregationalists and Baptists, Unitarians and Quakers, had become far more committed to the 'civilizing mission', and as such, found much more common ground with those of the Church of England clergy who showed concern about social problems. The new members of Bristol's social and cultural élite, the Liberal Nonconformists, now leading town councillors and philanthropists, were particularly committed to concern over the future of the social system.

They were to be outstanding examples of the kind of liberalism that Charles Marson, one of Stuart Headlam's friends and an extreme Christian Socialist, particularly disliked. He suspected such liberalism as involving 'a tendency to divide society into two classes, those who were to teach and those who were to be taught and improved.'[5] But 'teaching and improving' provided common ground between the different sects and offered a basis of co-operation amongst people in widely different social circumstances, which the epithet 'the middle classes' tends to disguise. In the absence of a system of secondary education for all, and the dearth of social institutions and amenities in the city, this 'teaching and improving' commitment provided a cultural impetus which was to reach and profoundly influence, though not necessarily convert, a significant proportion of Bristol's citizens. The attack was organized in basically four major directions: the work for temperance; education; youth work; and missionary work; the last including missionary activity of all kinds in the spectrum, from evangelical to 'civilizing' activities. They were all competing for a share in the leisure time of the workers. In the period 1880-1914, these activities reached new peaks in support and in resources devoted to them on a voluntary basis. It was the summit of the first phase of a widespread response to the changes brought by modern conditions of urbanization.

I TEMPERANCE WORK AND THE PROVISION OF LEISURE FACILITIES

The Temperance movement in Bristol in the late Victorian period was no longer the province alone of the Quakers, or even the Nonconformists. As levels of organization developed, the Church of England entered into the fray. The Bristol Temperance Society of 1836 was amalgamated to a new Nonconformist organization, the Gospel Temperance Union.[6] A branch of the British Women's Temperance Society was set up; the Total Abstinence Society and the Church of England Temperance Society began operations in the 1880s. There were further splinter groups such as the breakaway from the British Women's Temperance Association, which called itself the Women's Total Abstinence Society; and temperance societies aimed at specific occupations such as the Bristol Branch of the National Commercial Travellers League. Beyond this, there were Temperance Friendly Societies, the Independent Order of Good Templars (in Bristol in 1871), the Rechabites Order (in Bristol, 1881), the Great Western Railway Temperance Friendly Society (1884) and the Shaftesbury Crusade (1888). At the local level, the Bands of Hope continued to function. In 1897 an attempt was made to co-ordinate all these activities by the formation of a central advisory unit, and the Bristol United Temperance Council was set up.

All this activity and institutional growth suggests that the Temperance movement was strong in the city. But the temperance workers had no rosy path to follow, neither did they have a reliable indicator of the extent of their overall success or failure.[7] The success of the penny readings and temperance entertainments had launched them in a direction which some of them felt they could not control. By emphasizing the need to provide wholesome and unalcoholic recreational activities, they had instigated a transformation in what had been, at least in most Nonconformist circles, a well-established pattern of social life. Such a life was centred on the home and the family, daily Bible readings and prayers, and chapel three times on Sunday.[8] Yet such developments as the Quaker British Workman, the temperance coffee house, was opening up new possibilities. Not only was it a means for attracting would-be drinkers from the pub; it was also offering a new range of respectable activities for those already in the movement.

There was a direct confrontation between traditional Puritanism and the possibilities of pleasure now developing. 'Amusements: their use and abuse' was a controversial point amongst temperance workers and their attitudes to leisure for the rest of the century. In 1895 the West Bristol Gospel Temperance Society invited Mrs Ormistan

Chant of London to come and speak to them on the subject.[9] Mrs Chant was famous for her successful campaign to have the drink licence of the Empire Music Hall revoked, and her speech was mainly about the need for control over music halls by all those who cared for the Temperance movement and public morality. But she was quick to add, 'She was the last person in the world to feel anything except the extreme importance of multiplying the amusement of the people.' She was not a Puritan. 'Difference of tastes were no reason for objecting to anything', but she wanted to 'free the theatres from drink and white slaves as the U.S. had freed the negroes'. To emphasize her enthusiasm for new forms of recreation, she admitted she, herself, was the chairman of a ladies' cycling club and a strong believer in good exercise and fresh air.

Such a sophisticated approach seemed irrelevant to some, especially those of the smaller Nonconformist sects whose fervour for evangelism and Puritanism compensated for their relative lack of members. However, one of the most successful temperance activities in Bristol at this time was organized by just such a group, the Bible Christians, under the leadership of Mrs Terrett. In tune with American developments in mass evangelism, Mrs Terrett founded in 1878 in Bedminster, the White Ribbon Temperance Army which had, by 1890, developed into a large movement with forty-four town and country battalions. A campaign was fought in 1882 on behalf of the American-imported equivalent, the Blue Ribbon Temperance Movement; and the establishment of numerous branches of the Gospel Temperance Union, with its message of the direct connection between teetotalism and salvation were further examples of religious teetotalism. In their fervour to convert, they reinforced the Puritan response of abstinence to the problems of leisure, as well as drink.

But for all their misgivings about the impact of too much pleasure-seeking on the moral character, the Temperance workers still had to attract support. The formula of the 1860s, penny readings, concerts and entertainments, regular weekly meetings in clubs and mission rooms, remained the easiest and cheapest to organize and the least taxing on the Puritan conscience. Specific facilities available to club members or the public, such as billiard saloons, became very unpopular with temperance workers since they often lost control of the proceedings. Billiard saloons particularly, became 'dens of iniquity', attracting undesirable characters and gamblers. But the old formula of simple entertainments and lectures had now to compete against the facilities provided by other socio-religious workers, as well as the increasing commercial exploitation of the demand for entertainment.

It is therefore surprising in some ways to find that temperance entertainments were still attracting audiences in the 1880s and '90s. Partly this can probably be explained by the sub-culture of evangelical teetotalism and the 'institutionalizing' of the Temperance Year.[10] This was clearly evident in the Band of Hope, which had entertainments in the winter months, punctuated by a Christmas tea, usually provided by some philanthropic lady. Then in the summer months there were street processions, games and nature walks, with the annual outing providing the high water-mark of pleasure. A typical experience of this last development from many possible examples, was the 1880 Annual Outing of the Grove Band of Hope, Queen's Square. Members were taken by river to Hanham on August Bank Holiday, where they had a picnic tea.[11] Temperance workers also kept up support for their activities by dropping the title 'Penny Readings' and substituting instead, 'Happy Evenings for the People', or 'Pleasant Saturday Nights'.

They also used the latest lecturing techniques, particularly the magic lantern and this, together with the old combination of songs and music, appeared to work very well. There was a strong relationship between evangelizing and organizing temperance activities. For instance, in Counterslip, the Baptists found support for their chapel, rebuilt in 1878, declining in the 1880s. In 1887 the City Mission began evangelical operations in the area to feed the congregation, and temperance entertainments were started. A typical example was a Pleasant Saturday Night held in Counterslip in 1890. The programme was as follows: Address by Mr Dove Willcox on the need for these entertainments to keep up the fight against drink and to keep the workers happy (a view endorsed by enthusiastic support from the *Western Daily Press* in numerous leader articles).[12] The entertainment provided was a selection of Scotch airs and a serenade (Artot) played by Miss Mawer on the violin; Gounod's 'Meditation' (trio); 'The Broken Pitcher' sung by Miss Laura Metcalfe, who also sang 'After Sundown' (Bonheur); Miss Alice Hazell sang two songs, 'Sunshine and Rain' (Blumenthal) and 'Sissie' (Vernorkey); Mr G. P. Tresdian of Bristol Cathedral sang 'Vulcan's Song' (Gounod) and 'In a Sheltered Vale'; and Mr J. T. Brooks sang two songs, 'Heroes of Waterloo' and 'Road to Heaven'. The proceedings were concluded by a temperance address by the Rev. J. T. Briscoe of London on 'Yesterday and Today'.[13]

One thing about the temperance entertainment of the 1880s onwards seems reasonably clear. The cultural pretensions of the penny reading were to a large extent dropped, and the emphasis was placed on keeping the workers happy with respectable entertainment. As Mr Dove Willcox said in his address, their aim was 'to bring gleams of sunshine in the lives of the toilers and workers'. He continued,

> The present reduction in working hours meant either more time in the beerhouse or more time for recreational benefit and it seemed to him that not only did it rest upon the church to evangelise the masses but also to lead them into paths of thrift and encourage higher kinds of amusement and cultivate those tastes which would bring the largest amount of joy and gladness to the home. He was thankful that the people of Counterslip took such a practical view of the church's work; and they made it their business to look after the whole man.

He was mouthing as platitudes the vision of the 1860s, talking about 'caring for the whole man' without a sense of responsibility for social conditions.

The selfconsciousness of Mr Dove Willcox's speech was a reflection of changing conditions.[14] All the evangelical activity even of the highly organized 'modern' kind in the last quarter century had failed to reach the urban masses. Social and political pressures were generating a new fear. A leader writer in the *Western Daily Press* in 1896 sounded an uneasy note:

> Educational facilities are not all that is necessary to make crowded districts of great cities cheerful.... Although it is well to find that their duties as citizens are more than ever recognized by the working classes, it is not well to find that politics should absorb all the time not devoted to labour.

Support for Temperance entertainments by now had implications beyond the primary intention of character reformation and the salvation of the individual soul. The temperance work of churches and chapels had developed political overtones.

The change can be illustrated by the fortunes of the Quaker British Workman, at its opening in 1874, the ultimate in the contribution of temperance workers to the leisure facilities of the working classes. After its initial tremendous success, support for it began to decline markedly in the early 1880s, in spite of the efforts of the Gospel Temperance Society who used the premises regularly for their evangelical temperance meetings. In 1885 it was finally closed down, though the Quaker committee blamed new road developments which tended to cut off the British Workman, as well as increased competition from the development of other leisure facilities.[15] However, in 1887 a new start was made when an independent working man's club started to use the premises and a boy's club for older boys was developed. Real revival only took place in 1889, when the British Workman was used as a centre for discussions on the dock strike and labour questions. By now, the controlling Quaker committee remained very much in the background and considerable freedom was given to the superintendent of the Workman in determining the activities which went on there.

However, in 1898 a new superintendent, Henry Brabham, was appointed, who was also secretary of the Gas Workers and General Labour Union. Relations between the committee and Brabham gradually became more strained, and breaking point was reached in 1901 when the British Workman was used for the third year running as the meeting-place of the Union's Annual General Meeting, and it became the headquarters of the Tramway Strike of that year. The Quakers, of all the Nonconformist sects, were prepared to allow freedom to the members of their social institutions, but Brabham's actions dramatically revealed the limitations of the basic tenets of their religious and political philosophy. In religious terms, they believed in the freedom of individuals and equality of all men. This, translated into economic and political terms, meant a relationship between employer and worker where each respected the rights and duties of the other's position. Striking, and what was worse, disrupting a public service, cut at the heart of their philosophy. Demand for an increase in wages was, in any case, an unpopular cause with the Quaker committee (many of the 1874 Committee were still members), since an earlier superintendent had been sacked when he demanded an increase of weekly wages from 8s. to £1. The Committee felt in 1901, that the freedom they had given the superintendent had been abused and the British Workman was no longer allowed to operate as a separate institution. It was amalgamated with the Mission and both premises were used for the Quakers' most recently successful social experiment, the development of adult schools.

The conservative nature of the Happy Evenings for the People and the failure of the British Workman were both indications that the Temperance movement had nothing new to offer to the cultural environment of the city. The formative and influential time in this respect had been the 1860s and '70s. After that, the Temperance movement's main importance was to keep the need for leisure facilities in the public eye and to campaign against the attempts made by the Other Side to fulfil them. Cleaning up music halls, campaigning against the granting of fresh licences to new public houses or attempting to get the licences of rowdy and disreputable houses taken away was more or less its only contribution. For those within the movement it was a socially cohesive force, since teetotalism marked them out as belonging to a certain behavioural pattern. In the Edwardian period, enlightened social reformers still thought that Drink was the greatest social evil. But evangelical teetotalism was a non-starter as the social pattern for future urban civilization.[16]

II LEISURE PROVISIONS FOR YOUNG PEOPLE

The failure of the Temperance movement to develop a fresh approach to social life in the city left a void which was to be filled by a development, to be one of the most successful of all the socio-religious workers' attempts to shape the social system of the future. This was their work for youth. The connection between the Temperance movement and organizations for children was most marked in the national organizations developing in the 1880s in the form of voluntary armies. The Temperance Blue or White Ribbon Temperance Army organized into battalions provides a close parallel with the militaristic Boys' Brigade with their uniforms, white sashes and local battalions. Unlike Booth's Salvation Army dedicated to salvation and social relief, the Boys' Brigade, Church Lads' Brigade, and others of their ilk, were dedicated to standards of behaviour in a similar way to the Temperance movement. Just how close the connection was can be illustrated by the fortunes of the Shaftesbury Crusade in Bristol.

Founded in 1888 by a city missionary, supported by some influential businessmen, lay members of the Mission, the Shaftesbury Crusade was intended to be a Temperance coffee house, 'an agreeable place of reunion for conversation, instruction and recreation'.[17] Unlike the Quaker British Workman, there was little freedom in its management, and the project was a failure from the start. In the early 1890s, the Rev. U. R. Thomas of Redland Park Congregational Chapel was looking for a new project for his congregation, particularly for the young people who did not have the same commitment to the projects he had been running in the previous twenty-five years. With his usual flair for organization, he formed these young members into a Guild and suggested that they took the Shaftesbury Crusade as their base and concentrated their energies on the young people of the neighbourhood. Experience had shown that the best way of reaching young people was through providing recreational and leisure facilities, and the Redland Park Young People's Guild set about their work with a zest.

They started conventionally enough with a Bible and scripture reading class and a temperance band, but extended their activities to include cultural and sports projects. There was a reading circle, a literary and discussion class, a music class, and outdoor sports activities including athletics, tennis, cycling and country walks. To attract larger numbers of children, a Boys' Brigade was formed which was soon to be the largest in the city. These activities were supervised by a small group of adult socio-religious workers drawn from one or two families, particularly the Harris family and the Tribes, and the Rev. U. R. Thomas was able to persuade wealthy Congregationalists to support this initiative with funds for expanding the Crusade buildings. By 1900 the building had a new wing which included two large club rooms for youths, another for girls, a gymnasium, a skittle alley and classrooms. It had cost £6,000, of which £2,000 had been contributed by Sir W. H. Wills Bart and £500 from Mr Tribe, the rest being raised by smaller donations and fund-raising activities. The number involved in the Mission peaked in the next few years, 4,000 a week using the premises, and by 1908 the Shaftesbury Crusade was fielding seven football teams every Saturday on top of all its other activities.

The justification of the Mission was the competition it gave to the pubs of the area, which actually declined in numbers; though the decline was probably related to the emigration of residents as the land became increasingly used for industrial and commercial purposes. But there is no doubt that its success rested largely on the work of the Redland Park Young People's Guild and the youth organization. How was it that the Boys' Brigade, particularly, was able to gain such a response here? On the face of it, it was hardly an attractive proposition. Its aim was 'the advancement of Christ's Kingdom amongst boys and the promotion of habits of obedience, reverence, discipline, self-respect, and all that tends towards a true Christian manliness'. In practice, it was highly disciplinarian with much emphasis on drill and little concern for the development of individual character.

Yet for the boys who flocked to join, such indoctrination of the need for obedience and discipline was probably, after all, only what they had been used to in their Board Schools. Meanwhile the Brigade had some obvious attractions and excitement to offer. The army organization, with uniforms and brass, bugle, fife and drum bands, and street processions through one's own neighbourhood gave status, and the recognition of that status, to boys who had never had it before. Even all the drill exercises could be endured since membership also offered facilities for playing football and cricket, using the gym for physical training, and in the summer there were summer camps – for some town boys, their first experience of staying in the countryside. The success of the Shaftesbury Boys' Brigade gave a considerable impetus to the movement in the city and many other missions, churches and chapels began to organize battalions, though those of the Church of England were likely to be branches of the Church Lads' Brigade.

Baden-Powell's Boy Scouts provided the most violent reaction against the militarism of the Boys' Brigade and the habits of blind obedience that they were supposed to inculcate.[18] Baden-Powell returned to the much older socio-religious concept, of concern with the moral development of the individual. Yet, whatever the origins of his ideology – his experiences in the Boer War, the advances being made in educational theory, his commitment to improving the quality of life for under-privileged children – one thing is abundantly evident: Baden-Powell turned against the city environment as the suitable conditions in which to nurture children. The entire commitment of the Boy Scouts and, later, the Woodcraft Folk, was to the countryside and to nature. The summer camp became, not an escape for town children, but the starting point of new dimensions of cultural experience. Baden-Powell contributed his part to the socio-religious workers', and particularly the Temperance workers', message that the city was an evil place; that social relationships with any but like-minded people were contaminating, and that true Beauty, the ultimate of cultural experience, was to be found only in the pure, 'unpolluted' countryside.

The anti-urbanism of the socio-religious workers was reinforced by the threat they considered the city posed on the central ideal of home and family life. It was a constant theme and illustrated most clearly in the provisions made for women and girls. In the early missions, mothers had been taught hygiene and infant care, but even in the missions aimed at evolving a new urban civilization such as the St Agnes mission, women and girls were left out of activities, their place being the home. Their cultural role, if they had one, was to bring elements of beauty into the home, and Kyrle societies run by many missions and socio-religious groups devoted their energies to showing women how to grow flowers in window boxes or to arrange flowers in their homes. A vase of flowers in the front window was a talisman of Respectability, an indication that the woman of the household was fulfilling her function.

Schemes to encourage women in the home and family role became quite elaborate from the mid 1870s with the development of Home Encouragement Societies. These societies organized annual shows, such as the Redland and Kingsdown Home Encouragement and Flower Show first held in 1875, and the Bedminster Home Encouragement Exhibition and Flower Show first held in 1877. At these events, classes were held for neat and tidy homes; for window gardening, for cookery, and for the best cultivated allotment land. At a Home Encouragement Society Exhibition in Hotwells in 1881, forty houses were entered for the neat and tidy home competition (there is no evidence though, of how many of these were being run by young lady rent collectors on the Octavia Hill pattern). The judges were Miss Fry, Miss Woolcombe, Miss Roberts and Mrs H. Taylor.

The unfortunate judges of the cookery class had the problem of finding which were the best cooked potatoes and peas, other culinary delights being outside the range of the competitors' financial resources.[19] Home Encouragement Exhibitions began to die out in the early 1880s as the novelty of such activities wore off, though flower shows remained popular.[20] But the relentless propaganda about home and family life continued to dominate the leisure facilities for girls.

Working Girls' Clubs began to be developed from the late 1880s, and the activities approved by the national association of Working Girls' Clubs, which came into being on the ground swell of new organizations for girls in 1895, were 'singing, needlework, cookery, Swedish drill, folk dancing, hygiene, and elementary nursing'. A Young Women's Christian Association branch had been established in Bristol in 1855, two years after the YMCA. But its subsequent development in the next half-century, in contrast with the YMCA, could not make clearer the distinction considered proper between the sexes. There were no facilities for sport. Evening entertainments, if held, consisted of some singing and reciting poetry. There were no facilities for educational classes of a more exacting kind. The hostel facilities for young men established in the 1870s were developed also for young women, and this, in fact, became the central contribution of the YWCA for its members. Two hostels, 9 Berkeley Square and 17 Portland Square, were acquired. Regulations for inmates were extremely strict, rather similar to those endured by young female servants. By the turn of the century though, attitudes were thawing a little, and in 1909 the Bristol YWCA acquired a new building which contained club facilities and a restaurant as well as hostel facilities.

The basic concern remained however, as with other socio-religious institutions for girls, mainly concerned with keeping young girls, away from home, safe from the dangers of the streets. The Bristol Free Churches combined to found a Girls' Guild for younger children in 1902 which had hostel facilities and a restaurant for factory girls. In view of their younger age, the Guild was prepared to offer sports facilities such as hockey, swimming and gymnastics (in its own gym). From the late 1880s to 1900, about thirty girls' clubs had been formed in the city and they obviously were well supported. George Hare Leonard, in his speech at the annual exhibition of the Bristol and District Working Girls' Clubs, congratulated them on their achievement at being so numerous, since many men's clubs founded by the same socio-religious organizations now no longer existed.[21] In 1908 the Bristol and District branch of the National Association of Working Girls' Clubs was founded, twenty-four clubs were affiliated with a total membership of about 1,500. Two popular girls' and women's organizations usually organized in the parish by the Church of England vicar's wife, were the Girls' Friendly Society and Mothers' Union, the first directed mainly towards girls in domestic service, the second towards GFS girls after their marriage.[22]

The theme of youth work is a recurring one in socio-religious work, some missions starting with the youth of a rough neighbourhood such as the Clifton College Mission; others turning to youth work as their temperance activities dwindled through lack of support. Whatever the varieties of objective and the type of activities instituted, socio-religious workers were pioneers in highlighting the needs of children from the time they left elementary school at ten or twelve years of age until they reached adulthood. The lack of educational facilities, low pay, and the dead-end nature of much juvenile employment had, by the Edwardian period, become recognized social evils. On a local level, the activities designed 'to keep young people from

Detailed list of organisations for Bedminster[23]
(population figures from 1911 Census)

1. *Bedminster East*
   Population 19,120 One-sixth between ages of 10–17 inclusive.
   Activities: (a) St. Michaels Parish Scouts (Parish Hall)
   (b) Branch of Y.M.C.A. (with branches of Boys' Brigade and Boy Scouts)
   (c) St. Luke's Parish Boys' Brigade (Mission Hall)
   (d) Windmill Hill Senior School Football Club.
   (e) Railwayman's Institute, Junior Section Boys' Club.
   (f) Mission Room Spring St. Girl Guides and Girls' Club.
   (g) Girl's Friendly Society (run by Vicar's wife).

2. *Bedminster West*
   Population 23,061 One-sixth between ages of 10–17 inclusive.
   Activities: (a) St. Peter's Parish – Brass Band, Cricket Club, Football Club, Lads' Club, etc.
   (b) Clifton High School for Girls Mission, Working Girls' Club.

(total number of youths in Bedminster East and West c. 7,000).

going to the bad' were quite extensive by this time. A measure of just how extensive can be illustrated by listing the activities in one working-class area, Bedminster East and West, in 1910.

Yet although socio-religious work was flourishing, this apparent success hid many problems. The Boy Scouts and Girl Guides were the last of the new national movements for youth, and there was no fresh impetus towards further developments. New clubs, if they were established, were all on existing patterns. A team of young men at Toynbee Hall under the leadership of E. J. Urwick, undertook an investigation into Boys' Clubs which they published in 1904 under the title *Studies of Boy Life in our Cities*.[24] Their findings were not reassuring. Though large numbers of clubs existed, they reached only a minority of children. Of those they did reach, the boys from good backgrounds really had no need of a club and would be better occupied, in their opinion, studying at evening classes in the hope of better employment. Those from bad backgrounds were often rarely in contact with a club. One or two might be 'saved'. But unruly members in any club were troublemakers and likely to be expelled. Furthermore, club organization totally segregated the sexes, and girls in Girls' Clubs were no longer content to be excluded from the recreational facilities offered to boys. The contributors to the survey argued amongst themselves whether clubs for boys or girls were conducive to family life, or hampered it. Once again there was confusion, as the extent of the problems of adolescents in large cities was recognized, and in socio-religious circles the sense of direction was lost. As in philanthropic work at this time, there was a demand for centralization and co-ordination of effort, and a Bristol Recreation Council was set up, which promoted in 1916 a Juvenile Organizations Committee, under Frank Sheppard, soon to be the first Labour mayor in the city.

III PROVISIONS FOR EDUCATION OUTSIDE THE FORMAL SCHOOL SYSTEM

As confusion about the contribution of socio-religious workers to youth work gained ground, one hardy perennial continued to thrive. This was the general belief, which extended well beyond the ranks of the socio-religious workers, that education was the true medium of the 'civilizing mission'. What was meant by 'education' extended well beyond the limitations of an elementary school system. As a leader in the *Western Daily Press* said in 1869: the need for education of all kinds was so great that 'the friends of education are glad to welcome any new movement which supplements the ordinary schools in whatever quarter these movements may be originated.'[25] The writer presumably had in mind the sectarian disputes over education which had divided local communities up and down the country. Here Bristol was fortunate. The good relationships between clergy of different denominations and the acceptance of the Liberal Nonconformist élite amongst the city's social and cultural élite, minimized sectarian dispute in education in the second half of the century.

The first School Board, elected in 1870, reflected this balance. Seven members were Anglican, seven Nonconformist and one Roman Catholic. Splits in voting on policy were not often on sectarian lines; questions of economy versus bold new ventures were more likely to split the Board, and then individuals voted according to their own personal opinions. Two things, though, related the School Board to the socio-religious work in the city. The first was that the Board began with far fewer children in their care than socio-religious bodies. In the course of the next fifteen years this was to change, but there remained a close relationship between the socio-religious workers' discoveries of educational need and the School Board's attempts to meet it. The setting up of the Newfoundland Road School in St Agnes at the instigation of the Rev. J. M. Wilson is a case in point. The second contact was that many Board members were important figures in the socio-religious, philanthropic, cultural and educational life of the city. There was Lewis Fry and Mark Whitwill, the Rev. J. Percival, the Revs J. W. Caldicott and Gotch, W. Proctor Baker (alderman and member of the original committee for founding the University College) and other leading citizens devoted to social reform on all fronts, particularly, though, education.

The activities of the School Board, or even the philanthropic attempts to establish secondary schools for boys and girls, were by no means the sum total of educational effort in the city. There was much provision for education outside the formal school system in many different forms and organizations. Most socio-religious activities were supposed to have educational potential and many educational activities, socio-religious objectives. Yet this diversity can, for the purpose of analysis, be sorted into three broad categories; those 'educational' activities aimed at the general public at large; those specifically designed to bring secondary education within the reach of all and to encourage scientific and technical education; and those which stemmed directly from socio-religious activities and were aimed at character-building and the provision of recreational facilities. Since the personnel involved in organizing these activities were often the same, the distinctions between socio-religious and educational work were rather blurred. In practical terms, the main organizations in these three different categories were industrial exhibitions, evening classes and adult schools. But divisions were not always hard and fast.

In view of the fact that in the many discussions about the need for more educational facilities in the 1860s and '70s, the needs of industry were constantly stressed, it is surprising to find in Bristol that there was no very specific response. Bristol had acquired a trade school long before other industrial cities, in the 1840s. It had been started by the shipping interest in the city concerned about training boys in navigation and the nautical arts.[26] The Liberal Nonconformist, Handel Cossham, had tried to develop this institution in the 1860s to meet wider industrial requirements. He organized classes on mining engineering, many of which he gave himself.[27] But there was little general support for this. There was considerable response, however, for a much less precise method of advancing scientific and technical knowledge. This was the Industrial Exhibition.

The success of the Great Exhibition of 1851, the numbers of people who saw it, the shattering impact it must have had on those who had neither been to such an exhibition before or even travelled to London, opened up possibilities which were not lost on some Bristol businessmen.[28] The very first annual outing at the Wills tobacco factory had been to the Crystal Palace. Another businessman, Liberal Nonconformist, socio-religious worker and philanthropist, Joseph Dodge Weston, became a great advocate of industrial exhibitions, both large civic exhibitions and small parochial ones, usually run by socio-religious missions. Socio-religious workers became involved in these activities since a local industrial exhibition was ranked with the penny reading and the spelling bee as an ideal method of combining public instruction with entertainment.

It was not only a matter of cultural diffusion brought about in terms of encouraging better levels of social behaviour and providing edifying spectacles. Weston believed firmly that such exhibitions could stimulate the interest and inventiveness of working men, and by this method an effective solution to technological problems in industry would be found. As he said himself:

> There was nothing more important to the interests of the working men and in the interests of the community than that they should seek to obtain knowledge of everything excellent in their own trades and then try to produce something that would be equal to it or be even in advance of it. If workmen sought for knowledge in the articles they made and were always striving to produce something better, he was sure the outcome would be a considerable improvement.[29]

He was speaking in his capacity as Mayor, at the Clifton Exhibition in 1881, and his comments seem even more like wishful thinking in view of the exhibits from working men which were on display. These included:

> models of steam and sailing ships; picture frames; miniature inlaid marble tables; a case of hats; model obelisques; choice collections of china; diminutive tea, coffee and cocoa urns; models of drawing room furniture; a set of fine-toned handbells; a combined fountain, fernery and acquarium; cases of butterflies; a glass necklace; artistically designed flower stands; bird cages in wire; models of houses and churches; tables and workboxes inlaid with horn; oil paintings; a model of a working comb factory; models of steam engines at work; model of a brass founders shop; wax flowers, and a large number of miscellaneous articles too numerous to mention.[30]

But Weston's comments begin to make sense in the cultural context to which he belonged. He was a successful businessman. He was a Liberal Nonconformist. As an individual, he had achieved integration with the social and cultural élite, being Mayor of the city for half the decade of the 1880s for which he received a knighthood. Of all people, he must have been aware of the need for more education, particularly technical education.

But this concern was secondary to his social and political concern, to create contentment among the workers. After all, a rule of thumb approach and a competitive spirit had been successful in his own case. What he considered needed developing, was a sense of fulfilment and contentment amongst the working classes. As he continued in his speech:

> He felt, he was sure all present felt, that if they could only make their artisan classes have more regard for their homes; if they could but teach them to introduce the elements of beauty into them, they should make the inmates far more comfortable and less likely to be tempted by outside excitements.

The socio-religious ideal of home and family life, gilded birdcage and all, was being extended into the industrial sphere. After all, Liberal Culture was on Weston's side. The proposal for a technical institute had been transformed into a university college because of the importance of Culture as a civilizing force. The Sheriff replied to the Mayor at this same meeting: 'The civilizing effect of art had long been a matter of commonplace remark, and thanks to the efforts of that good man – Prince Albert – (cheers) they had ever since been testing its virtue.'[31]

The 'technical instruction' aspect of industrial exhibitions, however, began to diminish as they developed dimensions beyond their educational intentions. The socio-religious element became replaced by a more commercial approach as industrial exhibitions were used to advertise wares. The parallel was made by contemporaries between the Royal South and West of England Agricultural Show (held on the Downs) and major local industrial exhibitions which displayed the products of the city's industries.[32] These exhibitions were not district exhibitions of hand-made items, the outcome of efforts by the City Missionaries to find something for the non-intellectual working men to do in the winter months. They were city exhibitions and only three major ones were held before the First World War, in 1865, 1884 and 1893.[33] The first had actually been opened by Lord Palmerston and 116,926 people passed through the turnstiles to see such wonders as that displayed by Thatcher, the printer, of College Green. His firm had printed the Lord's Prayer in 132 languages.

However, the importance of these exhibitions, particularly those of

1884 and 1893, was much greater than the nature of some of the exhibits would suggest. They were thresholds in civic experience, of importance in convincing citizens that they lived in a large industrial city. The great International Expositions, the Chicago Exhibition of 1893, the Brussels International Exhibition of 1898, and the Paris Exposition of 1900, were having similar propaganda and consciousness-raising effects.[34] Mark Whitwill, junior, was sent by the Bristol Chamber of Commerce to represent the city at the Brussels Exhibition. Apart from all the propaganda and social junketings which attended these events, they were the only occasions when there was an overall view provided of the nature and extent of technological and industrial changes taking place.

Patrick Geddes, the pioneer sociologist and town planner, seized upon the possibilities of this method of educating people into an understanding of the industrial urban environment in which they had to live. Indeed, he developed the idea of civic exhibitions of all aspects of the city's life, industrial, social, cultural, geological and botanical, etc. as the basis for working out town planning schemes.[35] The results of regional and civic surveys had to be shown in the form of an exhibition to enable the individual to understand the multi-dimensional aspects of city life. His ideas were taken up at the time of the passing of the Town Planning Act of 1909 by those interested in town planning. A Towns and Cities Exhibition was set up in London which was attended by representatives from all large cities, including Bristol. However, without Geddes, Bristol's two main exhibitions of 1884 and 1893, sponsored by two leading Liberal Nonconformist citizens, Joseph Weston and Charles Wathen, did not move as far as they might have done in this direction. The socio-religious tendencies of the sponsors, perhaps, hid the possibilities.

But if Bristol's industrial exhibitions did little more than persuade people that Bristol was now a flourishing industrial city, other socio-religious agencies were at work to provide technical instruction on a more mundane and academic basis. The need for it was obvious. As the press commented: 'It is becoming more and more evident that the U.S. and the Continent are running us a close race in some of the industries which we were wont to regard as specially our need.'[36] This particular article concludes, however, by stating that there was no need for us to be second to any nation in technological invention, if only working men would use the facilities already available to them. The writer was probably referring to the evening classes run by the Trade School and the University College, and the fortunes of these institutions clearly illustrate the social and educational problems which had to be faced in developing technical instruction.

Evening classes were the only way that working people could be reached. Yet the classes run by the University College in 1876 had been almost a total failure. Few people turned up, and amongst those that did, were people without even an adequate elementary education. In the 1880s the University College hired local schoolmasters in Board Schools to give lessons in the three Rs to those who had, for some reason, not acquired a grounding in them when young. This was hardly an extension of technical and scientific education. Classes at the Trade School fared a little better. The School had been taken over by the Society of Merchant Venturers as part of their philanthropic contribution to secondary education in the city. Money was spent on improving facilities and increasing the staff, and this support kept the School's evening classes going. The Trade School, with the YMCA was the main provider of evening classes at this time.

Socio-religious work of the 1880s was opening up new possibilities for education through evening classes. The first lesson learnt, for instance, by the YMCA in 1883 was that the way to increase support was to open up district branches, and the second, was the possibility of attracting support by providing classes which were recreational and attractive. If further education in the city was to be run on a voluntary basis, in the leisure time of working people, then something had to be done to counteract the attraction of other forms of entertainment. The answer came in 1884 with the formation of the Bristol branch of the Evening Class and Recreation Society. Its aim was 'to assist and supplement by evening classes and otherwise, efforts already made for the intellectual, moral and religious improvement of Boys and Girls.'[37]

The organizational framework of the society, however, was not a religious denomination or a mission. It was to operate around the Board School system, now well established in the city. The aim was to reach the children in the schools and persuade them to join the evening classes run by the Society, automatically, as a continuation of their education. The Society thus had to cater for all intellectual abilities and it needed a large force of voluntary workers to set up a city-wide network. For this latter task, considerable numbers of young ladies were recruited to act as district visitors, the city having been divided into administrative districts, each running their own classes, co-ordinated by the central body. The failure of other evening-class facilities to gain adequate support was to be reversed, it was hoped, by the efficiency and enthusiasm of the district visitors and the attractiveness of the classes offered.

A sample of what was offered can be taken from the 1885 session. There were classes on practical cookery and domestic economy; wood-carving; fretwork; clay-modelling; needlework; painting and drawing. Each week entertainments were held with games of various kinds and music and singing were encouraged. The enthusiasm of lady visitors extended to fund-raising schemes, and some middle-class ladies in Clifton took cookery lessons themselves, for fun, on Saturday mornings. They paid handsomely for the privilege, the money going towards defraying the cost of cookery classes at the Society's different centres. But in the organization of this Society, one thing appears to have been overlooked: the need for more provision of scientific and technical education and the fact that evening classes were the only means which were possible for this.

In 1883 the Rev. J. Percival had been invited back to Bristol by the Trades Council to give them their annual address. The core of his speech was the need for more education at every level, especially the need for more scientific and technical education. He suggested that the Trades Council should petition the Education Department to finance evening classes in Bristol for this latter purpose. The suggestion was taken up and by 1885, the money was forthcoming. The old problems of attracting students and coping with differing academic standards, however, remained. The solution was the setting up of an Evening School Committee in the city, representing those concerned with the problem. It was made up of nine members of the School Board, four members of the Trades Council and four members of the Evening Class and Recreation Society. The Board Schools provided the administrative framework, the Trades Council members were concerned to develop scientific and technical education, and the Recreation Society had to attract support.

It was a great social compromise, on a voluntary basis, to ensure that some educational facilities were widely available even within the limitations of meagre financial resources. The Education Department would only pay for evening classes in strictly academic subjects

The Reading Room

laid down in the Evening School Code. Further, the money was paid in a small fixed grant given according to the number of weeks the classes were operating, and a further grant was given in ratio to the number of candidates who were successful in examinations conducted by Her Majesty's Inspectors. It was a pretty dismal prospect for those who pinned their faith on further education through evening classes.

The Committee, though, started efficiently.[38] The administrative districts set up by the Recreation Society were slightly adjusted so that three centres, the Castle, Windmill Hill and Newfoundland Road (in St Agnes) could become centres of higher education, offering advanced courses. In other centres, instruction was still fairly elementary, though classes in science were held in all centres. Children showing promise in these courses were encouraged to attend the classes of the Merchant Venturers School or the University College, and the Evening Class and Recreation Society offered a few 'scholarships' of ten shillings each to pay for an advanced course at one of these institutions. There was no formal administrative co-operation however, between these institutions and the Evening School Committee, and there was some overlap in courses provided.

With all this effort to promote evening-class education in the 1880s, what was the result? The sixth triennial Report of the School Board (1888–9) shows that achievements were not spectacular. Table 7.1 shows the numbers reached. Table 7.2, showing the amount earned in these years, shows the burden that fell on voluntary effort. In three years, the amount which had had to be raised by voluntary effort had risen from £124 13s. 10d. to £254 12s. 11d. to £470 19s. 10d., thus almost doubling every year. In spite of this and all the effort of district visitors, the numbers reached had not been very large.

TABLE 7.1

Date	No. admitted	Average attendance	Total cost
1885–6	641	361	£304 17s. 10d.
1886–7	1,250	889	532 4s. 11d.
1887–8	1,415	630	760 1s. 10d.
1888–9	1,424		Not yet assessed

TABLE 7.2

Date	Centres	Departments	Boys/Girls/Adults: proportional nos	Examined by H.M. inspector	Grant earned
1885–6	6	9	4:4:1	355	£180 4s. 0d.
1886–7	9	12	5:5:2	519	277 12s. 0d.
1887–8	8	13	6:5:2	678	289 2s. 0d.
1888–9	9	15	7:6:2	Not known – total registered 1,424	

The work of the Evening School Committee was circumscribed by lack of money and students.

These limitations were so depressing that not even a fresh initiative from Clifton College to promote education in the city was enough, though the headmaster, the Rev. J. M. Wilson did try. In 1888 he called a meeting to set up a General Educational Council in the city and 300 people attended. A Committee was formed from representatives of the University College, Merchant Venturers School, Endowed Schools of Bristol, Clifton and Redland High Schools, Bristol School Board, nine representatives from elementary schools and, in line with the socio-religious civic tradition, three general citizens of Bristol. A weighty committee, and its objectives were equally weighty and comprehensive, relating to all aspects of the city's educational system. Deficiencies were to be highlighted by propaganda, and co-operation between all educational institutions encouraged. This comprehensive approach was rounded off by an expressed desire that all members of the council would find encouragement, intellectual stimulation and a means for social intercourse through the social activities the council intended to organize. But the problems faced by the educationalists on every level were too great for the council ever to be effective or indeed, long-lived. Records of its existence last only from April to October 1888.

As far as evening classes and scientific and technical education were concerned, rescue operations from a desperate situation were begun in the early 1890s, by increasing initiatives from the Central Education department. The 'whisky money' of 1891 brought welcome relief to technical instruction classes within the formal educational system, especially to the newly developing Merchant Venturers Technical College, emerging from the embryo of the Trade School.[39] Evening classes in the city were given a new lease of life when in 1893 there was a further extension of subjects which could be fee-earning. This marked the end of the need for the Evening Class and Recreation Society, and the Society decided first that 'in consequence of the great alterations made by the Education Department, the council considered that there was no necessity for the society to continue its connection with the School Board.'[40] The Society finally went into liquidation in 1895.

Its demise, however, did not mean an end of the traditions in which it had been nurtured. These still continued to make their influence felt in the organization of evening classes for the rest of the century and beyond. The social objective of socio-religious workers' interest in education had been the encouragement of morality and upright character through knowledge of the Bible and membership of some religious congregation. The non-sectarian approach of the Evening Class and Recreation Society had converted religious commitment to sect to a question of the 'common good'. Under the secular control of the Evening Class committee of the School Board after 1893, the objective became, not a generalized religiosity, but commitment to the city and ideas of social citizenship. Throughout the 1890s, an evening class was held entitled 'the life and duties of a citizen', to which eminent citizens gave their services free as part of their contribution to this new social objective.[41]

The other tradition of socio-religious educational work had been the recognition that educational facilities had to attract as well as instruct. With the new freedom given by the range of subjects now grant-earning, the Evening School Committee pursued this tradition with enthusiasm. In the 1890s, their initiatives expanded with the favourable response that they received. People from a wider age group were encouraged to come and facilities were offered that were completely new. Shorthand and typing classes became important, candidates being examined by the Pitman's Association and the Society of Arts. There was a class for constables (a success in spite of the Boer War) and a St John's Ambulance class. Cultural activities were not neglected. A central choral class was built up and so much enthusiasm shown for it that the Evening School Committee was petitioned to allow it to meet in the holidays. A love of the countryside and local fauna and flora was encouraged by the organization of a Rambling Club, to visit places of interest. The curator of the museum agreed to give supplementary expositions on Saturday afternoons to the lectures held at the museum during the week on local history and botany, and he quite often had an audience of 300 students. An indication of the nature and extent of evening school work in the city towards the end of the century can be gained from the Tables 7.3 and 7.4.

In fact, by now the future outlines of evening-class work had become defined. It was recognized that it could never be the means

TABLE 7.3 *Some statistics of Evening School work for the Year 1896–7 – selected to give some indication of the impact of evening school work in Bristol towards the end of the century*
(taken from Reports of Evening School Committee)
October 1896 – 1,293 enrolled first week, average attendance 1,166
October 1897 – 2,032 enrolled first week, average attendance 1,754

Subjects taught 1896 – 7 Government grants paid

Subjects	Total no. of students taught
Reading and recitation	869
Writing and composition	883
Reading and writing	207
Arithmetic	1,428
English	183
Geography	100
History	235
'Life and Duties of a Citizen'	91
French	198
Algebra and Mensuration	31
Ambulance	392
Book-keeping	396
Shorthand	872
Vocal Music	440
Domestic Economy	78
Needlework	363
Cookery	319
Manual Instruction	567
Drawing, Elementary	627
Drill	108

TABLE 7.4 Statistics of ages of those at evening schools for session 1896–7

School		Under 13 years	13 to 14	14 to 15	15 to 16	16 to 17	17 to 18	18 to 19	19 to 20	20 to 21	21 and over	Total
Anglesea Place	Boys	3	7	11	6	7	5	8	4	2	16	69
Avonmouth	Mixed	18	17	20	15	10	6	2	6	3	21	118
Barleyfields	Boys	13	24	22	45	14	13	7	3	3	15	159
Barton Hill	Boys	12	13	36	31	24	14	10	1	3	12	156
Barton Hill	Girls	12	16	13	11	7	2	1	1	2	6	71
Castle Comm.	Mixed	13	37	61	55	56	41	38	25	15	62	403
Newfoundland Rd.	Boys	13	28	26	53	22	19	12	2	2	34	211
Newfoundland Rd.	Girls	4	12	23	19	14	11	5	5	3	8	104
South Street	Boys	18	28	26	32	25	13	11	7	5	26	191
South Street	Girls	6	14	33	28	15	12	10	2	1	1	122
Windmill Hill Comm.	Mixed	3	15	30	36	22	16	12	10	6	16	166
Windmill Hill Lower Grade		—	34	41	20	16	7	3	6	9	14	150
		115	245	342	351	232	159	119	72	54	231	1,920

of providing secondary education to the masses. As the School Board Report of 1898–1901 stated:

> Evening school work has its special difficulties. Indifference to progress, late hours of employment, overtime, clubs, the multiplication of places of amusement and even such organizations as Boys' Brigades, Band of Hope and Church of England societies, all tend to keep down the number of students.

Evening classes could not fulfil the demands of industry for more scientific technical education, nor could they compete with the purely recreational facilities of the city. But somewhere in the middle, they had found a role. A certain amount of vocational training, largely geared to the demands of shops and offices, particularly secretarial and accounting work and technical drawing, was offered to the working-class boy or girl with enough dedication to pursue such courses, in the evenings after work. There was a smattering of general cultural education available in foreign languages and the arts, and recreational facilities were provided for those who wished to join in organized activities.

As an achievement, it fell far short of the idealistic aspirations of the Rev. J. Percival, his Association for the Promotion of Evening Classes, and his desire to create an adult education movement which would lead to new levels of civilization and cultural experience. Those aspirations had to find a fresh context and a different group of men in which to flourish. The link Percival had encouraged between socio-religious workers' provision for education, university extension and workers' own educational aspirations, particularly in the Co-operative movement, was being forged in the 1890s which was to lead to the founding of the Workers' Educational Association in 1902, and the opening up of a new dimension of adult education. But these developments took place on the whole, quite outside the system of education through evening classes, built up in co-operation with, and finally in the control of the School Board.

IV DEVELOPMENTS IN ADULT EDUCATION

The socio-religious workers' provisions for education however, were to play an important part in the events which led up to the Workers'

Educational Association and kindred developments. At the centre of their contribution was the idea of adult schools which was to gain great popularity in the city, especially in the 1890s. Adult schools though, belonged to a much older tradition. They grew out of Sunday School work for children which the Quakers, particularly, were ready to extend to adults as well. This development did not take place until the mid-nineteenth century – the Quakers' First Day School for Men was not founded until 1857 – but Bible Classes and Mutual Improvement Societies had been flourishing long before then and contributed their part to the Adult School movement. Two factors were of outstanding importance in determining the direction the movement was to take. These were, that adults could not be treated like children at a Sunday School, particularly if adult schools wished to gain members and support; second, the Quakers played by far the most important part in establishing the movement in the city, and by inclination and practice they were far more willing than other Nonconformist bodies to take a non-doctrinaire line.

The result was that adult schools gained, of all socio-religious institutions for the social, moral and educational welfare of the masses, an independence which does much to explain their popularity in the 1890s and 1900s, when Men's Clubs and other institutions were failing through lack of support. The man who probably did most to achieve this result was Joseph Storrs Fry, Secretary to the Adult School Association 1874–98, whom we have already met as Chairman of the family firm, member of the cultural and social élite, Hon. Treasurer of the Bristol Museum and Library Society, and in his socio-religious work, member of the Quaker Mission and President of the Bristol YMCA. Since his contribution to the Adult School movement was so vital, it is worth briefly describing how he became involved in it.

He had begun as a class superintendent of the Friends' First Day School for Boys in 1852. This school had been founded in 1810 and was very much in the strict Sunday School tradition.[42] Fry, with one or two others, tried to break away from the inflexible Sunday School pattern, since Quakers had no vested interest in instilling such things as the catechism into unwilling minds. Instead they developed a wider range of activities at the Friends' School, extending to week-day evenings as well as Sundays and including Mutual Improvement Societies, a rambling club, and Bands of Hope and temperance groups. The aim was to nurture a spirit of friendliness and co-operation between teachers and scholars, and at Mutual Improvement Society meetings, strictly religious education was sometimes dropped and debates held instead. Even plays were read and discussed and elocution was practised. In a history of the school written in 1910, the author states: 'Many "old boys" now taking a prominent part in the City Council, acknowledge with thankfulness the help received while attending these educational classes.'[43] In all this activity, Fry was stepping beyond the well-defined limits of Sunday School work and met with growing opposition from Quaker elders. Finally, in 1874, he was stopped from pursuing these activities by his 'spiritual advisers' and prohibited from attending the school forthwith.

In this action, the Quaker elders were not only making a Puritan stand, they were in line with the policy of the Sunday School Union and the generally accepted view on the nature of Sunday School work. Throughout all the developments in socio-religious work in the nineteenth century, Sunday Schools remained the one institution in all denominations which was determinedly and dogmatically religious. At the centenary meeting of the Sunday School movement in 1880, this policy was reiterated as being the only one possible for such an institution, though there was condemnation of teachers who made the children recite sacred texts without understanding them in the least; and an expressed hope that in the future Sunday Schools 'should not be made places in which children should find weariness rather than pleasurable and profitable occupation.'[44] Sunday Schools, however, were never allowed to organize leisure activities on a regular basis. Their main contribution in this field was the passive one of providing a fertile recruiting ground for other youth organizations.

When J. S. Fry was stopped from pursuing his Sunday School work, he transferred his energies to the adult school, becoming secretary of the Bristol Adult School Association in 1874. Under his leadership, the movement grew rapidly. He wanted to continue the 'friendly and social' terms which had existed between teacher and scholar in his work in the Boys' School and he was also prepared to include educational and recreational activities, as well as religious instruction. In fact, religious instruction began to take a much smaller proportion of total time, and activities were more equally divided between the educational and recreational. Between 1890 and

1900 the Quakers opened fourteen branch schools in different districts in the city and suburbs, and their success and example encouraged other denominations to join in the work.

By 1900 there were forty-five schools for men, and in the Edwardian period, some schools acquired new purpose-built premises. An example of the latter provides a good insight into the nature and activities of an Adult School. The Hotwells Adult School Club gained a new building in 1908. The basement was given over entirely to indoor sporting activities; punch ball, quoits and a skittle alley were provided. On the ground-floor there was a reading room, refreshment bar, washhouses and the caretaker's room; whilst on the first floor there was a large assembly room used for school meetings on Sunday and any other function during the week which needed space, particularly plays, debates, recitations and indoor sports. Apart from the hall, there were four other rooms on the first floor. These were a draughts- and chess-room, a billiard-room with two full-sized billiard tables, a room for non-smokers and a meeting room for the management committee.

The formula appears to be very similar to that pioneered by the Rev. T. W. Harvey at St Agnes. Adult schools were local community centres providing education and recreation for near-by inhabitants. However, in theory at least, there was a big difference between Harvey's Working Men's Club and the adult schools. Harvey's ambition had been to provide, under the indirect influence of the church, a suitable environment in which cultural activities could be pursued and a new concept of urban civilization realized. Adult schools, on the other hand, had no specific ideological aspirations. They were simply the means whereby wholesome entertainment, recreation and educational facilities, under suitably moral influence, could be made widely available to the respectable poor. Mr Dove Willcox's phrase 'bringing gleams of sunshine into the lives of the toilers and workers' springs to mind. However, they were usually controlled by management committees drawn from amongst the ordinary membership and the overall control of the religious denominations who provided them was lightly exercised. 'Suitably moral influences' could be summed up as the common biblical culture which ran through all these organizations, though many members had no religious commitment and were even atheists. The career of William Straker provides one illustration of how the adult schools were able to operate freely, although ostensibly under the religious control of church or chapel.

Straker was a secularist who was to become the first district secretary of the Workers' Educational Association in the Western district. A native of St Agnes, he gained his first educational training in a Bible class and then a Quaker adult school, in spite of his antireligious views. He became 'an amateur of learning and an accomplished local botanist'.[45] He also happened to be an employee in the Fry factory, where his job was repairing the harness of the van horses. J. S. Fry, with his deep commitment to socio-religious work and the concept of 'caring for the whole man' was a paternalistic employer. Daily prayers were held at the factory in the city centre, in an old Wesleyan chapel that had become swallowed up by the firm's expansion. When the whole factory was moved to the southeast of the city, Fry provided sports facilities for his employees with a handsome pavilion on a near-by field to add to the facilities – restaurant, washing facilities and reading room – already provided for the staff. He then forbade the organization of trade unions amongst his employees. What need had they of these organizations since he was providing for their every need?

Resistance to this was led by Straker. He and a few others had the idea of forming within the firm, a branch of a union outside Fry's sphere of influence. Accordingly they set up the Confectionery Branch, which was affiliated to the Dockers' Union. It was to be the germ of the future Transport and General Workers' Union. Straker maintained support for this Confectionery Branch by organizing regular educational activities such as he had already been engaged in with local co-operators and the small group of men who founded the Bristol Sunday Society in the late 1880s, which was to gain considerable support in the 1890s. Thus Straker's early training in Bible class and adult school had both failed to make him a religious convert or a tool of those who organized such activities. He had gained a love of learning which was to be the mainstay of his life, and he found his true vocation in his work for the Workers' Educational Association.

Yet for all his independence of outlook, he was touched by the same idealism as Percival and Harvey. Percival indeed, 'extolled well-tried cooperators such as Mansbridge and Straker because they combined the vision of a moral movement with a public educational policy'.[46] Though a secularist, Straker was tolerant of the religious views of others and in his old age, when he had become a member of the Bristol Education Committee, he was much in demand at prize days in local schools, for handing out the scripture prizes. Straker's work for adult education, the Workers' Educational Association and the Co-operative movement only gathered momentum in the second half of the Edwardian period, and until then the adult schools played an important part in providing educational and recreational facilities. By 1908 the Quakers had been joined by the Baptists and Congregationalists in the provision of adult schools, and others had sprung up independently, such as the one at Barton Hill, which used the School Board buildings for its meetings. There were now about fifty schools with around 5,000 members. It was one of the few areas in which socio-religious workers found the response to their activities remained undiminished.

V THE SOCIAL WORK OF RELIGIOUS MISSIONS

Many of these adult schools were developed in fact, by missions who found that the limitations of their work were becoming ever more apparent. In the period 1890–1910 the mission movement split apart as its role came to be questioned. Not many socio-religious workers committed to mission work, though, were quite as rationally honest as the Quakers, who stated in their 1890 Report: 'And now it may be asked what are the results of this varied labour of your Missionary, your committee and the numerous Friends who have given time, and thought, and money, to the New St. Mission? and we can only answer – we cannot tell.' The great 'civilizing' mission had not obtained its socio-religious objective: the conversion of the urban masses. The Quakers continued however, to organize activities for the next decade, though the feelings of disillusionment grew ever more compelling, reinforced by the problems of the British Workman Coffee House and the trade unionist superintendent, Henry Brabham. Finally, in 1905, the Quaker Mission Committee decided to admit defeat, and the Mission, founded with such deep hope in 1865, ceased to function as a mission. But practical as ever, the Committee made plans to let the premises remain available for the social needs of the neighbourhood under the auspices of the Adult School Association.

Other missions, however, run by denominations committed to higher levels of socio-religious propaganda than the Quakers, were not prepared to give up so readily. Instead, the 1890s, particularly, mark a period of frenzied missionary activity, when all the well-worn paths of missionary work, straightforward evangelism, temperance work, youth work, and the provision of cultural facilities, were followed again by ever more vociferous missionaries. Only now such activity had ceased to be purely socio-religious. The political dimension of needing to keep the workers happy and occupied, away from the dangers of trade unionism and politics could not but be apparent to the businessmen who provided most of the financial resources needed to maintain socio-religious work.

Thus instead of concern over the social life of the urban poor developing towards an ever-increasing understanding of the impact of an urban environment on society, an insurmountable barrier to such an understanding was erected. Leisure facilities and concern for the environment as 'caring for the whole man' had become the moral basis of 'social citizenship', which in turn was part of the capitalist answer to socialist demands for greater economic as well as social equality. A significant split was opening up between cultural and political aspirations along class lines. Such a division was a grotesque development of the idealism of the 1860s and '70s.

What happened was a drying up of that creativity of the earlier period which had given such impetus to fresh institutional developments. Now there was some expansion in activity in the late 1890s, but nothing on bold new lines. Some dedicated Christians tried to force a way through the impasse. Stuart Headlam's Christian Socialist Guild of St Matthew had adopted a socialist position and the policy of land reforms proposed by Henry George. Other 'Christian Socialists' amongst the ranks, both of the Nonconformists and the Church of England, were not prepared for a political solution, and yet they were deeply concerned about economic and social questions. National associations were set up, the Nonconformist Christian Social Brotherhood and the Church of England Christian Social Union. It is significant that the Bristol branches of these associations met, the Nonconformists at the YMCA; the Church of England group at the St Agnes Parish Room.

The aims of the former were stated to be 'to emphasize the need of a deeper recognition of the relation of universal brotherhood implied in Christian discipleship and to study social problems'; whilst the latter was dedicated 'to the application of the Christian teaching to life, preceded by a careful study of the problems to be met'. Its studies were listed as the current phases of housing and temperance reform, commercial morality, trade unions, etc.; it had a woman's trades sub-committee; and it had issued leaflets on Dangerous Trades and 'Leadless Glaze'.[47] But both the Nonconformists and Church of England associations constituted nothing more than worthy attempts to meet political problems with religious solutions. There is little evidence to suggest that they were widely supported, though they were consulted from time to time on specific issues such as housing, for instance, when in 1907 the Bristol Trades Council were making their investigation into the housing problem.

A theoretical solution to the impasse, however, remained impossible without political commitment. Yet some practical ways around it were opened up by a few socio-religious workers who had got used to responding to needs and theorizing afterwards. This was particularly the case with the Settlement movement, especially the university settlements both in London and the provincial cities. Canon Barnett's career exemplifies this trend. He had, for example, early on in his career become deeply involved in the educational provisions for children in his parish. His ideas on what constituted an education were so far advanced, that his school lost its grant for not sticking rigidly to the authorized syllabus. But whatever liberal cultural ideals he may have had on the purpose of education, he was faced with an immediate practical problem. The children attending his school were often hungry and undernourished. Yet the solution of feeding them undercut socio-religious ideas about home and family life. In the 1880s, only those committed to a different set of principles, such as Annie Besant, in her socialist stage, and serving as a member of the Tower Hamlets School Board, were ready to advocate strenuously that schoolchildren should be fed.

Barnett, however, though initially with some reluctance, was prepared to put practicalities before ideology. As he wrote in *Towards Social Reform*:

Visitors to schools in poor neighbourhoods may convince themselves that, whether it be from poverty, ignorance or carelessness, many of the children are ill-nourished ... the obvious remedy is free meals. But family life owes much of its strength to the family meal, whose preparation and expectation keep together the heart of mother and children.[48]

By adopting this pragmatic approach, Barnett felt able to dodge the obvious conflict growing between socio-religious work and socialist ideas even to the extent of writing his last book, before his death in 1913, on *Religion and Politics*. This example of Barnett's, towards a pragmatic and practical approach to immediate problems was developed much more fully by the younger generation now involved in settlement work.

Bristol University settlement, which came into existence in 1910, had grown from some socio-religious work undertaken by Marian Pease, a Quaker, in the parish of St Luke's in the 1880s. Then she had organized clubs and societies for women and girls where the main activities were domestic economy and entertainments, interspersed with sewing classes in which students had to conduct 'improving' conversations with their benefactress whilst they sewed. In 1910 all these traditions were determinedly thrown away. The settlement run by Hilda Cashmore was devoted instead to what we should now recognize as social work. Gone were the entertainments and methods of 'civilizing' the poor. Now it was a matter of providing help and information to those in some kind of need about problems such as rents and housing, or sickness and unemployment. Settlement workers kept case histories and worked on practical problems as professionally as possible.

This was very much a development of the late Edwardian era and, meanwhile, many other missionaries were determined to have their last fling. The 1890s, in fact, superficially appears to have been one of the most religious decades in the city's history. The amount of newsprint devoted to the cause of making Bristol a Christian city was staggering. There were numerous religious, temperance and missionary publications. This was the decade of the *Bristol Christian Leader*, published between 1891 and 1896, and the high water-mark of the parish magazine. What they had to report was renewed attempts at missionary work by Nonconformists and Church of England alike, in both directions of socio-religious work, the straightforward evangelizing, and the 'civilizing' mission. In the former, the complexity and variety of methods used to get the working classes to partake in some form of religious worship had never been surpassed.

There were the mass evangelical techniques used by the Christian Brethren in the city, made popular by the Moody and Sankey crusades. There was the evangelical social work of the Salvation Army fighting against evil. Now there were also evangelical missions which were undenominational. It did not matter which way you approached your Saviour, as long as you believed. In 1893, for instance, some tents were put up in a field off Mina Road, and non-sectarian religious services held there on Sundays, which resulted in the formation of a new People's Mission. Other missions were started, not based on a district or parish, but on specific social groups; one even being started for that blasphemous crew, Bristol's cabmen. Every attempt was made to allay the suspicion and distrust of working men about religious propaganda. Musical services were held at the Colston Hall on Sundays when George Riseley, the Cathedral organist, played sacred music. These were non-sectarian, but Riseley was sponsored by the Nonconformists in his afternoon appearance, and the Church of England in the evenings. It was all rather frenetic and the impetus behind these missionary attempts usually petered out.

But the crusading spirit gave a new lease of life to some of the old established missions, particularly those of the Congregationalists, Baptists and Wesleyans. The Bristol City Mission was still operating as their evangelical watchdog, trying to keep up the strength of their congregations in inner-city areas and the working-class suburbs. One of the most successful of the city missionaries was C. R. Parsons, who built up a Bible Class to feed the Old Market St Wesleyan Chapel, which had more than 1,000 members. His avowed aim was 'To foster love of the word of God and Christlike sympathy with each other, to promote brotherliness, to win souls for the Saviour and to elevate the character of the members for time and eternity.' Parsons used directly evangelical methods, mass meetings, street canvassing and street processions with bands, and he maintained the evangelical impetus by encouraging members of the class to undertake their own missionary work. Since 1883 some of his class members had been involved in running a mission at Wesley Hall in St Philips.[49]

But in spite of this success, the city missionaries could not adequately cover every district in the city, and in 1888 the city missionary for Broad Plain, St Philips, had to be withdrawn. This had been an area where the Highbury Congregational Chapel and its members had been active since 1870, and the withdrawal of the city missionary left what they considered to be a vacuum, which they were determined to fill. Only this time the mission was to be the culmination of all the experience gained by the Highbury Congregationalists in many years of social work. They decided to plump for the 'civilizing mission' rather than evangelical work, and Broad Plain was to be the peak of their efforts. Highbury Chapel had been responsible since the 1870s for three missions in Bristol, at Kingsdown, Anvil Street and Southmead. But Broad Plain was designed to have the greatest impact on the social life of the neighbourhood; it was to transform the social environment.[50]

A resident warden was appointed, George Hare Leonard, later to be a Professor of History at the University College and a strong supporter of the University Settlement. He wanted Broad Plain to be a 'University College' for the people of St Philips (no church was to be built) and the educational classes there gained a high reputation as Leonard engaged the support of his friends and colleagues. Broad Plain never quite gained the same impetus as the St Agnes Working Men's Club. Leonard, for all his cultural idealism, was still firmly within the Nonconformist tradition of cultural diffusion rather than mutual co-operation which had been the keynote of the St Agnes Mission. Activities reminiscent of the early Kyrle Societies of the 1870s, flourished at Broad Plain.

As Leonard himself said:

> In our work we felt constantly the need of bringing beauty into the lives of those who spent their time in dull or ugly surroundings. Much was done to encourage the growth of flowers in window boxes which we made and gave to our neighbours. We had such success that it might be said that whole streets blossomed like a rose. We often had gifts from friends with suburban gardens, but still the demand was insatiable.[51]

To be fair to Leonard, his Mission did contain many elements of the kind of work to be undertaken later by the Bristol Settlement, which can be broadly termed as social work. Besides all the usual activities such as clubs for boys and girls and a working men's club, a penny bank and sickness benefit schemes, Broad Plain did offer facilities for cripples, it did have a district nurse attached to it, and its own poor man's lawyer. It certainly engaged the energies of many of the Highbury congregation in the 1890s, reconfirming their belief in the 'civilizing mission'.

For some, such as Mark Whitwill, it was the crowning touch of a lifetime's work for cultural improvement. As town councillor for St Philips, back in the 1870s, he had campaigned for a people's park, and for a free public library. His concern for temperance had led him to support warmly the Quakers and their British Workman Coffee House. Now Broad Plain was offering a community centre where intellectual, social and recreational needs could be met, its influence radiating visibly out through the streets, marked by the flowers in the rows of window boxes. Could this be, at last, the Nonconformist takeover from the Church of England as the dominant social and cultural influence in the parish? The Congregationalists, unlike the Quakers, were not prepared to admit defeat.

But by the turn of the century, it became obvious that the flow of energy and resources required to maintain such a mission could not be sustained indefinitely. The specific help the mission provided with social problems ensured that it met with some response. Yet the thinking behind the recreational and leisure facilities was dominated by the idea that if the poor were given the same kind of facilities as the rich, this would cure social unrest as all would be socially equal. It was an idea which had appealed to many socio-religious workers, though its ultimate absurdity had already been demonstrated in the 1880s with the failure of Walter Besant's People's Palace of Delight in the East End. This experiment is worth describing briefly as, in spite of its failure, the ideas behind it were to appear again and again not only in socio-religious work, but also in the town planning movement before the First World War.

Besant outlined his ideas in his novel *All Sorts and Conditions of Men*, which he published in 1882. His basic theme was that the discrepancy between the lives of the rich and the poor, the cause of so much social unrest, could be eliminated if the poor had the same social facilities and opportunities as the rich. He wrote:

in the Palace of Delight we are equal to the richest: there is nothing which we, too, cannot have: what they desire, we desire; what they have we shall have: we can all love, we can all laugh; we can all feel the power of music; we can dance and sing; or we can sit in peace and meditate.[52]

It was to be inter-class co-operation based on joy or delight. But it did not work. Rowdy elements with no interest in an applied use of leisure time caused difficulties and had to be eliminated by putting up entrance fees, which in turn lost the Palace popular support.

As for the recreational and educational ambitions of those who used the palace, they were not the same as those of the philanthropists. Instead of 'joy' and 'delight', there was a demand for excitement to be gained by gambling in the billiard saloon; instead of Liberal Culture and literary ambitions, those wanting educational classes showed greater demand for technical and vocational training. Within a few years the palace became financially unviable and its facilities were taken over by the draper's company to be run, in Besant's words, as 'a polytechnic and nothing else'.[53] Yet as a method for counteracting the social degradation of a poor environment, the idea lived on. An article on the 'Recreation of the Poorest' in the *Town Planning Review* of 1912, comes to the conclusion that the best answer for improving the environment of the poor was a people's palace.[54]

The fact that ideas remarkably similar to those of Besant's, could still be put forward seriously, thirty years after the publication of *All Sorts and Conditions of Men,* is an indication that there was little fresh thinking now on the environmental problems of the slums. By the 1890s, the ideas of those who had started from religious, social or cultural standpoints to combat the evils of the city, had been worked through. Whatever personal success or failure had attended their efforts, all had proved ultimately bankrupt in the face of economic inequality and the sheer weight of poverty. It was recognized, gradually, that to make an impact on slum conditions needed a new outlook and a fresh list of priorities, requiring resources largely outside the scope of voluntary work. The Quakers had begun to recognize this from the 1890s, benefiting from the fact that the freedom they allowed in their social institutions brought the realities of the situation more quickly to the fore.

The Congregationalists, Baptists and Wesleyans took another

twenty years to reach the same conclusion. The Wesleyans in Bristol had come to the 'civilizing' mission rather late. They had been shattered numerically by schism in the mid-century years, and their missionary efforts had tended to be more or less straightforward evangelizing. But in 1899, with new confidence in their own strength and security, a missionary campaign was started, to result in three new missions using some of the 'civilizing' techniques. One of the missions, operating from an old theatre building, was actually called the People's Palace, though whether this was a matter of direct competition with local music halls or a reference to Besant's idea is not clear.

What is clear, though, was that these missions, like all the 'civilizing' missions of the 1890s and 1900s, conformed to a distinct pattern. Recreational and educational work was carried out on strictly traditional lines. A biblical culture was common to all, and the precepts of Liberal Culture were the guiding influence on the choice of recreational and educational activities. Fresh air, healthy exercise and sport were also encouraged since they were popular and non-political; whilst summer camps and country rambling fed an idealism about nature and rural values to counteract the 'evils' of urban life. Support for these 'civilizing' missions however, was bolstered up increasingly, by the social work they undertook outside the 'cultural improvement' sphere. Even the Wesleyans, who tended to be more evangelical than the Congregationalists and merely larded their evangelical activities with doses of cultural improvement, were on an equal footing when it came to social work. They undertook 'social rescue' work and organized a Labour bureau. As the 'civilizing mission' ground slowly to a halt, it was this aspect of socio-religious work which remained as the kernel for future development. The difference between Broad Plain Mission of the 1890s and the University of Bristol Settlement of 1910 clearly illustrates this shift.

For the churches and chapels this really meant the end of the road, more or less, of the 'civilizing mission'. Justification for religious bodies undertaking social work had always been a sensitive question and once the objective of the ultimate salvation of souls was removed, or pushed ever further into the background, arguments against churches and chapels continuing this work became more convincing. However, total withdrawal was difficult. Clubs, societies and institutions continued to flourish in the years before the First World War.

The Clifton College Mission to St Agnes gained its last group of buildings in 1908. In this dilemma between present responsibilities and an ultimate desire to withdraw, the logic of the situation and practical requirements brought about the final flowering of the socio-religious traditions of the last half-century. Under the common banner of 'social citizenship', religious bodies found themselves able to co-operate with the municipal council, to co-ordinate, maintain and find aid for their activities. In 1908 the Lady Mayoress, Mrs Edward Robinson, launched the Social Service League for this purpose.

Municipal authorities, often in the control of the same people who were engaged on socio-religious work, had long appeared to be the ultimate refuge for those concerned with the social environment. At Toynbee Hall, Barnett's young men were deeply engaged in the administration of local government machinery in the cause of the common good. In 1893 Barnett was appointed a canon of Bristol Cathedral and he wrote a pamphlet entitled 'The Ideal City', lifting his head for the moment from the problems of the East End to contemplate the application of 'social citizenship' to a whole city. His enthusiasm is infectious as he begins to outline what he thinks could be achieved if the city's leaders really believed in this concept. The major base of his plan is close co-operation between the town council and voluntary socio-religious institutions in the city. The former was to extend its activities to meet every practical requirement, the latter would bring light, culture and close co-operation between the classes.

The city, through the activities of its rich and educated citizens, would become responsible for the total welfare of all citizens. The city, not the state, was the creative force in modern civilization. Poverty, want, hunger, ignorance and disease, could all be conquered in the city. The town council could, by application of the Artisan's Dwelling Act, replace dwellings; it would compel factories to consume their own smoke; it could provide a crematorium; it could make civic buildings enobling and inspiring and, by laying new, cheap tramlines to the hills surrounding the city, open these up to residential development. It could secure purity of all food and drink; complete the sewage system; make the river sweet; inspect, regulate and provide lodging houses; establish an art gallery; open museums and libraries on Sundays; suppress improper houses; make playgrounds; be a model employer; increase and develop the means for washing and bathing, and finally, increase street lighting and thus decrease the police rate. The town council's actions were to be supplemented by an enlightened School Board which not only made educational facilities more efficient, but also attractive as well; and an equally enlightened Board of Guardians which might organize a pension scheme, a training centre for the unemployed and hospital care for every sick person. Barnett knew his ideal city was a dream, for even if the will was there, the resources were not. He was not above retorting though, that 'the expense involved in such changes is not a necessary obstacle. The Japanese have made far greater changes.'[55]

But Barnett's vision was way beyond the aspirations and/or the capabilities of Bristol's social and cultural élite. By the middle of the Edwardian period, two important developments were encouraging them to seek a larger, less personal framework for their social work, and to place the fruits of their efforts under the wing of the municipal council. The first was the growing political and industrial power of the organized Labour movement. The second, the continuing growth of the city, which was leading to boundary extensions and administrative changes diluting the power and influence of the élite. In view of these developments and the experience of missionary work after 1900, with its increasing emphasis on social work, the setting up of a Social Service League in 1908 by the Lady Mayoress seemed a natural step. Between 1908 and 1910 the concept of a municipal welfare system was given practical form as Mrs Robinson's Social Service League was amalgamated with the Bristol Charity Organization Society to form the Bristol Civic League. The League was mainly concerned with social problems, particularly housing, but it did acquire a Juvenile Recreation Committee to co-ordinate and encourage the youth organizations founded by the socio-religious workers.

The establishment of this League marked the end of the socio-religious workers' hopes of solving the 'social problem' by providing for the social life of the working classes. Yet their work had uncovered some of the fundamental changes affecting the social life of the poor in an industrial urban environment. In at least three different fields they had pioneered important new facilities. These were first, the realization of the need for some sort of community centre or meeting place, particularly in newly built-up areas; second, the provision of facilities for adult education, vital to those excluded from a formal education, and vital as a means of communication on equal terms (albeit amongst very small groups) between different social classes; and finally, the emphasis socio-religious workers gave to work for young people. 'Muscular Christianity' had long been a joke, but poor children had never before been given facilities beyond those necessary to keep them disciplined and obedient.

8

URBANIZATION AND LEISURE — THE SECULAR CULTURE OF CITY AND SUBURB

The social reformers' attempts to fill the leisure time of the urban masses must be seen against the background of the major changes taking place in the development of leisure pursuits. Details of the counter-attractions of the largely secular, dominant, urban culture give a perspective to the leisure facilities provided by the religious sub-culture. An analysis of these changes, however, can only be given on a superficial level. Much day-to-day activity went unrecorded. Much popular entertainment was self-entertainment, made domestically and privately, leaving no traces for the historian. The complex relationship between urban growth, social change and leisure generates questions more easily than answers. How far did the changing use of land in the city affect the space available for leisure pursuits? What contribution did advancing technology make to entertainment? In what ways did Bristol's citizens respond to new opportunities? What indications do new leisure pursuits give of the kinds of social changes taking place? How did the leisure provisions of the socio-religious workers relate to changing trends in the use of leisure? The rest of this chapter will be devoted, not to answering these questions entirely, but to doing what can be done from sources such as newspapers, periodicals and the miscellaneous information to be found in the Bristol local collection, to outline the development of leisure facilities in the city.

I POPULAR AMUSEMENTS OF THE PEOPLE

Change was particularly dramatic in popular amusements. Popular entertainments before the nineteenth century, and in many rural areas and small towns well into the twentieth century, were based on rural and domestic life within small, well-defined communities. In a large city, such as Bristol, there was a high degree of segregation between parishes and districts, which again provided the close, social relationships of a small community.[1] The characteristics of popular entertainments were thus governed by a social context which was largely local, informally organized and traditionally inspired. Customs varied from region to region, between different crafts. There was a high level of socially tolerated physical violence, even cruelty; and a high degree of emotional spontaneity. Within this day-to-day pattern of activities, however, there were annual events and festivities often related to seasonal activities. Much popular amusement went unrecorded, since it belonged to the oral tradition, until the point of social change was reached which threatened its future existence, when minor masterpieces such as that of Joseph Strutt appeared.[2]

But it was not a simple matter, as Professor Malcolmson has brilliantly shown, of a rural-based popular culture succumbing to the impact of urbanization.[3] Popular entertainments have always reflected widely held social values. Old-fashioned paternalism was symptomatic of the traditional response; Puritanism and new attitudes to economic and social issues tended to lead to hostility to established social customs.

> These, in fact, were the two dominant types of social outlook, and both traditions were vigorously alive around the beginning of the eighteenth century; they offered competing standards for assessing social behaviour and they represented opposing models of the desirable society – the one essentially backward-looking, the other energetically 'progressive'.[4]

Gradually, however, in the course of the late eighteenth century, the latter became ever more victorious over the former. The final outcome, though, was largely lost as the process of urbanization, particularly from 1850, completely transformed the social and environmental context of the struggle.

Bristol, as the second largest city for much of the eighteenth century, and a port, was large enough to contain elements of both of the two dominant types of social outlook towards popular entertainments. In the early part of the century, local authorities such as the Mayor and Corporation positively encouraged popular pastimes, to the extent, for instance, of providing financial support for bull-baiting.[5] By the nineteenth century the city's local dignitaries appear to have shifted their views to the other dominant tradition, but bull-baiting remained very popular and was still practised in the city until the 1830s. The impact of the city on popular entertainments at this time seemed to be largely a matter of law and order. The larger the city, the larger the crowds involved in these activities and, on the traditional holidays of the year such as Easter, the local authorities were likely to be strictly repressive. No amount of disapprobation from local authorities though, was able to curtail the annual fairs, such as the horse fair in Wade Street, the fair at the Old Market and, most famous of all, the Bedminster 'revels'.

However, from the 1830s Bedminster became substantially developed as an industrial and residential suburb and this, with the hostility of the local magistrates, did put an end to the 'revels'. Yet visiting shows and circuses still came to Bedminster until the end of the century. By then, the area's close contacts with popular amusements took a new lease of life with the application of technology to entertainment leading eventually to the construction of the Bedminster Hippodrome in 1912.[6] This sequence of events provides, perhaps, a more general insight into the development of popular entertainments in the city in the nineteenth century. It is obvious that local authorities and building development between them would be enough, supplemented by changing working conditions, to alter popular amusements profoundly. But in spite of all this, the evidence suggests that Bristol's citizens enjoyed a vigorous popular culture, and the death knell of any activity only took place when demand for it had already declined, in favour of some new pursuits.

The old traditional elements of popular entertainment, the spontaneity and lack of formal organization, continued to flourish in spite of change. Most of Bristol's immigrants, even in the 1860s, were drawn from the surrounding rural counties where traditional attitudes remained largely untouched by the economic and political changes of the previous century.[7] Popular entertainments were considered a fundamental right and even that organ of middle-class antagonism to the freedom of citizens in this respect, the *Western Daily Press,* commented in 1869: 'The masses of English people have always been and always will be, so long as they preserve one of their best national characteristics, fond of amusement.'[8] Two of the traditional pastimes which survived well into the second half of the nineteenth century were pugilism and coursing. Reports of prize fights continued in the press until the 1890s, though in 1869 a crowd gathered to watch a fight had to disperse at the approach of police.[9] Coursing, however, remained within the law, and meets were frequently held at Long Ashton.[10]

The staple diet of the poorer citizens of Bristol in recreation and entertainment centred on drink, informal activities in the streets, and irregular visits from commercial entertainers, particularly circuses.[11] Dr Harrison has clearly shown the fundamental importance of inns, taverns and beer houses at every level of urban life.[12] Although the Temperance movement became established, and was pursued with much vigour, even the basic conditions of the city were against the reformers, let alone the inclinations of individuals. In 1845 only 5,000 of Bristol's 130,000 inhabitants had a water supply to their homes. Inns and taverns were the natural meeting-places for all social gatherings for whatever purpose. As conditions changed and old coaching inns lost their traffic to the railways, and the Temperance movement began its sustained attack, publicans responded by diversifying their attractions. The skittles, quoits and billiards used by the socio-religious workers in their clubs were all made popular in the first instance by publicans. The addition of singing, music and dancing was, of course, to lead to considerable development in the mid-century years of tavern music halls.

Singing and music were also an important part of street entertainment with organ-grinders and monkeys, street musicians, ballad singers and the bands which accompanied the processions undertaken by all kinds of different groups. At the anniversary in 1869, for instance, of the three old established Friendly Societies which made up the Berkeley Benefit Societies, all the members took to the streets for a procession. The weather was fine, the streets full of people, the bells of near-by churches were rung, banners carried, and after the procession there was dancing and amusements in the streets.[13] Street processions were the commonly used methods of advertising the arrival of circuses in the town, regular visitors to the city since the 1790s. One of the traditional sites used by circuses, the Grove to the south of Queen's Square, had been used since Elizabethan times for popular entertainments such as bear-baiting.[14] A new indoor site was provided in the 1860s with the construction of the Rifle Drill Hall, though the wooden building in Stokes Croft was lost to the Salvation Army in the 1880s.[15]

From the 1860s there were two main trends affecting commercial entertainment in the city. The first was the rapidly increasing number of public halls available for hire by enterprising entertainers; and the second was the development of technology for entertainment purposes. Both were to lead to a greater degree of formality and organization in popular amusements. The most important hall was the Colston Hall built in 1867 with its three auditoriums. The large hall was used mainly, at first, for musical concerts organized by many different groups, especially Friendly Societies and trade unions. Other entertainments such as the phantascope (magical and mysterious!) were also frequently organized.[16] The smaller Colston halls and the Broadmead rooms were the venue for minstrel shows, from Butterworth's Christy Minstrels at Broadmead to the Bohee and Livermore Troupes, and Moore and Burgess Minstrels, who undertook musical tableaux vivants at the Lesser Colston hall. Numerous other halls were built in the course of the 1870s and '80s and were used for entertainment. Even the YMCA hall which could seat 1,250 people, was available for hire.

The increasingly sophisticated levels of entertainment however, were achieved usually with the aid of technological advances. The latest novelty from the bioscope, eragraph, theatrograph, cinematograph, are obvious examples of this. These kinds of inventions were developed much more in the last decade of the century.[17] From the 1860s, though, technological advances in modes of transport indirectly affected popular amusements. This is particularly evident in the changing response to the traditional holidays, at Easter, Whitsun and the harvest home. Already by the mid-century, the railways had opened up the possibility of day excursions and the surrounding seaside villages had responded to the potential. Clevedon decided to aim for the middle-class market, built a small pier and remained a select resort. Avonmouth, with fewer natural attractions, established some pleasure gardens where every form of popular entertainment, then in fashion, was to be found. There were 'vocalists, negro-delineators, comic singers, dancers, comedians etc, hay making and rustic sports, brass band and string band for dancing, trapeze and rope walking acts, outdoor amusements, swings, whirl-abouts, quoits, croquet, American bowling alleys and a new skittle alley',[18] and admission to the Gardens only cost 4*d*.

It was one long succession of spectacle and amusement for two or three days of the holiday. If the out-of-town rail journey to Avonmouth was too much, the suburban train to Horfield was cheaper and closer, and some pleasure gardens were established there. The Downs were also extensively used by fairs and entertainers. In the period 1869-71, however, when the problem of popular holidays had reached national proportions and they were to be curtailed and regulated finally by the 1871 Bank Holiday Act, much concern was shown by local authorities about public behaviour on these occasions. On the Easter holiday of 1870, the *Western Daily Press* devoted a leader article to a long homily on the need for self-discipline amongst holiday-makers and the desirability of returning to work without a headache.[19] But blanket repression of all amusement was not considered to be the answer. An article written a year earlier, most clearly illustrates the response, which was to improve, not destroy, popular entertainment. Entitled 'the Pulpit and Popular Amusements' it was an attack on the repressive attitudes of church and chapel to the amusement of the poor and a plea that the only way to attack the 'low music hall, redolent of tobacco smoke, vile cigars and the fumes of execrable liquor' was to provide good, wholesome, musical concerts, say Handel's music, at the same low price as the music hall.[20]

There was a new self-consciousness though, about the use of leisure which was not confined to the would-be social reformers. The press again reflects this change with an article on the 'Rationale of Holiday-Making'. The conclusion is drawn that what constitutes a good holiday is a change of scene and pleasant companionship.[21] Popular demand in the next two decades was to prove that this was a widely held view. An attempt was made to revive an age-old popular pastime in the teeth of change. In 1873 the Prince of Wales was induced to come to Bristol to open the Knowle race-course. But attending race-meetings did not have the massive popular appeal that was hoped for. The course shut down because of financial difficulties by 1880. However, train trips and day trips out of Bristol became far more popular as the great annual events of the year. Visits to Weston-super-Mare, Clevedon, Portishead, Avonmouth, and further south-west for those who could stay away a night or two, became far more popular. It was a two-way traffic, since country folk poured into the city, usually to wend their way to the Zoo Gardens or the Downs.

The annual outing became an important event, outstripping in some respects the traditional holidays. The Wills firm took their workers on the first annual outing to London in 1851 to the Great Exhibition. Annually, thereafter, the whole firm embarked on a train for some destination, usually by the sea, for the annual outing. The practice still continued when the firm's employees were numbered in thousands and three special trains had to be booked. The 'wayzgoose' of the *Western Daily Press* workers was a similarly well-loved occasion.[22] By the end of the 1860s, the social behaviour and attitudes of the workers had already been much changed. One Bristol citizen concerned with social conditions, is willing to explain this change in terms of a great diminishing of the poverty and brutality of the people. At the Paulton Harvest Home in 1869, Henry Milward concluded his speech, saying: 'I have lived amongst middle and working classes of this neighbourhood for nearly 28 years and in that time the change for the better is so wonderful that indeed we have to thank God for the past and work more heartily.'[23]

Between 1870 and 1890, changes in popular entertainments continued, though in an unspectacular fashion. Old established popular amusements remained alongside the new developments, though by 1890 there was no hint of alarm in the press, as there was twenty years earlier, about standards of social behaviour on Bank holidays. Instead the leader article places emphasis on how Bank holidays, generally, provide a big boost to the holiday movement, underlining the need for more holidays for everyone on a far greater scale. The need for mass entertainment is taken for granted, not only on public holidays, but all the year round.[24] The commercial realization of this demand was to transform popular entertainments in this decade. As Miss Barker points out: 'in 1890, the pattern was essentially still that of twenty years earlier'; 'by 1900 much of this pattern of entertainment had already broken up or was on the verge of doing so.'[25]

The 1890s were to see the end of the old tavern music halls and the beginning of 'family' entertainment with the large new music halls, the People's Palace Baldwin Street and the Empire Theatre of Varieties at Old Market. The city's two theatres, the eighteenth-century King Street theatre and the 1867 Prince's Theatre were in their last period of local ownership before being taken over by national concerns. The size of these establishments, particularly the two new music halls of the 1890s which could seat around 3,000 people, and the lavishness of the entertainment provided, meant that their programmes had to be based on the broadest popular appeal. The new music halls were teetotal, though in the case of the Empire, this was a nominal gesture since the entrance to the hall was through the White Hart Hotel. Teetotalism was a bow in the direction of the Nonconformists who had always been the enemies of the theatre and drama, and it appears to have worked, since theatre-going lost its sinful overtones. A leader in the press of 1910, reviewing the progress of drama since the 1870s, points to the intellectual improvements brought by the new dramatists, Ibsen, Barrie, Shaw and Galsworthy; to the high standards of acting now achieved; 'indeed half the London stage is filled with University men'; whilst 'perhaps even more wonderful still has been the advance in the class of music hall entertainment.'[26]

The advance of the latter was maintained by technical innovation, as well as the quality of the artistes that the large new halls could afford. The comment of the drama critic of the programme at the Tivoli theatre in January 1901, isolates for special praise the contribution made by the cinematograph and the concertophone, the latter giving songs of Dan Leno and others 'so distinctly as to admit of every word being heard in any part of the hall'.[27] It was obvious as the techniques developed in the Edwardian period that these innovations had the potential to continually draw an audience. As Miss Barker points out, they had the key elements formerly confined to live entertainment: 'pictorial interest, topicality, amusement *verismo*'.[28] They also had the power of reducing audience participation to the passive response of silent spectators, although the early films were certainly not greeted in this way. Emotional spontaneity in this respect was possibly the last and strongest link with the behavioural response to the traditional popular amusements of the past.

The development and strength of the music halls and other popular commercial entertainment testify to the fact that the tradition of popular amusement could survive both the hostility of social reformers and magistrates, and the process of urbanization. Traditions might be transformed in a physical sense by the new context but the importance of popular amusements in the community sustained institutions and activities through the transitional period. Although social reformers tended to consider popular amusements as a necessary 'safety valve' in any society, yet they had a far more significant role than that. They could perpetuate certain values of the community, define the social identity of those who participated in or supported them, and help to guarantee the survival of social independence. The fact that in the 1890s the music halls for instance, became respectable, even teetotal, was not evidence of a capitulation of their independent role, rather it was an indication of their ability to reach larger numbers of people. They had become an integral part of the dominant secular culture of the city, available to all classes in a way which signified virtually a social revolution.

II THE LABOUR MOVEMENT AND LEISURE

Social attitudes to leisure though, were neither uniform nor class bound. Many of the people actively concerned in the Labour movement for instance, were, for different reasons, as enthusiastic for socially improving activities as any socio-religious worker. They showed an interest in education, in the growth of public libraries and the diffusion of knowledge. In Bristol in the 1860s and '70s, this had led to close co-operation between middle-class reformers, like the Rev. J. Percival, and working-class leaders of the Bristol Trades Council and the Co-operative Movement. The latter's educational programme had received a boost in 1869, when their secretary, Mr J. W. H. Wall, helped Percival to launch his Association for the Promotion of Evening Classes for Young Men.

The subsequent history of the activities of the Bristol Co-operative Education Committee, however, shows considerable differences of opinion and objective between the Co-operators and Percival. The main concern of the Co-operators was not Liberal Culture, though they were eager for knowledge; their main concern remained propaganda on behalf of the movement and training of members in business administration for the benefit of their commercial activities. In fact, the sole contribution of the Bristol Co-operative Education Committee in the 1880s, apart from the provision of practical instruction, was a series of lectures at the Athenaeum on 'Co-operation and

Capitalism.'[29] The activities of the Education Committee then lapsed again until the late 1890s when a new propaganda campaign was launched, mainly directed to children. They were invited to enter a competition by submitting an essay on the subject 'What I think of Co-operation'. A small prize went to the winner.

By 1902, the importance of stepping up propaganda and also providing for the education of their members, became more apparent. Classes on the history of the movement were held at most Co-operative branches in Bristol and outlying areas. The Bristol and District branch went further, and founded a discussion class and the nucleus of a library, largely devoted to economics. New subjects were added to those examined by the Committee so that the list now read: co-operative history, co-operative management, co-operative bookkeeping, economics and industrial history. To become a co-operator could involve both the working and leisure hours of members. It was a life of some dedication. The overall impact of the activities of the Education Committee on those outside the Co-operative movement was probably small even after 1902. An indication of the range of these activities can be gauged from a sample financial statement of the Committee for the year 1908-9 (see Table 8.1).

In two respects however, the co-operators' interest in education did have important effects. First, simply by virtue of the fact that they were interested in education, members of the Co-operative Education Committee were consulted whilst negotiations were afoot to transform the University College to a full, independent University. When it was agreed to allot eight seats on the court of the new University to the working classes, two of the seats went to the co-operators. Second, they offered equal status and opportunities to women at a time when working-class women had few other facilities directed towards them.

Working-class girls and women could, and did, attend evening classes run by the Bristol School Board and later the local education authority. But the Co-operative movement offered them training and practical experience in all aspects of business management alongside the men. The historian of the movement in Bristol, writing in 1910, said of the people who had developed co-operation in the city:

> A large proportion of these are women who, through their Guilds, have been for the past sixteen years studying problems

TABLE 8.1 *Bristol and District Branch: financial statement 1908–9*

INCOME	£	s.	d.	£	s.	d.
Balance brought forward				106	10	0
Grants from current profits				489	14	0
Special grant for Propaganda				19	17	6
Women's Subscription to Guild				7	2	6
				623	4	0

EXPENDITURE						
Propaganda						
Concerts	66	13	0			
Children's Fetes	114	15	10			
Piano Purchase	28	1	3			
Subscrip. to 'Right to Work' Comm.	16	8	6			
				225	18	7
Educational						
Subscriptions WEA, etc.	9	0	0			
'Wheatsheaf'	65	7	4			
Lectures and Lantern Expenses	1	6	5			
Purchases – Literature	1	8	9			
Classes	26	17	8			
Choir	7	18	7			
				111	18	9
Administration						
Printing and Postage	50	14	2			
Rents of Rooms	36	4	0			
Delegates Fees and Fares	28	2	8			
Secretary	10	0	0			
				125	0	10
Sundries				9	4	0
Balance at end of year				151	1	10
				£623	4	0

of citizenship, preparing themselves for the time when they will be called upon to exercise themselves in a practical manner in affairs of state, even as they have done from the commencement in the cooperative movement.[30]

The National Women's Co-operative Guild had gained such a large membership by 1893 that it began to hold its annual meeting separately from the Co-operative Congress. The Guild, officially described as a 'self-governing organization of 25,942 women who work through cooperation for the welfare of the people, seeking freedom for their own purposes, and the Equal Fellowship of men and women in the Home, the Store, the Workshop and the State' was definitely a 'progressive' cultural experience for its members.

The 'Brave New World' spirit was evident in the cultural activities organized by the women of the Bristol Guild for their leisure hours. In the first three months of 1910, for instance, a course of lectures was held. In January the series began on a serious note with weekly lectures on the following subjects: 'Infant Management', 'Suffrage', 'CWS Production', and 'Hygiene Talks'. But by February a wider cultural context was sought. There was one lecture on 'Palestine', two on 'Mazzini', and the fourth was entitled 'Chats with John Gregory's Poems'. By March, any flagging enthusiasm could be rekindled by two lectures devoted to the achievements of women, the subjects being Elizabeth Fry and Christina Rossetti. The last lecture of the series was devoted to reports of all the activities of the Bristol Women's Guild; their contribution, on however small a scale, to redefining the role of women in contemporary society.

The mixture of education, propaganda and entertainment which the co-operators used in the organization of their leisure facilities was a popular one amongst many other groups in the labour movement. William Straker, the man who had led the opposition to Joseph Storrs Fry's edict forbidding Trade Unionism in his factory, had helped to build up support for his union by organizing educational entertainments for members. He was also one of a group of working men whose Sunday leisure activities mushroomed by the end of the 1880s into the Bristol Sunday Society, supported by thousands at its regular weekly meetings in winter months. The formula for success was the same mixture of education, entertainment and propaganda, this time in the socialist cause.[31]

The original nucleus of the organization was a group of five friends who decided in the winter months of 1887/8 to meet together on Sundays, to help each other learn shorthand. They met each week in the sitting-room over J. W. D. Marshall's barber's shop at 16 Peter Street, but their enthusiasm for shorthand diminished as they found greater pleasure in literary discussion. They read and discussed Mazzini, Carlyle and Emerson.[32] By the following winter, they considered that their activities could be enjoyed by a wider group of people, the 'respectable' working class who had virtually no entertainment available to them on Sundays, their only free day. Debates in the town council about the Sunday opening of the libraries, and in 1893, the museum, had been won by adherents of the Lord's Day Observance Society.[33] The group of friends decided to step into the breach by organizing the Bristol Sunday Society which would not only provide entertainment, but would also popularize socialist ideas.

The Empire Theatre of Varieties was booked and lecture courses organized. Some of the lecturers were particularly distinguished, including George Bernard Shaw, Annie Besant, R. H. Haldane and Graham Wallas.[34] But the lectures were not all devoted to promoting socialist ideas. All kinds of topic were on the programme, such as natural phenomena, 'Experience in Search of Volcanos' or 'The Mighty Ocean'; or travelogues, 'Malta, Ancient and Modern' and 'The New Far East'.[35] The lectures were illustrated with lantern slides and preceded and concluded with musical items. In the range of lecture topics, the programme of the Bristol Sunday Society much resembled the popular lecture series run by the University College, the Merchant Venturers Technical College and the YMCA. Yet the venue at the music hall, the meetings on Sundays and the political commitment of the organizers, gave the Society an independence, even if its activities appeared identical to those run by social reformers as part of the 'civilizing process'.

Those working within the labour movement were willing to take a 'progressive' view of popular entertainments and to condemn ignorance, brutality and lack of behavioural restraint. From 1901, the Co-operative societies in the city joined forces with the Trades Council to organize labour festivals and fêtes. These were held annually at the Colston Hall and included a wide range of entertainments and social activities. There were musical concerts of high quality interspersed with speeches, followed by games and dancing, as well as the diffusion of information on wider spheres of labour activity.[36] Classical music, since the opening years of the Colston Hall, had become a leisure pursuit of the organized labour movement in the city. It was an indication, amongst many others, that the working classes could now claim, as their own, the heritage of liberal cultural activities from which they had formerly been excluded.

III THE PASSION FOR MUSIC

One of the most dramatic changes in the leisure pursuits of all classes in the second half of the nineteenth century was to be found in music-making. One contributor to the *Bristol Argus* in 1886 wrote,

> music now plays such an important part in our everyday life, that there is scarcely a household that does not contain either a singer or a player amongst its members. In no part of the world's history has there been such a development both of taste and talent for music.[37]

Basic to such a development were numerous technological changes, particularly in the design and manufacture of musical instruments, higher levels of popular education and an increase in the number of halls or rooms where musical concerts could take place. These were all changes encouraged by the growth of large cities. The musical life of Bristol was to reflect the full spectrum of the changes that were to take place in the nineteenth century as the organized pursuit of music spread from the rich, to encompass inhabitants of every suburb of the expanding city.

In the early Victorian period, Bristol's middle classes took part in the musical 'revolution' encouraged by Prince Albert.[38] In 1843 the Victoria Rooms in Clifton were built to house concerts and musical soirées, and chamber concerts of German music were held. Serious attention had been paid to religious choral music since the eighteenth century, and choral music festivals had been instituted in a number of places around the country, the pioneer being the Three Choirs Festival of the Cathedral choirs of Worcester, Hereford and Gloucester established early in the eighteenth century.[39] Bristol had no choral festival of her own before 1873, but choral concerts were held in aid of charity. The new interest in music in the 1830s and '40s encouraged amateur music-making, especially the formation of choral societies and an antiquarian interest in music, reflected in the formation of the Bristol Madrigal Society and various glee clubs.

All these activities however, were confined to the rich and educated. The vocal score of the *Messiah* in the 1830s still cost about three guineas, and few people could read music.[40] However, court patronage, and the popularization of musical techniques, gained increasing influence in the mid-century years. Prince Albert was far more than a patron. He was active in promoting musical activities. He himself played the organ at Windsor. He attempted to improve English musical taste by becoming director of Ancient Concerts (a scheme whereby no music written in the last twenty years was played, in an attempt to stamp out the vogue for novelty, rather than good music, in concert programmes). Above all, he encouraged the organization of music at the Crystal Palace; a Crystal Palace Orchestra was set up in 1854 and concerts were cheap to encourage the widest possible audience.

The response which followed Prince Albert's initiatives were manifold and reached out in the following decades to the provincial cities. The Crystal Palace, W. S. Jevons wrote: 'was the most admirable institution in the country. It has been of infinite service in showing what a rich nation might do in uniting Science, and Art and Nature for the entertainment and civilization of the people.'[41] A Musical Union was set up at the Crystal Palace, later to become the Monday Popular Concerts at which music, such as Beethoven's piano sonatas, played by Charles Hallé, conducted by John Ella, could be heard. The huge enclosed space of the Palace was particularly suited, after its move to Sydenham, to full-scale choral performances with very large choirs, to thrill and impress audiences.

The popularity of all these activities had been one of the major stimuli to the group of Nonconformist businessmen who formed the Colston Hall Company in Bristol, for the purpose of building a hall large enough to be able to contain the greatest orchestras and choirs then in fashion. From its opening in 1867, the Colston Hall became the focal point of the musical life of the city. George Riseley, appointed cathedral organist in 1875, began from that time to imitate the Monday Popular Concerts held at the Crystal Palace, with similar concerts at the Colston Hall. In the 1880s and '90s, he expanded his activities to include popular concerts on Saturday nights as well, less 'high brow' than the Monday concerts. These were extremely well-supported, playing to large audiences in the winter months.

Religious music, especially large choral works, was popular amongst the middle classes, and the size of the Colston Hall provided a new potential for the mounting of major performances. Handel's

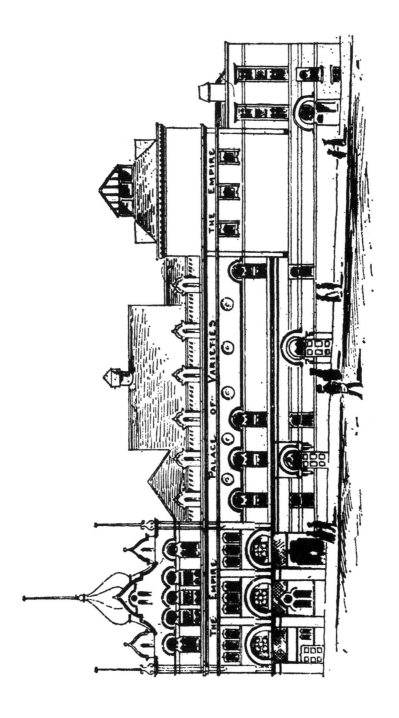

Messiah, Mendelssohn's *Elijah*, Costa's *Eli* and Spohr's *Fall of Babylon*, were the favourite pieces, choruses numbering hundreds of voices collected together to perform them. In London in 1862, the Sacred Harmonic Society had organized a monster festival at the Crystal Palace, using no less than 3,625 performers.[42] Music festivals established in Leeds and Birmingham began to undertake huge-scale performances. With the building of the Colston Hall, Bristol's middle classes were ready to join the vogue. When the idea was put forward for a music festival in the city in 1873, enthusiasm was so great that in only a few weeks from the date when the idea was first mooted, a choir was hastily got together, the hall booked, and Charles Hallé invited to come and conduct the performances.

These music festivals then continued to be held at three-year intervals until 1905; though a small interruption was caused when the Colston Hall got burnt down in 1898. This socially exclusive and limited form of music-making, though, was not an unqualified success. Out of the total of eleven festivals which were held, five made financial losses, those from 1885–93 fairly serious losses. Attendance figures, built up in the early festivals of the 1870s, began to decline in the 1880s, reaching an all time low of 8,000 in 1893, which was the total of attendances for all concerts and performances. There was some improvement in the last two festivals held, 1902 and 1905, when the figures were 13,956 and 15,821, though the rebuilt Colston Hall could hold larger audiences than the old one. But these figures were not enough to offset the waning popularity of large scale oratorio concerts. As the music critic of the *Western Daily Press* wrote in 1905, 'High class concerts are not drawing the crowds whilst the ballad type programmes are increasing in popularity.'[43] 'Popular' taste was being formed by commercial entertainment.

The organization of the music festivals in the city, however, over thirty years, did have some small spin-off on the musical life of the city, again in an area much encouraged by the late Prince Albert. He had been most concerned about the training of young musicians and the Royal College of Music had been set up to honour his memory, in 1875.[44] George Riseley founded a local School of Music for budding professionals but he was unable to get enough support. He petitioned the town council many times without success. In Bristol, there remained few facilities for training musicians. Piano and violin playing were taught in middle-class secondary schools, including Clifton College. The Music Festival Committee did come to the aid of those wishing to learn instrument playing, who were excluded from these meagre facilities. Classes for adults were organized by the Committee, costing threepence a lesson, and 1,140 people made use of this opportunity.

Much of the demand for facilities of this kind was due, however, to astonishing developments in the musical life of the city, far beyond the exclusive levels touched by the music festivals. Methods of bringing written music within the reach of the people and the means to make it possible, had been found in the mid-century years. The last quarter of the century was to mark the widespread growth of musical clubs and societies devoted to serious music, in every suburb of the city. Most of these organizations undertook choral music, since the breakthrough in teaching people to read music had been designed for this purpose. From the 1830s increasing concern over popular education, and the growing demand for choirs to sing hymns and anthems in numerous other socio-religious activities, had focused the attention of interested parties on the means of teaching people to read music.[45] The most successful system was that popularized by the Congregational minister, the Rev. John Curwen; it was known as the Tonic Sol-fa method.

The impact this method was to have, being easy to learn and easy to teach, was backed up by some important technical breakthroughs. Published music became far cheaper to produce with improved methods and thus, cheaper to buy. The *Messiah* by 1866 could be bought for one shilling, and four-page part songs for one halfpenny. The manufacture of pianos was similarly transformed and with mass production became cheap enough to be found in working-class homes. The result was not only to give a boost to the enormous popularity of certain music hall songs; it was to put serious music-making within reach of many more people than before.

Much of the initial impetus to fulfil this potential in Bristol came from the middle-class, socio-religious workers. A Church Choral Union was founded in 1879 which held special festivals to encourage competitions between parish choirs from 1880 onwards. Temperance choral societies flourished, particularly among Bands of Hope such as the one run by the Unitarians at St James Back. The 1880s mark the peak of socio-religious inspired, working-class choirs. Examples around the city included the St John Choral Society, the Choral

Society at the Clifton College Mission in St Agnes, and the Æolian Male Voice Choir in St Philips, which was still flourishing in the decade before the First World War.

In the course of the 1880s, however, music-making had broken out beyond the confines of socio-religious activity. The most vigorous new element was the development of the brass band movement in the city, considerably later than in other, more northern cities. Yet by the 1880s, many large factories and works had their own bands. There was more demand for their music as well as growing enthusiasm amongst players. Annual outings, for instance, with street processions, were not complete without a band. Roger Till writes in his history of Wills, 'A typical Wills outing at the end of the 1880s began with the employees trooping to Temple Meads station at six or seven in the morning with the newly formed Wills Workpeople's Band playing a lively air down Victoria Street.'[46] One member of the Wills Band, Mr Godfrey who played the euphonium, also ran the band which played at the football matches of the Bristol City Club. The county ground was able to draw on the services of the Post Office Band to entertain the crowds.[47] Again technical advances made on brass instruments, particularly the cornet-à-pistons, made the popular development of brass bands possible; and cheap rail fares to attend competitions and festivals encouraged a national movement.[48]

The playing of musical instruments however, remained a mainly middle-class, amateur activity, apart from the brass bands. The YMCA did form an orchestra in 1890, but the cost of a musical training in both time and resources, put such a possibility largely beyond the reach of the poorer sections of the community. The Society of Instrumentalists, which was founded in 1888, grew rapidly to a membership of 200, and was described as 'the largest amateur orchestral society in the kingdom', drawing its strength from the middle classes.[49] At least in choral music, though, there were no such economic and social barriers for the enthusiast. In the late 1890s there was a fresh growth of choral societies. The initiative for their establishment appears to have come from institutions or simply groups of people who enjoyed singing, and the camaraderie of a communal activity. The choirs became known by the district of the city in which they operated, the first big choir established being the East Bristol Choral Society of 1900.[50]

It was quickly followed by the North Bristol Society in 1901 and the Railwayman's choir, which had been meeting for some years in the Totterdam YMCA, changed its name to the Bristol South Choral Society. A Bristol Harmonic Male Voice Choir used the old Quaker Mission building in St Judes. Other choirs such as the Central YMCA Choral Society of 1899 and the Knowle and Totterdam Choral Society, run by the local vicar, did still have a socio-religious flavour. But choral singing had reached new heights in popularity. The choral society run by the Evening School Committee of the Bristol School Board generated enormous enthusiasm and support. In 1899 the Bristol Co-operative Choir, 120 strong, under their conductor Mr E. T. Morgan of the Bristol Cathedral Choir, carried off the second prize at the National Co-operative Festival at the Crystal Palace.[51] Choirs flourished in districts, among trade unions, co-operative and friendly societies, in factories and educational institutions. The considerable development of serious amateur music-making in the two decades before the First World War indicates a popular new dimension in the leisure activities of the urban masses, originally nurtured by socio-religious organizations, but developing on its own, once facilities and expertise were more widely available.

IV THE PURSUIT OF ORGANIZED SPORT

Another dimension, of perhaps even greater significance in the new uses of leisure, was the growth of organized sport. This too, gained impetus initially at the hands of the socio-religious workers, with their belief in 'Muscular Christianity' and healthy, harmless ways of using leisure time. But the development of all kinds of sport struck a response from the English public and, as part of it, Bristol's citizens, which far exceeded the intentions of any conscious, deliberate social engineering. Why was it that the world's most urbanized nation should have initiated a revolution in sport which, subsequently, was to spread round the world? The social significance of this phenomenon has been used by sociologists to indicate the levels of social change taking place in an industrialized, urban society.[52] Modern organized sport is the very antithesis of the popular recreations of pre-industrial society. How did organization and rules permeate age-old social customs? How was greater discipline achieved, and with what results? Two significant factors determining these developments were the role played by the middle classes, in their public schools, universities and sporting clubs; and the rapid advance of technology which, applied to sport, meant better and cheaper equipment was more readily available.

The latter, the impact of technological advances on sporting life was, perhaps, the most dramatic. By far and away the most important technological breakthrough was in transport, since cheap and rapid travel facilities opened up sports on a national and international basis and helped to stimulate national interest in the outcome of sporting contests. The Great Western Railway, in Bristol's case, was the backbone of the Southern and South-Western leagues which flourished in football, cricket, athletics and bicycling. Better communications, such as the telegraph, also meant that reports of race meetings and hare coursing, with the latest betting results, were reported in the press with increasing frequency from the 1880s.

Interest generated by these means was reinforced on a wider scale by the cheap press and sporting publications, such as almanacs, made possible by further technological advances in printing and publishing. In 1869 English sporting news was sent direct by Atlantic cable (laid in 1866) to the USA, when a crack Harvard rowing team had a contest with Oxford University.[53] The local press in Bristol responded to demand by devoting more and more space to sporting activities, the key change in policy becoming more apparent in the decade of the 1880s. By 1890 a whole page every day in the sedate *Western Daily Press* was devoted to sporting news, which was enlarged again to two and sometimes three pages by 1900. The *Bristol Argus*, founded in 1886, devoted a section in every issue to sport since 'For some years it has been felt that the increasing importance of all kinds of manly exercise and recreation amongst the young men of Bristol and the locality demanded some recognition in the press.'[54] In 1889 a new publication, *Amateur Sport*, was founded locally; and by 1887 supporters of a single sport, bicycling, were enough to maintain, for a while, the *Bristol Bicycle and Tricycle Club Monthly Gazette*.

'Bicycling,' wrote a contributor to the latter publication, 'what visions the word recalls! Viewed in the light of a pastime alone, cycling has opened a new experience to the youth and manhood of the world and by more recent development, the womanhood as well!'[55] The implications of that technical breakthrough, especially the advances made in the safety and manufacturing methods of bicycles, was certainly destined to extend the range of experiences of more individuals than any other product of the Industrial Revolution. Progress was slow in the early years. The cumbersome machines that generated the 'Velocipede Mania'[56] of 1869 were both expensive and extremely difficult to ride, the toys of athletic gentlemen. Enthusiasm was enough though, in the 1870s, to stimulate the organization of clubs such as the Clifton Cycling Club and the Bristol Tricycle and Bicycle Club itself, formed from the amalgamation of two smaller clubs in 1876.

The main purpose of these clubs was to organize meets and races and to constantly work away at breaking time and speed records. With this intention, they gradually introduced into a leisure activity, attitudes and aspirations which closely resembled the new work-discipline of modern industry.[57] To break records needed greater self-discipline, an application to technology and a methodical approach to getting the best out of machine and man. Some of the feats achieved by members of the Bristol Tricycle and Bicycle Club were evidence of the results of the new approach. In 1888 E. Moon created a record by covering 235¾ miles on the solid-tyred safety bicycle (without any pacing) in the phenomenal time of twenty-four hours. Perhaps old-fashioned brute strength still had something to do with it after all. But the bicyclist was the 'modern' man, eager to exploit technological possibilities, and another member of the club had the enterprise to travel to the American championship races, from which he emerged the overall victor.

The bicycle, however, was far more than a sporting toy, it was a revolutionary means of personal transport. The new opportunities now available for pleasure for the non-sporting bicyclist were considerable. Dr Dunlop invented the pneumatic tyre in 1888, which made cycling on bumpy country roads less of a physical torture. Enthusiasts for the countryside could quickly reach the remotest areas by using the train out of the large city, stopping at some country station and then bicycling through the lanes.[58] Technological spin-offs from bicycle manufacture, apart from pneumatic tyres, were numerous, and were to be used in the manufacture of motor vehicles. The invention of ball-bearings was used in the manufacture of other sporting equipment, particularly the new roller-skate, which initiated one of the first nationwide sporting crazes.

In the 1870s 'rinkomania' became a passion. Its significance was that it was one of the first crazes which affected middle-class girls as well as young men. Three rinks were opened up in, or close by, Clifton. T. H. S. Escott, mindful of the fears of mothers whose daughters could be 'twirled round in the arms of some youth just introduced', was rather disparaging about the craze. 'Any available buildings', he wrote, 'were laid down with floors more or less lubricated, on which the sons and daughters of the various sections of the great middle class, shod with a peculiar adaptation of wheels, slipped about, and called it skating.'[59] The impact of technological advances on sports equipment led to constant innovations and improvements which were evident in many sports. The use of rubber in the manufacture of tennis- and golf-balls; the mass production in the manufacture of billiard-tables; revolutions in the design of diverse things from guns to the sliding seats of a rowing skiff, continually fed the growing interest in sport in the same way as the technical breakthroughs in the modern hi-fi industry create an ever-growing demand.

Yet equipment cost money which usually placed it out of the reach of all but the middle classes. Perhaps the real sporting revolution of the late nineteenth century lies in the social implication of this fact. The sporting pastimes of country and town, in the days before technological breakthroughs, had traditionally cut across class barriers.[60] But new sports depending on expensive equipment left few complementary roles for different social classes; though, paradoxically, for the growing numbers of people with middle-class incomes, more sporting activities were within their reach than ever before. Largely outside the hunting, shooting and fishing pattern of the landed aristocracy, the urban middle classes, guided by the lead from the public schools, began a sports cult which was to reach alarming proportions. As Escott pointed out: 'It signified the revolt of the sons and daughters of the middle class against their exclusion from modes of social enjoyment that to their contemporaries slightly above them in the social scale had long been allowed.'[61]

The two features of this cult that were evident in Bristol, were the passionate enthusiasm it roused, and the attempt that was made to control, socially, sporting organizations, in recognition of the fact that sport had important social, as well as athletic dimensions. The result of this latter concern was most clearly seen in the distinctions that were made between amateur and professional sport; and the fact that the city's response in providing sports facilities was fragmented by countless bodies attempting, on a private basis and in competition with each other, to secure their own facilities. Good sporting facilities were the privilege of the wealthy few. Not surprisingly, the earliest organization of the fastest growing sports of the early Victorian period, cricket and athletics, were to be found in the more affluent areas. Clifton Cricket Club was established in the 1830s, Knowle and Bedminster Cricket Club in the 1840s. The Zoological Gardens had been used since its inception as a venue for athletic meetings. Class prejudice was actually reported in the *Western Daily Press* in 1869, when a gentleman refused to run against an artisan at one of the athletic Meets at the Zoo Gardens.[62]

Athletics, however, was one activity which could not be socially contained. Running, for instance, did not require any special equipment. There was thus some attempt to meet popular demand on a broader basis, and the pleasure grounds at Avonmouth and Horfield were equipped with suitable tracks. Athletic meetings in the last quarter of the century became the main spectator sport in the city.[63] Gentlemen fearing defeat by the lower classses could turn their attention to bicycling (still too expensive in the 1870s to be common); to rowing (the Ariel Rowing Club was founded in 1870 and regattas held annually thereafter on the Avon at Shirehampton and Saltford); to cricket (in their exclusive clubs); and to Rugby football (enthusiastically taken up by the Clifton College boys who played the first Rugby football match between schools in a match against Marlborough in 1865: Clifton Rugby Football Club was founded in 1872).

The public school cult created a sporting ideology which in turn led to an adulation of sportsmen and their achievements which had formerly been more the preserve of eminent clerics or preachers in middle-class homes. Bristol was the home-ground of W. G. Grace, whose father had been a member of the Clifton Cricket Club and who had helped to form the Gloucestershire County Cricket Club which originally played on the Downs. W.G.'s exploits in these formative years of county cricket (by 1870, twenty-two matches were played; by 1880, it had reached fifty) are well known. An indication of the adulation he received comes from the pen of the Bishop of Hereford:

Had Grace been born in ancient Greece, the *Iliad* would have been a different book. Had he lived in the Middle Ages, he would have been a crusader and would have been lying with his legs crossed in some ancient abbey, having founded a great family. As he was born when the world was older he was the best known of all Englishmen and the King of that English game least spoilt by any form of vice.[64]

Emphasis on the moral value of sporting activities was an important element in popularizing sport amongst the middle classes. Sometimes it reached extremes as when one stalwart Bristol vicar, a keen cyclist on his Humber tricycle, went as far as exhorting his parishioners to join him in forming the Bristol Crusaders' Cycling Club for their mutual spiritual benefit.[65] Such moral approbation however, did provide a shield behind which 'modern' middle-class young ladies could find greater personal freedom in the pursuit of sport. The emancipation of women by the bicycle is a familiar theme. It was not accomplished before the 1890s, even though the first chain-driven safety model bicycle was invented in 1879. By 1896 the Bristol Bicycle and Tricycle Club organized a series of mixed groups for bicycle rides, and from then on, women were included in the social bicycling activities of the club, though the serious business of racing remained a masculine affair.

Lawn tennis and archery were sports which women found particularly suitable, and clubs for women were developed in Clifton and Weston-super-Mare.[66] In 1890 twenty-two ladies in Clifton decided to storm the masculine stronghold and organize a game of cricket.[67] They had to bowl underarm because of their clothes, but perhaps the greatest freedom for women, gained through sport, was the development of special clothes for sporting activities which gave them a greater physical freedom. Obviously sporting clothes, bicycles, sports equipment, etc. all required capital expenditure, which meant that only the daughters of the affluent middle classes could enjoy this freedom. But developments in medical knowledge about the benefits of loose-fitting clothing, fresh air and exercise did have an impact on challenging social inhibitions which largely controlled the lives of middle-class females.[68]

By the turn of the century, the numbers of different sports pursued by both men and women which were reported in the press were legion. To those already mentioned can be added hockey, lacrosse, quoits, croquet, golf, rifle-shooting, billiards, swimming and model yachting, though perhaps the latter is a hobby rather than a sport. The sports reporter of the *Bristol Argus* in 1887, rather overcome by the rapid development of interest in sport, wrote: 'Legitimate sport or exercise for the grave and gay, for the young and old, for the rich and poor, for the male and female is the great order of the day.'[69] The key word here is 'legitimate', which the writer found necessary to include, presumably to contrast the new middle-class pursuit of sport from old popular pastimes. But the dividing line was, in many respects, largely social.

The old popular pastime of prize fighting was made illegal, though it was still practised in the city. Yet the middle-class Bicycle and Tricycle Club could hold a fund-raising 'Assault-at-Arms' in the gymnasium attached to the private swimming baths at Kingsdown in 1887. At this event there were boxing matches, fencing and quarterstaff, and a tug-of-war between different cycling clubs, easily distinguishable since they all wore uniforms. The 'Assault-at-Arms' was supposed to be a 'quaint' affair deliberately recalling old popular pastimes, socially acceptable because it was decorously organized. Yet even decorum was thrown to the winds by other middle-class sports enthusiasts. The traditions of social behaviour which grew up amongst Rugby football players would suggest that all the elements frowned upon in old popular amusements were dealt with leniently when the activists were obviously middle-class young men from the best families. In the process of the 'modernization' of sport, the middle classes had made a bid for exclusive rights in the kind of activities which traditionally had cut across class barriers.

The role of the Bristol Bicycle and Tricycle Club in the late 1880s and 1890s provides ample evidence of the drive towards exclusiveness in sport. It was a social as well as a bicycling club, and it catered for the social as well as bicycling needs of its members. In the course of one year, 1897, besides all the racing and bicycling activities, there was the breakthrough in including women in bicycle rides; an athletic sports was held by the club in aid of charity; and the club's annual dinner was presided over by the Mayor, attended by the Dean of Bristol, many other local dignitaries and also delegates from top London clubs.

It was in vain that one local reporter suggested that what was really needed was the amalgamation of all the clubs in one sport, such as bicycling, which could then have a central clubhouse in the city. The advantages would be 'a store home for your machine, a clubhouse centrally situated wherein you can find papers, periodicals, chess, draughts, billiards, etc. and a gymnasium.' But he gave his own reasons for the impossibility of the scheme: class distinction between Clifton and Bristol, and the competitive rivalry between clubs.[70] The development of sport was trapped in the social context. Bicycling broke through the barrier, as technological innovations led to the manufacture of cheap bicycles. But growth in popularity of the sport led to the decline of organizations such as the Bristol Bicycle and Tricycle Club. Now motor-cars became the new toy of the rich.

However there were sports which gained and maintained popular appeal at all social levels. By far the most common sport was football, and the names on the fixture list, published in the press, give an indication of the origin of the teams. They vary from old boys' teams, socio-religious teams of church, chapel and the YMCA, firms' teams,

Association Football Fixture List[71]

Location	Teams
Coalpit Heath	Cotham Amateurs v. Coalpit Heath
Bower Ashton	Hebron v. Redcliff O. Boys
Tytherington	Thornbury v. Tytherington
Thornbury	Thornbury 2nd v. Slimbridge
Camerton	Clifton Wanderers v. Camerton
Wickwar	Stonehouse v. Wickwar
Whitehall	Milford v. Whitehall
New Brislington	Barton Hill Adult School v. Redcliff Thistle
,,	St. Matthews v. Riverside (Cardiff)
Paulton	Clifton Glendale v. Paulton Reserves
Bedminster	St. Lukes v. Southmead
Downs	Grosvenor v. Dominican Reserves
,,	Coronation v. Clifton Trinity
,,	Distillery v. Rosevery Athletic
,,	Sneyd Park v. Gaunt House
,,	Lodway v. Westbury Park
Eastville	Bethesda United v. Knowle Social Reserves
,,	Seymour v. M. C. Memorial Reserves
,,	Grenville v. Redding United
,,	Victoria Athletic v. Newtown
,,	Easton Athletic v. Wellington
,,	Easton Athletic Reserves v. St. Paul's P.S.

and trade union teams. The fixture list of 1901 gives some indication of the range. This list was by no means inclusive of all matches played in the city that day. The clubs belonging to leagues which enjoyed press coverage were well-established, usually with middle-class connections.

Football had universal appeal and there were no class barriers to actually playing the game. Association football had not received the blessing of the socio-religious workers in Bristol as happened in other towns. Many of the famous clubs up and down the country, such as Everton, Fulham, Burnley, Barnsley, Aston Villa or Queen's Park Rangers could trace their origin to a Sunday School side, or a mission, or an enthusiastic clergyman at a local Board School.[72] But the middle-class game in Bristol was Rugby, and the west of England became a stronghold of the game. However, Association Football did gain a following in the city, more and more teams being organized in the course of the 1880s. For the many who did not either belong to some organization or work in a firm or factory where sporting activities flourished, there was still the local community. In the course of the football seasons of 1880-3, several district teams emerged. Equally rapidly, many of them disappeared again, as their organizational problems, particularly the lack of suitable pitches, were too great.

Of the two major teams which were later to survive as professionals, the Eastville Rovers had the advantage of a suitable pitch in a field off Fishponds Road, as yet undeveloped, and they widened their support to include all East Bristol. It was a local honour to be selected to play for the 'Blackshirts', and the boys and young men who assiduously practised in Eastville Park provided the major proportion of the team.[73] The other team to survive, Bristol City, had a broad area of local support since the club was formed from the amalgamation of two smaller district teams, the Bristol South End and the Bedminster Club. The big step of turning professional was not taken until the 1897/8 season when four of the district teams still in existence, St George's, Warmley, Bristol City and the Bristol Rovers (the new name for the Eastville Rovers) took the plunge. Of these, only the latter two were to survive.

The Rovers started well, getting Aston Villa as their first fixture and working their way through the Southern League to emerge as the champions in the 1903/4 season. But success was relative, since their spectators numbered only about 5–6,000 throughout this period, and Club members had to exercise considerable ingenuity in fundraising activities. City, on the other hand, after a few lean years and much desperate fund-raising, did manage to have a run of fairly successful seasons, culminating in their highest achievement of reaching the Cup Final against Manchester United in 1909, which they lost. However, this meteoric rise earned the club a band of between 25,000 and 30,000 supporters, which helped to pay for the stadium at Ashton Gate. The size of the crowd meant that professional football, as a spectator sport, had arrived in Bristol and the great divide between amateur and professional was to be firmly cemented.

In the early days of organized football, particularly in the 1860s and '70s, it had appeared that, at least on the sports field, class differences might be overlooked. But the history of the Football Association Cup Championships shows that the great divide, to be made absolute by the distinctions made between the amateur and professional, only took time to surface. The point of final confrontation was reached in 1883, the year that Toynbee Hall was founded to bridge the gap between the Two Nations; the year that the Clifton College Mission in Bristol built the working men's club. That year the working-class team, the Blackburn Olympic, beat the Old Etonians in the final of the FA Cup, played at the Crystal Palace. From that moment, the public school teams withdrew from the competition, to devote their energies towards building up the amateur tradition of the privileged.[74] Professional football was left to develop as a spectator sport for the urban masses.

Its significance in this respect, in the context of the industrial urban city, is a matter of debate. There is no doubt that far more people watched football than could have played it because of the dearth of pitches and open spaces in the most densely populated areas. Some sociologists have seen the development of football fanatics, and the life-style that ensued from this, as a significant subculture as all-embracing as anything ever produced by the religious sub-culture. Others have suggested that football as a spectator sport was like a 'safety valve' performing the same function as the popular pastimes of old. Gerth and Mills write:

Many mass audience situations, with their 'vicarious' enjoyments, serve psychologically, the unintended function of channelling and releasing otherwise unplaceable emotions. Thus great volumes of aggression are 'cathartically' released by crowds of spectators cheering their favourite stars of sport – and jeering the umpire.[75]

T. H. S. Escott, who was making stringent comments on football as a mass spectator sport in 1897, would not have believed a word of it. He did liken football to an old popular pastime, pugilism. But he did so to denounce it. He believed that football did not release aggression, it created it. Describing the arguments about the rules and regulations controlling the game he wrote:

> the feuds among football legislators are thus as varied and violent as the forms of muscular ferocity which the game itself allows. That these can be minimised by a strenuous and keen referee is probable; that when this functionary is slack, professional football resembles the revival of the prize ring in disguise, admitted.

He profoundly laments 'the fashionable brutality not only of the players but the spectators'.[76] The size of the problem in Bristol though, can hardly have been acute since the crowds at the matches of the two professional clubs remained modest in size. Bigger crowds before the turn of the century were to be found at the County Cricket Ground at Ashley Down, opened in 1888. Here there were facilities for athletics and bicycle racing and a crowd of 10,000 turned up to the first meet held there in 1888 by the Bicycle and Tricycle Club.

For the majority of Bristol's urban poor, organized sport probably had very little impact on their lives, Unless they could belong to a club, a trade union, or a large firm which supplied sporting facilities,[77] there was little chance of actively participating in sport. Space was always expensive and even Bristol's natural facilities, the Downs and the river, were already over-utilized by middle-class clubs.[78] Further, the increasingly sophisticated levels of organization in sport put them beyond reach of the poor. Sporting activities were not encouraged at school, many schools not even possessing playgrounds, though a voluntary Physical Recreation Society was set up in 1890 to promote this cause.[79]

The success of the sporting facilities provided by the socio-religious groups, particularly the YMCA, is easily explicable in this context. But these facilities, again, were spread very unevenly on the ground. In spite of the universal appeal of sport, middle-class enthusiasts were too busily engaged on the survival of their own clubs and activities to take a civic view. The result was that land which may have had potential as playing fields was rapidly built over and the 'sporting revolution' belonged, in the main, to the middle classes in their more spacious suburbs. Thus organized sport took its place alongside other voluntary leisure pursuits, not as a means for promoting social integration and the civic spirit, but as a reflection of the socio-economic division in society.

9

SOCIAL DEVELOPMENT AND THE CITY

The main purpose of this book has been to illustrate that the modernization of the city contributed to a new self-consciousness about urban civilization. The public health movement had made the first and most lasting contribution to the raising of that consciousness. Problems of dirt, disease, pollution and mortality were pressed home in Chadwick's Blue Books and taken up with dedication and a sense of mission by a new breed of professionals, Medical Officers of Health, Borough Surveyors and Engineers, Inspectors of Nuisances, men who were to do the ground-work for the evolution of a municipal civil service in all large cities. But the next step beyond public health, the social and cultural response to mass urbanization, required above all things, imagination; the ability to transcend the ugly facts and to work towards a vision of a future civilization which would bring greater happiness to a greater number.

I THE SOCIO-RELIGIOUS RESPONSE

The vision which emerged amongst groups of men and women in many large cities in the 1860s and '70s was of a civilization based on morality and culture. They tried to solve the social problems of the city by transforming the social environment and improving the social relationships between rich and poor. Yet in spite of many successes, the Evil Giants: Want, Ignorance, Idleness, Squalor and Disease, refused to go away.[1] Indeed, they were brought ever more to the foreground by the statistical studies of the social scientists.[2] In the course of the Edwardian period it became obvious, under mounting industrial and political pressure, that a radically new approach was required.[3] The developments which took place had the effect of undermining the autonomy of the city and the sense of individual, urban communities, which had been the foundation of the 'culture and morality' response. Lloyd George and Churchill introduced measures of state responsibility for social conditions.[4] The Fabians, and especially the Webbs, talked in terms of creating vast national bureaucracies to deal with education, sickness and want. The Royal Commission on the Poor Laws, deliberating in these years of change from 1904-9, was unable to agree on a new approach to poor relief or a new role for private philanthropy, that kingpin in the cities of the philosophy of 'social citizenship'.

One thing was certain though, the city was not, and never could be, an independent community, responsible for its own development, for meeting its own social needs. The propensity of large towns to go on getting bigger and the increasing complexity of the administrative units they required was leading towards a fresh response to urbanization. The emphasis was now on a conception of the city as merely a reservoir of people, each with rights and needs to be met, rather than the city as a single community. Gradually the sense of responsibility for the social environment based on the idea of an urban community, which had seemed such a comprehensive schema for attacking the social problems of urban life, began to appear irrelevant. So irrelevant in fact, that even modifications and amendments to the institutions and organizations developed under its influence could not restore that sense of importance once attached to these activities.

In the subsequent disillusion, however, a vital element was lost. Never again were those concerned with the city to have such firsthand experience of the relationships between environment and social problems. The socio-religious workers had begun their work at a time when little was understood about the process of urbanization. The many individuals involved in this unspecialized response had been goaded to action by numerous different stimuli. Yet thirty years of personal experience in many different voluntary activities, which had to attract support to survive, had taught them to be responsive. They uncovered specific social needs, formerly unrecognized, especially in their work for children and young people, social clubs and community centres, and their contribution to further education. Above all, both because of their idealistic outlook and because their practical activities had to be concentrated in this way, they had explored a crucial dimension for future social development, the provision of facilities for the use of leisure.

In this period, in the last quarter of the nineteenth century, when it was becoming obvious that, both in Western Europe and America, the majority of the nations were becoming urbanized, the importance of this factor was widely recognized. Arthur M. Schlesinger in his book *The Rise of the City* quotes from a US presidential campaign address made by J. A. Garfield in 1880.[5] Garfield said: 'We may divide the whole struggle of the human race into two chapters; first, the fight to get leisure; and then the second fight of civilization – what shall we do with our leisure when we get it.' Schlesinger then points out: 'it was in the city that the people were squarely engaged in the "second fight of civilization" for it was in the city that the first fight was being won.' But unfortunately, at the turn of the century, this analysis seemed no longer so clear nor so obvious. Partly this was because of the discrediting of socio-religious work which had been supremely concerned with this issue.

But partly it was also due to the challenge that was being provided by the transformation of working and living conditions, and the constant pressure of social and material advances, to an understanding of the importance of leisure.[6] The socio-religious workers had responded initially to the idea of providing leisure facilities as a means of attracting support, and exercising an influence over social behaviour. Some of them went further and began to appreciate the new importance of leisure activities themselves as compensation for difficult working conditions and to counteract the 'evil' influences of an urban environment. But there was little pressure to investigate in depth the full complexity of the changing relationship between work and leisure in both the home and work environments. Perhaps the possibility of having two well-established social environments, at home and at work, where social contacts could be made, social and leisure elements shared, was one of the more important changes of the late Victorian period. More people than before, working in large institutions or manufacturing units, had the chance of belonging to a 'community' not regulated by home or family ties.

The idea of community, so central to much socio-religious work, was as hard to pin down in practical form as concepts of leisure. Why did some missions, such as the Clifton College Mission in St Agnes, manage to succeed in creating a 'community spirit' whilst others, like the early days of the Shaftesbury Crusade, fail? Differences of approach and ideology can provide some explanation. But even these do not cover the fact that communities developed in areas untouched by socio-religious work.[7] Perhaps a broader based explanation of this phenomenon had much to do with the physical development of towns, the scale of building, the suitability of the terrace house for meeting the main family and social requirements of those who lived in them. Nineteenth-century speculative development may have been as responsible as changing economic patterns in destroying the range of social contacts and experiences possible in a pre-industrial city. Yet houses were built by local builders, who used the most readily available local materials and, unconsciously perhaps, incorporated some local traditions in their design and layout, as any comparison of nineteenth-century working-class housing in Bristol, with that in Birmingham, Nottingham or Sheffield immediately makes obvious.[8] Working-class housing which had not actually begun as jerry-built slums (and after 1875 this was only a small proportion of the total) reflected clear social aspirations and attitudes, adapted to the practicalities of urban living.

Such practicalities also had a vital, determining, influence on the use of leisure. The time not spent at work or asleep could not easily be spent in leisure institutions, even by the most enthusiastic supporter of such activities. The difference between work and play, especially for working-class women, was not always clear. Moments of relaxation and entertainment had to be snatched in the constant round of work and chores. For men, the types and choices of leisure activity were influenced by many factors, such as satisfaction of boredom at work, or the degree of physical and mental fatigue arising from work. The space and privacy of the terrace house, though limited, was enough to encourage the pursuit of personal hobbies such as the keeping of animals, birds and fish, growing flowers and vegetables, or keeping the small modicum of equipment necessary for hobbies as diverse as woodwork, bicycling or fishing. Evidence from the local newspapers in Bristol suggests that these activities were gaining rapidly in popularity from the 1890s.[9] The leisure experiences even for the people of St Agnes, who enjoyed the most developed range of social facilities that socio-religious work could offer, were made up of far more than the influences they received through contact with these institutions. Cultural experiences and social life could not be so easily equated in the way envisaged by Canon Barnett in his view of the 'Ideal City'.

The cultural institutions of the socio-religious workers were never the controlling factors in the social environment. But they did succeed in one respect, in that they were responsible for creating facilities where none had been before. This largely accounts for much of their success, since prior to the 1860s and '70s, no attempt had been made to provide a range of institutions and facilities in all areas of the city. The attempt was comprehensive because the same people worked at providing facilities in their different roles as philanthropists, socio-religious workers and town councillors. The ultimate objective, beyond the vested interests of particular organizations, had been to make a contribution to overall social development as part of an ideal of what could be achieved in an urban civilization.

In the circumstances it is hardly surprising that the end of the 'culture and morality' response should mark also the end of the ideal of a great urban civilization in large provincial cities. Now the suburb became the focus of attention, rather than the city.[10] Social development was left to state organizations, particularly education, and to private enterprise. City development was dominated by housing, and the most convenient location for industries and services. It was as if the nascent anti-urbanism of the middle classes, evident in the countrified environment of the affluent suburbs, was finally released. In Bristol, as in other large cities, further boundary extensions encouraged the shift of interest from the centre outwards. The city became fragmented by this suburban development, too large and amorphous to stimulate an individual response any more. Greatest casualty of all, was the interruption of a systematic search for a solution to the 'second fight' of an urbanized and industrial nation: what to do with leisure time after it has been won.

II LEISURE AND SOCIAL CHANGE

Changing attitudes to leisure in the late Victorian period have further significance in that they provide an indication of the degree of social change taking place in the city. Sociologists and others have described this social change as no less than the evolution of a 'mass society'.[11] A 'mass' society, Edward Shils suggests, exists when the whole of society is drawn within the pales of civilizations; when 'the center of society – the central institutions, and the central value systems which guide and legitimate these institutions – has extended its boundaries.' A 'mass' society comes into being when most of the population establishes a closer relationship with the centre than had been achieved in earlier forms of Western society.[12]

This development should have begun to take place in Bristol, as in other large cities, since large cities contained the kind of central institutions, economic, social, and political, which provided the nodal points, in society at large, to which people could relate. As Louis Wirth wrote, in his inimitable way:

> What we call civilization as distinguished from culture has been cradled in the city, the city is the centre from which the influences of modern civilized life radiate to the ends of the earth and the point from which they are controlled; the persistent problems of contemporary society take their most acute form in the city.[13]

Ultimately, the most pressing social problem of the future was how to achieve closer integration of the population and create a new social order in which people could relate to the central institutions of society. In circumstances of considerable social and economic inequality, the ideal of cultural unity, promoted by Canon Barnett and pursued by many reformers in Bristol and elsewhere, was a logical, if Utopian, response to the challenge.

The evidence from the activities of the reformers in Bristol, however, make abundantly clear that their conception of what constituted 'cultural unity' had no hope of succeeding. And yet, in spite of the failure of the reformers, in the course of the forty years or so from 1870–1914, a considerable degree of social change seems to have taken place which, superficially at any rate, gives the impression of a growing social consensus, even the development of a 'mass' society. Random references to this change can be found in many newspaper and periodical articles, one example being a report on a Saturday popular concert at the Colston Hall, published in the *Bristol Argus* of November 1886. The writer describes the audience derisively as mainly young people 'belonging to that fungous growth of the nineteenth century – "a genteel appearance" – which includes everyone from scavengers to the great middle class.'[14]

Not much weight can be given to such a biased and isolated example, but behind the derision, the writer was illuminating an important historical fact. A profound change in social behaviour and outward appearance was spreading amongst all classes of citizens. Its development was most clearly evident in the new institutions and organizations devoted to leisure, many unrelated to the efforts of the socio-religious workers. Since, one suspects, many generalizations about 'mass' society stem from the observation of this phenomenon, some aspects of the nature of this change appear to be worth investigating. The evidence from this study of Bristol can, perhaps, throw some light on the process of cultural diffusion; the attempt to achieve a cultural consensus; and the evolution of new patterns of social behaviour.

The normal pattern of cultural diffusion, as Georges Duby suggests,[15]

> is that the cultural patterns of the upper classes in society tend to become popularized, to spread and to move down, step by step, to the most deprived social groups. If we take the word 'culture' in its narrowest sense, beginning, that is, in the realm of literacy and artistic creation, of religious knowledge, beliefs and attitudes, it is very easy to discern this phenomenon of popularisation.

This was the process as understood by Canon Barnett, and in Bristol, by the Rev. J. Percival. But they were also aware that the context of a modern city subtly disrupts the 'normal' pattern of cultural diffusion. Basic developments of universal literacy, improvements in transport and communications, and the speed with which changes were now taking place, meant that even the socially deprived in the city were not an isolated community, waiting for influences from above to reach them.

All levels of society were subject to a far wider range of influences, above all, those generated by their own experiences and own response to change. It was appreciation of this which led the Rev. T. W. Harvey to follow Percival's ideal at St Agnes, by merely creating a more favourable institutional framework within which an independent culture could flourish. Of course, Harvey's outlook was quite rare amongst the socio-religious workers in the city. Most preferred to

expend their energies on transmitting the values and standards that they held dear. But the ultimate failure of the religious sub-culture to dominate even the leisure patterns of the city, though Bristol had a larger proportion, statistically, of religious adherents than any other large city, indicates the problems of diffusing a value-system. That such an attempt was made had the immediate result of stimulating social and cultural activity. This was evident in the transformation which took place in all the major propaganda campaigns aimed at gaining the widest possible social support, from political parties, religious sects, to the great Temperance movement. All turned to entertainment, laced their exhortations with music and verse; developing, from the institution of penny readings amongst the general public in the 1860s and '70s, ever more sophisticated techniques of combining propaganda, education and entertainment. From the point of view of social form, there was little difference between meetings organized by Temperance societies to reform behaviour, and meetings of the Bristol Sunday Society to promote socialism. Both used music, lantern lectures and other entertainments to maintain interest.

The impact of this social and cultural activity, which extended virtually to all organizations which had to attract support from people during their leisure hours, must have been substantial. This does not mean, however, that it was a hey-day for the propagandists, though one aspect of this activity was important. This was its immediacy. Meetings which brought people into physical and social contact with each other, and the medium of the spoken word, with its direct emotional appeal, could exert a considerable influence. As Professor Handlin points out: 'the intense involvement of the masses with their culture at the turn of the century' was due to the direct forms of communication that existed in the absence of mass media.[16]

This social and cultural activity did not necessarily bring the majority of the population, however, into closer relationship with the central institutions of society, a vital prerequisite for a 'mass' society. Political and economic institutions were still dominated by the small group of the ruling élite. The élite believed the way to bring the majority to support or acquiesce in the 'central value systems which guide and legitimate these institutions' was by achieving a cultural consensus amongst an educated population. The history of the dominant cultural institutions in the city bears witness to this belief.

These cultural institutions had played a significant part in the early nineteenth century, in encouraging social integration amongst the educated. Why should they not play the same role in an era of mass literacy? Indeed, the stages of development of these institutions, from their creation by a small band of enthusiasts to their subsequent takeover by the town council, for the benefit of the community at large, mirrors the steps which were taken to try and achieve a cultural consensus.

But it is clear from this study of Bristol, that these institutions were not able to promote a cultural consensus in the city. Of the three leading cultural institutions, the library system, museum and art gallery, only the libraries met with a widespread response. Yet even that response was not intimately related to a belief in Liberal Culture and new cultural interests. A demand for entertainment and the ever-growing needs of young people and students, faced with examinations, provided some of the main drives behind further institutional development. The museum and art gallery, without popular support, had reached an impasse. Their takeover by the town council in the decade 1895–1905 was the embodiment of the ideal of a cultural consensus, based on the precepts of Liberal Culture. But by that time, social developments had made such an ideal appear somewhat anachronistic.

New ways of seeking excitement and pleasure, particularly sport and commercial entertainment, had quickly established themselves as a more popular prospect of the 'good life'. Relaxation, entertainment and informal social activities were also much more immediately attractive than the austere, intellectual demands of the Liberal Culture ideal. As Edward Shils points out, sensibly: 'No society can ever achieve a complete cultural consensus',[17] and the Liberal Culture ideal was ill-suited to attract more than a minority. Thus the takeover by the town council of the cultural institutions of the city marked, not the achievement of a cultural consensus, but the abandonment of responsibility for that ideal by the élite, who had formerly supported such institutions. Cultural diffusion was left to the professional educationalists, involved in the long-term process of social development. Any direct influence of the élite over the leisure institutions of the city came to an end, finally, with the introduction of technology to entertainment.

Professor Asa Briggs has suggested that the cluster of inventions of the last quarter of the century

> were as basic to new ways of life in the twentieth century as were the inventions of the last quarter of the eighteenth century in textiles, iron and power, to the new industrial patterns of the nineteenth century. The difference between them is that the eighteenth century inventions transformed the material standard of living and the nineteenth century inventions, the forms of culture.[18]

Yet this technological transformation of cultural life did not immediately cancel out the impact made by the attempt to achieve a cultural consensus. The definition of Liberal Culture made in the 1860s and '70s, coupled with the ideal of 'social citizenship', remained the most influential in the educational field. A new departure in education, the 'progressive school' movement, ushered in by Abbotsholme in 1889 and Bedales in 1893, were deeply imbued with these ideals. The movement in England projected an image of the 'good life' based on a deeply moral view of the individual and his role in society. Self-development and social development through Liberal Culture and social citizenship were doubly reaffirmed.[19]

One of the more lasting results of the Liberal Culture campaign, however, was to come with the development of mass media. The men who were to control the media, particularly the radio, were confronted with exactly the same problem, in a different context, as the social reformers of the 1860s and '70s. They had to achieve a cultural consensus within which they could operate. The compromise solution of labelling activities 'highbrow', 'middlebrow' and 'lowbrow' was a fresh response to the difference between the vision of the ideal and social reality. It was a response of some significance in a so-called 'mass' society, since the terminology highlights the social snobbery and élitism which had come to dominate all cultural responses.

It illustrates, as the history of the cultural institutions of the city illustrates, the fact that the social context of cultural diffusion had gained an importance beyond the process of widening the cultural experience of the masses. The result was a self-conscious fragmentation of cultural influences along class lines. In this process, opposing value systems became far more broadly based since they were adopted as synonymous with class consciousness. The result, in practical terms, on the cultural life of the city, was to leave the recognized institutions and pursuits of Liberal Culture to the middle classes. By a supreme irony, Matthew Arnold's attack on the Philistines could be relegated to the past and regardless of the truth, the middle classes identified their outlook with an appreciation of classical art, music and literature.

Their superiority in terms of the appreciation of Liberal Culture was maintained by the exclusion of nearly all but the affluent from recognized institutions of secondary and tertiary education. An appreciation of the liberal arts had become related to class, wealth and social behaviour. The cultural institutions of the city lingered on as symbols of excellence, and of the tradition of culture, and a few, not barred by political or social prejudice, were able to use and enjoy them. The seed of the 'cultural renaissance' of the 1860s and '70s had fallen on somewhat stony ground. Perhaps the main achievement of the Arnoldian vision of culture had been to stir the ruling élite, whose economic and social success might have left them complacent and dedicated to personal ostentation, towards a concern for their city and an ideal of urban civilization.

However, cultural institutions had not provided that hoped-for link between the masses and the central institutions of society. In this sense, the prerequisites of a mass society as outlined by Shils had not been met in Bristol at any time between 1870 and 1914. The relationship of the masses with the 'centre' may have become more complex, now that 'civilizing' influences extended to the boundaries of society, but it was not much closer. To say this goes against the views of contemporaries, especially the views of the socio-religious workers. Archdeacon Wilson who, as the second headmaster of Clifton College, had been responsible for appointing the Rev. T. W. Harvey, gave a speech at the Working Men's Club at St Agnes in 1893, to mark the tenth anniversary of the founding of the club.

He said:

Possibly a future historian writing the history of the English people in this period will think much less of the legislative and even of the commercial and scientific progress of the period than of the remarkable social movement by which there has been an effort made, by a thousand agencies, to bring about unity of feeling between different classes, and to wage war against conditions of life which earlier generations seem to have tolerated. The national importance of individual and, so to speak, local effort in this connection, the aggregate strength and value of all such agencies as Boys' Clubs, Children's Help Societies and the like, can hardly be overestimated. Squalor and neglect are far too general now in some districts of every great city, but there are few cities where the new ideas of what constitutes duty to a neighbour have not provided schools, clubs, reading rooms and libraries, swimming baths, parks and similar wholesome influences, which a generation ago were non-existent except for the rich. It is this social progress that encourages bright hopes for the future.[20]

However, an historical evaluation of the achievements of 'neighbourliness' outlined by Wilson does not bear out his thesis. Wilson appears to believe that these institutions and societies did provide the hoped-for link between classes and thus between all citizens and the central organizations of the city. But he failed to appreciate the important distinction between facilities which would result in a widening of cultural experience and which represented a rational response to the conditions of mass urbanization, and the development of a new social order, which depended not on such improvements, but on the total experience of all individuals.

The factors creating a new social order and contributing to changes in social behaviour are only 'cultural' factors, if the word is used in its widest rather than its narrowest sense. Because the socio-religious workers generally concentrated on the narrower view of culture, much of their effort was wasted and what they did achieve has been roundly criticized. Indeed, one recent assessment is that the whole attempt to create a new social order, based on a common cultural consensus, was nothing but a narrow-based, class-biased attempt by the middle classes to win over the masses. Describing the new towns and 'modernizing' towns of the nineteenth century, Harrison writes:

> A great poverty of social life at all levels marked the new towns;

and a process of social disintegration paralleled the physical break-up of the town into a series of concentric suburbs based on social distinction. The initiative in the solution of these problems lay with the dominant middle class and they had only one answer – to make the whole of society in their own image.[21]

There is no doubt that an attempt was made by middle-class reformers to define a code of values for society at large which was termed Respectable and which had political and cultural connotations. The question is, how were these universal values arrived at even amongst the middle classes themselves, and how successful were they in transmitting them? In the second half of the century, the scale of change demanded ever greater levels of endeavour by all social groups. One of the major objectives of such an endeavour was to create a measure of order in the social environment. This had been recognized in the 1860s and '70s as one of the basic challenges of mass urbanization. W. S. Jevons was voicing a widely held view when he wrote that to conceive of creating a social order by increasing levels of social discipline, was only of limited value.[22] The real problem was to create a social order, based on commonly accepted social values, which was sufficiently definite to allow prediction and yet sufficiently flexible to allow for change and for differences between individuals.

Dr Kelvin, as a social psychologist, provides an analysis of how such an order can be established.[23] He suggests it is largely a matter of practice and principle. People are born into a social system, but acceptance of the norms of the community, the social values, depends on the judgment of the individual. Such values are formed from a combination of principle related to actual experience. The social environment is thus ordered in a two-way interaction between socially accepted terms of probability and the basis of values held by groups and individuals. For this process to proceed smoothly and to encompass social change and development, two factors are necessary – a mixture of conformity and non-conformity and the creation of stereotypes and reference groups.[24] For historians, this mixture of conformity and non-conformity and the image of stereotypes can prove a stumbling block in social analysis.

For example, it is easy to pick up the evidence of Samuel Smiles's book *Self-Help* (published in 1859), which provides all the values and stereotypes of the middle-class ideological propaganda of Respectability, and then point to the numbers of copies that were sold.[25] But what is not so easy, is to assume that the result was mass indoctrination. As Dr Brian Harrison points out in his study of the great Temperance movement, the decline in drunkenness and violence in the streets can hardly be claimed as a great victory for the teetotalists. It was much more the result of improved economic and social conditions, alternative sources of excitement and a greater stability and security in social life.[26] Thus as far as the ethic of Respectability is concerned, it is probably more accurate to suggest that different social groups responded to that particular stereotype in ways which appeared relevant to them.[27] Certainly, as far as leisure pursuits were concerned, newer activities such as a wider pursuit of music, organized sport and commercial entertainment gained the status of Respectability, with little reference to middle-class ideology.

In some ways, then, the vision of a social order based on commonly accepted values was realized in this period without a loss of social independence for those in inferior economic and social positions.[28] The desire for order was universal, though the city itself produced a social environment which was too complex for any one social group to be completely dominant. In Bristol, in the 1860s and 70s at least, it had been possible to have close collaboration between leaders from different social backgrounds in the pursuit of social and cultural objectives. The Rev. Percival's close links with the Co-operative movement and the Trades Council, and the common demands from middle-class Radicals and working men for libraries, reading rooms and parks, illustrates a readiness to co-operate in face of the challenge of 'modern' urbanization. The fact that this co-operation inspired the ideal of a cultural consensus in the minds of the socio-religious workers was an unfortunate distortion, which simply illustrates the dangers of starting from an intellectual premise, such as Arnold's *Culture and Anarchy,* and misreading the situation. Demands for knowledge, self-improvement and entertainment had been the basis for collaboration, not acquiescence in any ideology alien to the experience of the working classes.

When social and political tensions grew in the Edwardian period, those who had benefited most from this collaboration were often the leaders of the opposition.[29] In the ensuing bitterness, so-called middle-class cultural values were eschewed and battle lines drawn on a cultural, as well as a political and economic basis. But however fervently delineations were made, there could be no invasion of territory since both middle-class and working-class culture belonged to the same civilization, and in some cultural aspects, the influence of the city superseded the class struggle.

In one crucial dimension at least, the influence of the city was paramount. This was on the use of leisure which was gaining ever greater levels of social significance. Leisure was becoming more than an antidote to work. For some it could even be the major source of emotional and intellectual satisfaction in their lives.[30] A key challenge for the future was not simply a matter of merely finding new ways of filling the leisure hours that were available; it was, much more importantly, finding an answer to the question: 'what will be the capacity for experience of the men who have this undirected time to live?'[31] In practical terms, the 'modern' city was an important containing factor. A beneficial or hostile influence, varying according to society's capacity to understand and control its own self-made environment.

ABBREVIATIONS

AJS	*American Journal of Sociology*
BJS	*British Journal of Sociology*
EcHR	*Economic History Review*
Eng HR	*English Historical Review*
ISSB	*International Social Science Bulletin*
IRSH	*International Review of Social History*
JSH	*Journal of Social History*
JRSS	*Journal Royal Statistical Society*
P&P	*Past and Present*
TIBG	*Transactions of the Institute of British Geographers*
TRHS	*Transactions of the Royal Historical Society*
VS	*Victorian Studies*
WDP	*Western Daily Press*

NOTES

CHAPTER 1: INTRODUCTION

1. See A. F. Weber, *The Growth of Cities in the Nineteenth Century*, 1899, pp. 147–51.
2. George Tucker, quoted *ibid.*, p.v.
3. 'The Modern city as a field of historical study', in O. Handlin and J. Burchard (eds), *The Historian and the City*, 1966. pp. 1–27.
4. *Ibid.*, p. 3.
5. See W. Ashworth, *The Genesis of Modern British Town Planning*, 1954, pp. 72–7.
6. See W. Ashworth, *An Economic History of England: 1870–1939*, 1960, pp. 25–45.
7. A. Briggs, *Friends of the People: the centenary history of Lewis's*, 1956, Introduction, pp. 19–22.
8. J. R. Kellett, *The Impact of Railways on Victorian Cities*, 1969, p. 337.
9. P. S. Bagwell, *The Transport Revolution from 1770*, 1974, pp. 151–6.
10. J. A. R. Pimlott, *The Englishman's Holiday: A Social History*, 1947, p. 164.
11. Lewis Mumford, *The City in History*, 1966, pp. 508–12; criticized by Asa Briggs, 'Historians and the study of cities', *George Judah Cohen Memorial Lecture*, 1960, pp. 8–15.
12. N. Elias and E. Dunning, 'Leisure in the sparetime spectrum', in R. Albonico and K. Pfister-Bing (eds), *Sociologie des Sports*, 1971, p. 28.
13. Reprinted in W. S. Jevons, *Methods of Social Reform*, 1904, p. 1.
14. E. E. Lampard, 'Historical aspects of urbanisation', in P. M. Hauser and L. F. Schnore (eds), *The Story of Urbanisation*, 1965, p. 521.
15. Quoted in L. Mumford, *The Culture of Cities*, 1940, pp. 6–7.

16. Although these three held very different social and political views, Raymond Williams links them together as products of the nineteenth-century intellectual tradition in which it was commonplace for aesthetic, moral and social judgments to be closely interrelated. R. Williams, *Culture and Society 1780–1950*, 1963, pp. 137–61.
17. L. Mumford, *The City in History*, 1966. Graphic section three, plates 42–3 and pp. 558–61.
18. Quoted in Williams, *op. cit.*, p. 109.
19. See W. Ashworth, *op. cit.*, pp. 118–64, and G. E. Cherry, *Urban Change and Planning*, 1972, pp. 108–25.
20. S. A. Barnett, 'The Ideal City', p. 10.
21. E. P. Hennock, *Fit and Proper Persons: Ideal and Reality in Nineteenth Century Urban Government*, 1973, pp. 61–178.
22. R. A. Nisbet, *The Sociological Tradition*, 1970, pp. 47–106.
23. *WDP*, 11 March 1895.
24. T. H. S. Escott, *Social Transformations of the Victorian Age: a survey of court and country*, 1897, pp. 67–76.
25. This is a central theme in much of his writing. See particularly a series of articles in the *Nineteenth Century*: 'Practical Socialism', April 1883; 'Town councils and social reform', November 1883; 'University settlements', February 1884; 'Great cities and social reforms', October 1884.
26. Quoted from M. Richter, *The Politics of Conscience: T. H. Green and his age*, 1964, p. 344.
27. *Ibid.*, p. 355.
28. See Evening School Reports of the Bristol School Board 1895–99, Local Government Records (Bristol).
29. Geddes explained the sociological and planning importance of survey work in his article 'The city survey: a first step', *Garden Cities and Town Planning*, vol. I, 1911.
30. See H. L. Beales, 'The making of social policy', *Hobhouse Memorial Lecture*, 1952.
31. Described by Stedman Jones as the 'theory of demoralization', it was an updating of the 1834 Poor Law attitude to poverty. G. Stedman Jones, *Outcast London: A Study in the Relationship between Classes in Victorian Society*, 1971, pp. 241–70.
32. R. Pemble, 'The National Association for the Promotion of Social Science 1857–1886: Some Sociological Aspects' (unpub. MA thesis, University of Nottingham, 1968).
33. Werner Conze, 'Social history', *JSH*, vol. I, 1967–8.
34. Stedman Jones, *op. cit.*, pp. 67–98.

35. D. C. Marsh, *The Changing Social Structure of England and Wales 1871–1961*, 1965 edn, pp. 111–30.
36. B. S. Rowntree, *Poverty: a study of town life*, 1901, pp. 136–9.
37. See, for example, Chiozza Money, *Riches and Poverty*, 1905, and A. L. Bowley and A. R. Burnett-Hurst, *Livelihood and Poverty*, 1915.
38. J. W. Burrow, *Evolution and Society: A Study in Victorian Social Theory*, 1970, p. 263.
39. Nisbet, *op. cit.*, p. 315.
40. Burrow, *op. cit.*, p. 219.
41. J. S. Mill, *Autobiography*, pp. 136 and 144–5, quoted by Burrow, *op. cit.*, p. 266.
42. M. Arnold, *Culture and Anarchy*, ed. by J. Dover Wilson, 1969, p. 11.
43. M. Arnold, *Schools and Universities on the Continent*, 1868, p. 276.
44. M. Arnold, *Culture and Anarchy*, pp. 35–6.
45. An illustration of this is the connection between Edward Denison's pioneer activities in London's East End in the 1860s (to bring the civilizing influence of resident gentry into the neighbourhood) and the bringing of Samuel Barnett to be first warden of Toynbee Hall in 1884, to St Judes, Whitechapel, through the influence of Edmund Hollond, Denison's friend. See Stedman Jones, *op. cit.*, p. 259.
46. Jevons, *op. cit.*, chapter 1.
47. *Ibid.*, p. 7.
48. Though the Temperance movement was not particularly successful in creating new recreational patterns; see B. Harrison and B. Trinder, 'Drink and sobriety in an early Victorian town, Banbury 1830–60', *Eng HR*, Supplement 4, 1969, pp. 46–63.
49. C. L. Mowat, *The Charity Organisation Society 1863–1913. Its ideas and work*, 1961, pp. 8–18.
50. Charles Kingsley, *Sanitary and Social Lectures and Essays*, 1880, p. 5.
51. R. W. Malcolmson, *Popular Recreations in English Society 1700–1850*, 1973, p. 159.
52. E. Dunning, 'The development of modern football', in E. Dunning (ed.), *The Sociology of Sport: a selection of readings*, 1971, pp. 133–51.
53. A. Briggs, 'Mass entertainment: the origins of a modern industry', *29th Joseph Fisher Lecture in Commerce*, 1960.

CHAPTER 2: BRISTOL IN THE LATE NINETEENTH CENTURY

1. P. McGrath, 'Bristol since 1497', in C. M. MacInnes and W. F. Whittard (eds), *Bristol and its Adjoining Counties*, 1955, p. 210.
2. W. E. Minchinton, 'Bristol – metropolis of the west in the 18th century', *TRHS*, 5th series, IV, 1954, pp. 69-89.
3. W. Ison, *The Georgian Buildings of Bristol*, 1952, p. 25.
4. H. A. Shannon and E. Grebenik, *Population of Bristol*, 1943, p. 6.
5. *Ibid.*
6. *Royal Commission on the Housing of the Working Classes* (C4402, vol. XXX), p. 315.
7. *Royal Commission on the Health of Towns*, 2nd Report 1845 (XVIII, I, 299), Appendix on Bristol, p. 68.
8. *Ibid.*, p. 71.
9. *Ibid.*, p. 75.
10. S. E. Finer, *The Life and Times of Sir Edwin Chadwick*, 1952, p. 217.
11. J. Redlich and F. W. Hirst, *Local Government in England*, 1903, vol. I, pp. 174-279.
12. J. Latimer, *Annals of Bristol in the Nineteenth Century*, 1887, p. 291.
13. N. A. Ferguson, 'Working Class Housing in Bristol and Nottingham 1868-1919' (unpub. Ph.D. thesis, University of Oregon, 1971, university microfilm no. 72-923), p. 107.
14. J. C. Tarn, *Five Per Cent Philanthropy: an account of housing in urban areas between 1840-1914*, 1973, pp. 123-4.
15. *Board of Trade Enquiry into Working Class Rents, Housing and Retail Prices*, 1908 (Cd. 3864), p. 117.
16. *Ibid.*, p. 116.
17. *Bristol Hovels*, Report from the Bristol Housing Reform Committee, October 1907 (Bristol, 1907), p. 7.
18. Ashworth, *The Genesis of Modern British Town Planning*, pp. 176-80.
19. Weber, *The Growth of Cities in the Nineteenth Century*, 1899, p. 49.
20. Ashworth, *op. cit.*, 12.
21. T. A. Welton, *England's Recent Progress: An investigation of the statistics of Migrations, Mortality etc. in the twenty years from 1881-1901, as indicating tendencies towards the growth or decay of particular communities* (1911), pp. 15-16.
22. Shannon and Grebenik, *op. cit.*, pp. 11-12.
23. *Ibid.*, p. 11.

24. C. M. Law, 'The growth of urban population in England and Wales 1801–1911', *TIBG*, vol. 41 (1967), p. 138.
25. B. W. E. Alford has a forthcoming article on Bristol's population and occupation structure in the nineteenth century for the centenary volume of the *Transactions of the Bristol and Gloucestershire Archaeological Society*, 1976.
26. See two pamphlets by G. Farr, *The Steamship 'Great Britain'* (1965), and *Bristol Shipbuilding in the 19th Century* (1971).
27. J. H. Clapham, *An Economic History of Modern Britain*, 1932, vol. 3, p. 386.
28. *Handbook for British Association visit to Bristol 1898.*
29. S. Hutton (pseudonym for A. E. Tilling), *Bristol and its Famous Associations*, gives numerous details.
30. Anon., *A Few Plain Words about Bristol* – by one who has scribbled at a desk, c. 1860.
31. Anon., *A Word in season to the Municipal Burgesses of Bristol*, 1860.
32. *A Few Plain Words...*, p. 4.
33. See B. Atkinson, 'The Bristol Labour Movement 1868–1906' (unpub. Ph.D., University of Oxford, 1969), p. 222.

CHAPTER 3: THE CITY AND ITS CULTURAL INSTITUTIONS

1. Addison's *Cato*.
2. See V. G. Kiernan, *The Lords of Human Kind: European attitudes to the outside world in the Imperial Age*, 1969.
3. J. A. Symonds, 'Ten Years 1851–61: own inaugural lecture delivered at the Bristol Institution, 14 January 1861' (Bristol pamphlet, n.d.), p. 1, Bristol Local History Collection.
4. See A. Briggs, *Victorian Cities*, 1963, p. 208.
5. The importance of voluntary organizations in periods of rapid urbanization are explored in a different cultural context in K. Little, *West African Urbanisation: a study of voluntary associations in social change*, 1965, see esp. p. 163.
6. C. Wright Mills, *The Power Elite*, 1956, pp. 31–4.
7. W. J. Reader, *Professional Men: The Rise of the Professional Classes in Nineteenth Century England*, p. 146.
8. Leaflet prepared for intended subscribers of a building for Literary and Philosophical Purposes, with plans of intended rooms (Bristol, 1811).

9. See W. H. G. Armytage, *A Social History of Engineering*, 1961, p. 122.
10. W. R. Barker, *History of the Bristol Museum and Art Gallery*, 1906, pp. 16–31.
11. H. J. Price, 'Adult Education in Bristol during the Nineteenth Century' (unpub. MA thesis, Institute of Education, University of Bristol, 1965), p. 54.
12. For a history of the British Association, see O. J. R. Howarth, *The British Association for the Advancement of Science: A retrospect 1831–1931*, 1931.
13. See *History of the Bristol Madrigal Society* (Jubilee pamphlet, Bristol 1887), and H. Byard, *History of the Bristol Madrigal Society* (Bristol Historical Association pamphlet, 1966).
14. See P. Grosskurth, *John Addington Symonds: a biography*, 1964, pp. 5–7.
15. H. J. Price, *op. cit.*, pp. 32–7.
16. M. Arnold, *Culture and Anarchy*, 1869. J. Dover Wilson edn, 1969, p. 102.
17. *Ibid.*, p. 121.
18. *Ibid.*, p. 69.
19. R. Williams, *Culture and Society 1780–1950*, 1963, p. 134.
20. J. M. Wilson, *Autobiography 1826–1931*, 1932, p. 141.
21. See R. Johnson, 'Educational policy and social control in early Victorian England', *P&P*, no. 49, November 1970, pp. 96–119.
22. See for example, the attitudes of the Winkworth sisters in M. Shaen, *Memorials of Two Sisters*, 1908.
23. E. Sturge, *Reminiscences of My Life, and some account of the children of William and Charlotte Sturge and the Sturge family of Bristol*, 1928, pp. 15–16.
24. Miss Sturge herself took courses on the natural sciences, elementary logic, astronomy, history, Greek literature and the Italian Renaissance (course given by J. Addington Symonds).
25. Josephine Butler, *Woman's Work and Woman's Culture*, 1869, preface, p. xv.
26. E. Sturge, *op. cit.*, p. 80.
27. B. Cottle and J. Sherborne, *Life of a University*, 1959, p. 16.
28. J. Butler, *op. cit.*, p. xii.
29. P. Geddes and J. A. Thomson, *The Evolution of Sex*, 1889, p. 259, quoted from J. Conway, 'Stereotypes of femininity in a theory of sexual evolution', *VS*, September 1970, vol. XIV, no. 1, pp. 54–5.
30. The National Anti-Contagious Diseases Acts Association was formed immediately after the SSA meeting; see Jean L'Esperance, 'The work

of the ladies' National Association for the Repeal of the Contagious Diseases Acts', in *Bulletin for the Study of Labour History*, no. 26, Spring 1973, pp. 13–15.
31. J. W. Burrow, *Evolution and Society: A Study in Victorian Social Theory*, 1970, pp. 93–100.
32. For a full description of building, see W. R. Barker, *op. cit.*, pp. 51–4.
33. O. J. R. Howarth, *op. cit.*, p. 95.
34. T. Veblen, *The Theory of the Leisure Class: An economic study of institutions*, 1925, p. 364.
35. Quotations from Percival's pamphlet are taken from W. Temple, *The Life of Bishop Percival*, 1921, p. 259.
36. M. Arnold, *Schools and Universities on the Continent*, 1868, p. 276.
37. His speech is reported verbatim in a *Report of a Public Meeting Held at Bristol to Promote the Establishment of a School of Science and Literature for the West of England, 11 June 1874*, 1874.
38. N. Elias and E. Dunning, 'The quest for excitement in unexciting societies', in G. Lüsdren (ed.), *The Cross-Cultural Analysis of Sport and Games*, 1970, p. 35.
39. S. A. Barnett, 'The Ideal City', pp. 13 and 14.
40. Quoted in *Report of a Public Meeting ..., op. cit.*
41. In Bristol Local Collection, Bristol Central Reference Library.
42. A. Briggs, 'The language of "class" in early nineteenth century England', in A. Briggs and J. Saville (eds), *Essays in Labour History*, revised edn, 1967, p. 59.
43. According to the first extant set of Club rules dated 1893.
44. *Clifton Antiquarian Club Proceedings*, 1893.
45. J. Burt, *The Bristol Chess Club – its History, Chief Players and Twenty-Three Years' Record of Principal Events*, 1833, p. 3.
46. O. Handlin and J. Burchard (eds), *The Historian and the City*, 1966, p. 22.
47. E.g. article entitled 'A discussion on the purpose and efficiency of the Bristol Academy of Fine Arts', in *Art Life in the West of England*, June 1863; and regular comments each year in *WDP* on occasion of art exhibitions.
48. The Museum and Library Society had been losing financially with a decline in its major source of income, library subscriptions, with the development of the free public library system. In 1893 its debts amounted to £6,000.
49. Reprinted in W. S. Jevons, *Methods of Social Reform*, 1904, pp. 52–79. Jevons points out that the role of museums had been frequently discussed at BA and SSA Congresses, see pp. 59 and 63.

NOTES TO PAGES 67–75

50. E. Norris Matthews, *Survey of Bristol Public Libraries* (Bristol pamphlet, 1900), written for Library Association visit.
51. Even the local press admits: 'In the present pressure of local responsibilities, we might not as a community have been able to afford the luxury of an Art Gallery', *WDP*, 3 January 1905.
52. *Library Committee Reports*, 1900–6.
53. Frank W. Wills, FRIBA in conjunction with Messrs Houston of London.
54. W. R. Barker, *op. cit.*, p. 74.
55. Barker wrote (*op. cit.*, p. 73): 'the Committee went on in faith, and they were not wrong in feeling sure that in order to adorn so beautiful a building the kindly assistance of private benefactors would not be wanting.' 373 paintings, water-colours and drawings were temporarily loaned for the opening. But a year later the Gallery had acquired 75 paintings in a permanent collection.
56. They came 9 July 1908 for the opening of the Royal Edward Dock, Avonmouth.
57. The complete list of activities and programme of the visit, with much other material relating to the visit, is preserved in the Bristol Central Reference Library.

CHAPTER 4: BRISTOL'S LEADING CITIZENS – A GOVERNING ELITE?

1. S. F. Nadel, 'The concept of social elites', *ISSB*, VIII (3), 1956, p. 417.
2. G. Kitson Clark, *An Expanding Society: Britain 1830–1900*, 1967, p. 134.
3. E. E. Butcher, *Bristol Corporation of the Poor 1696–1898*, 1972, p. 22.
4. In his first year of office, he raised a 'handsome' sum for the relief of sufferers from the Pontypridd Colliery disaster. He was re-elected Mayor in 1894, 1896 and 1897. He raised £5,000 to relieve unemployed in 1896 and £6,000 towards the Indian Famine Relief Fund in 1897. He paid for the civic celebrations for the Queen's Diamond Jubilee and was knighted in 1898.
5. See for example, the *Report of the Bishop's Committee into the condition of the poor* (Bristol, 1884).
6. See C. L. Mowat, *The Charity Organisation Society 1869–1913. Its Ideas and Works*, 1961.

7. The breakdown of the figures was as follows:

The Poor Law in and out-door relief	£55,500
Endowed Charities	50,000
Subscription Charities	38,000
Colston Charities	3,000
Almsgiving	50,000
	£196,500

Bishop's Committee Report, pp. 179–80.
8. A. Briggs, *Victorian Cities*, 1963, chapter V, p. 185.
9. See discussion of the LDOS in B. Harrison, 'Religion and recreation in nineteenth century England', *P&P*, no. 38, December 1967, pp. 98–125.
10. See J. H. S. Kent, 'The role of religion in the cultural structure of the later Victorian city', *TRHS*, 1973, pp. 153–73.
11. G. F. Stone, *Bristol as it was and as it is: A record of fifty years progress* (reprinted with additions, from articles in the *Bristol Evening News*, 1908–9), 1909, p. 139.
12. There was a pronounced evangelical tradition amongst Bristol's Anglicans. See D. J. Carter, 'The Social and Political Influences of the Bristol Churches 1830–1914' (unpub. M. of Letters, University of Bristol, 1971), p. 51.
13. Kent, *op. cit.*, 154.
14. Figures given by D. J. Carter, *op. cit.*, p. 94.
15. Miall's figures are quoted in O. Chadwick, *The Victorian Church*, part II, 1970, p. 226.
16. *Ibid.*, p. 219.
17. There were seven new parishes added to the city's total which J. H. S. Kent describes as 'part of the nineteenth century drive to extend the small-parish system which was the bane of Anglican planning', *op. cit.*, p. 156.
18. Fund-raising to build a new nave and two west towers was begun in 1866. In 1877 the nave was finished, in 1888, the two west towers, total cost £80,000.
19. For information of Bristol's religious life, see G. F. Stone, *op. cit.*; J. F. Nicholls and J. Taylor, *Bristol Past and Present*, vol. II, 1881, which includes in an appendix, pp. 305–8, a reprint of the religious census of 1881 taken by the *WDP*; and the unpub. thesis of D. J. Carter, *op. cit.*
20. There are several biographies of outstanding Bristol churchmen. See particularly H. C. A. Colville, *Thomas William Harvey, Prophet and Priest*, 1918, and H. A. Thomas, *Memorials of David Thomas*

(Minister at Highbury Chapel, Bristol), (London, 1876), and D. M. Thomas, *Urijah Rees Thomas: his life and work*, 1902.
21. See D. Timms, *The Urban Mosaic: Towards a theory of Residential Differentiation*, 1971.
22. J. H. S. Kent makes the point that 'In the late Victorian period institutionalized religion ... came so frequently into conflict with other institutions which affected the other elements in the urban culture ... that ... it becomes necessary to ignore denominational differences to some extent and think instead in terms of a religious sub-culture which was slowly separating itself, institutionally, from the dominant, largely secular culture', *op. cit.*, p. 158.
23. E. P. Hennock, 'The social compositions of borough councils in two large cities 1835–1914', in H. J. Dyos (ed.), *The Study of Urban History*, 1968, esp. pp. 332–4. See also E. P. Hennock, *Fit and Proper Persons*, 1973, esp. part II, chapter 5.
24. See E. P. Thompson, 'Homage to Tom Maguire', in A. Briggs and J. Saville (eds), *Essays in Labour History*, revised edn 1967, pp. 276–316. In Bristol there was a close relationship between Liberal Councillors, e.g. Lewis Fry, Mark Whitwell and, above all, F. Gilmore Barnett, brother of Canon S. A. Barnett, all advocates of 'social citizenship' and organized Labour movements. Barnett devoted his time in the 1880s to trade union and political organization, and was supported by the city's most radical group, the Bristol Radical Reform Association.
25. Quoted from N. A. Ferguson, 'Working-Class Housing in Bristol and Nottingham, 1868–1919' (unpub. Ph.D., Oregon, 1971, university microfilm 72-923), p. 177.
26. Figures from Rev. A. B. Beaven, *Bristol Lists: Municipal and Miscellaneous*, 1899, p. 59.
27. *Contemporary Biographies; 1898*, vols. I and II, 1898–9, provides some biographical material on most leading citizens at that date.
28. One major thesis has so far been completed on the town council in the nineteenth century. A study of the impact of the 1835 Reform Act, G. W. A. Bush, 'The old and the new: the Corporation of Bristol 1820–51' (unpub. Ph.D. thesis, University of Bristol, 1965), in which the main conclusion is that even the 1835 Act had remarkably little effect on the personnel of the town council.
29. Professor Briggs has emphasized that leadership was a key factor in local councils. 'Deficiencies of leadership,' he writes, 'were more serious than biases of social composition.' A. Briggs, *Victorian Cities*, 1963, p. 238.

NOTES TO PAGES 90–101

30. Calculated from lists of names of councillors. *Local Government Records* (Bristol City Archives).
31. There are no major biographies of members of either family. Information about the Frys can be found in the Quaker Papers, Bristol City Archive Office. Biographical outlines of the Wills family history are given in B. W. E. Alford, *W. D. & H. O. Wills and the Development of the U.K. Tobacco Industry, 1786–1965*, 1973.
32. W. L. Guttsman, 'The changing social structure of the British political élite 1886–1935', *ISSB*, 8 (3), 1956, p. 129.
33. *WDP*, 13 February 1905.
34. B. W. E. Alford, *op. cit.*, p. 279.
35. *Ibid.*, p. 279.
36. M. F. Pease, *Notes on the Fry family of Sutton Benger and Bristol 1627–1921* (July 1951), Quaker Papers, Bristol City Archives.

CHAPTER 5: MUNICIPAL FACILITIES FOR LEISURE AND PLEASURE

1. Comparative material for this purpose from: Manchester (Salford), Liverpool, Birmingham, Leeds, Plymouth, Sheffield, Rochdale, Nottingham, Portsmouth, Newcastle, Stoke-on-Trent, Bradford, Huddersfield, Birkenhead, Southampton, Norwich, Cheltenham, Exeter, Cardiff and Aberdeen.
2. See A. Briggs, *History of Birmingham*, vol. II, 1952, chapter 4.
3. Canon and Mrs S. A. Barnett, *Towards Social Reform*, 1909, p. 31.
4. See T. H. Mawson, *The Life and Work of an English Landscape Architect: An Autobiography* (London, The Richards Press, 1928). Mawson was a landscape gardener whose career was boosted when he got the job of designing a public park for the people of Hanley. He subsequently made himself a landscape architect with a special interest in town planning and published a manual on the subject, *Civic Art*, in 1910.
5. See the introduction by P. Green to a reprint edition of this work (Shannon, Irish University Press, 1973).
6. See W. A. Munford, *Penny Rate: aspects of British Public Library History 1850–1950*, 1951.
7. For a biography of Ewart see W. A. Munford, *William Ewart M.P. 1798–1869. Portrait of a radical* (London, Grafton, 1960).
8. For a biography of Edwards see W. A. Munford, *Edward Edwards 1812–1886: portrait of a Librarian*, 1963.

9. T. Greenwood, *Public Libraries, their organisation, uses and management*, 1890, 3rd edn, p. 24.
10. Canon and Mrs S. A. Barnett, *op. cit.*, pp. 237–8.
11. Not only reading books, but actually using public libraries was an exercise in social behaviour. No talking was allowed and a high level of discipline and respect was expected from borrowers. There was no direct access to bookshelves.
12. As he wrote himself, 'the citizens could not be aroused from their indifference to the advantages resulting from Public Libraries and my book remained unsold.' C. Tovey, *Bristol City Library: its founders and benefactors; its present position in connection with the Library Society, etc.*, 1853.
13. Local information is taken from the Library Committee Reports, *Local Government Records*.
14. Speech reported in the press. *WDP*, 9 June 1885.
15. Reported in *Bristol Evening News*, January 1887.
16. Thomas Greenwood, *op. cit.*, p. 211.
17. *Ibid.* (1889), p. 212.
18. *Ibid.*, p. 224.
19. W. J. Harte, *Gleanings from the manuscript of Richard Izacke's Antiquities of the City of Exeter* (City Library, Exeter).
20. Quoted from J. D. Chambers, 'Nottingham in the early nineteenth century', *Trans. of the Thoroton Society*, vol. 45, 1941. Nottingham had at that time a population of 10,000, about 2,000 houses and an area of 2,610 acres.
21. See G. F. Chadwick, *The Park and the Town*, 1966.
22. See L. Mumford, *The City in History*, 1966, chapter 16, esp. plates 4 and 44 and commentaries.
23. G. E. Cherry, *Urban Change and Planning*, 1972, p. 49.
24. E. H. Roberts, 'A study of the growth of the provision of public facilities for leisure time occupation, by local authorities of the Merseyside' (unpub. MA thesis, University of Liverpool, 1933), p. 64.
25. In *WDP*, 6 November 1872.
26. Information from W. Nelmes, 'A brief history of the Cardiff parks', *The Cardiff Naturalists' Society Reports and Transactions*, vol. 87, 1957–8, pp. 5–12.
27. See W. Creese, *The Search for Environment. The Garden City: before and after*, 1966.
28. *City of Birmingham Handbook*, 1938, p. 87.
29. To mark the opening of this hall as an art gallery, an Inaugural Exhibition of Art Treasures was held in 1904 opened by the Prince and Princess of Wales. See J. Bentley, *Illustrated Handbook of the*

Bradford City Parks, Recreation Grounds and Open Spaces (Bradford, 1926), p. 25.
30. It was named, inevitably, Victoria Park.
31. See article by A. Briggs, 'Cholera and society in the nineteenth century', *P&P*, no. 19, 1961, p. 76.
32. Details from Reports of the Baths and Washhouses Committee, *Local Government Records*.
33. It had become a matter of philanthropic concern. The Bristol Humane Society had begun to encourage swimming amongst elementary school children, holding annual competitions at the private swimming baths in Kingsdown. In 1883, out of the 10,305 boys in public elementary schools in the city, only 384 could swim. Within the year, the Society had encouraged a further 414 to pass the test distance. *Bishop's Committee Report*, 1884, p. 136.
34. For example see match between Bristol Leander swimming club and the club at Kingsdown Baths reported in the *WDP*, 16 June 1880.
35. The plans included a swimming bath not less than eighty feet in length, six first-class and eighteen second-class private baths for men, four private baths for women. There were no laundry facilities.
36. See T. H. Mawson, *op. cit.*, preface, p. xiv.
37. For a detailed analysis of what Geddes meant by 'conservative surgery' see J. Tyrwhitt (ed.), *Patrick Geddes in India* (London, Lund Humphries, 1947), pp. 40–59.
38. The attendance at Calderstones Park on Whit Monday 1911 was 15,288, and in the summer of 1912, 73 school treats were held there. E. H. Roberts, *op. cit.*, p. 74.
39. J. S. Nettlefold, *Practical Housing*, 1908, p. 46.
40. *Sociological Papers* (1905), p. 133.

CHAPTER 6: THE 'CIVILIZING MISSION' TO THE POOR

1. B. Harrison, *Drink and the Victorians*, 1971, esp. chapters 8 and 9.
2. Records of 'British Workman' are to be found in the Quaker Papers, Bristol City Archives.
3. C. B. P. Bosenquet, *London: some account of its growth, charitable agencies and wants*, 1868, p. 82.
4. T. Ostler, 'The antecedents and history of the Bristol Young Men's Christian Association', *Bristol and District Y.M.C.A. Record* (July 1898).

5. Records of the Quaker Missions are in the Quaker Papers, Bristol City Archives.
6. C. R. Parsons, *Records of Mission Work in Bristol 1878-83*, 1883, p. 25.
7. Annual Report 1865, Quaker New Street Mission, Quaker Papers.
8. For an account of the Penny reading movement see H. P. Smith, 'Literature and the people – a forgotten movement', in *Literature and Adult Education a Century Ago: Pantopragmatics and Penny Readings*, 1960.
9. *Ibid.*, p. 35.
10. *WDP*, 18 November 1870.
11. *WDP*, 6 January 1870.
12. Reported in press, *WDP*, 12 May 1869.
13. See D. J. Carter, 'The Social and Political Influence of the Bristol Churches 1830-1914' (unpub. M. of Letters thesis, University of Bristol, 1971), p. 164.
14. See D. Large and R. Whitfield, *The Bristol Trades Council*, 1973.
15. See John Taylor, *From Self-Help to Glamour: the working man's club 1860-1972* (History Workshop Pamphlet no. 7, 1972), p. 19.
16. Reported *WDP*, 1 December 1880.
17. The account of Riley's activities is taken from Samson Bryher (pseudonym for Samuel Bale), *An Account of the Labour and Socialist Movement in Bristol*, 1931, p. 25.
18. In a letter from Percival to the local press, *WDP*, 11 October 1869.
19. Quoted from H. C. A. Colville's biography, *Thomas William Harvey: Prophet and Priest*, 1918.
20. *Ibid.*, p. 32.
21. See particularly Canon and Mrs S. A. Barnett, *Towards Social Reform*, 1909, esp. last three sections of part III, pp. 239-88.
22. Not before he had compiled a *Book of Bristol Sonnets* (London, Hamilton Adams, 1877), which contained a poem, 'Bristol University College', outlining the new vision of the relationship between academics and workers when 'The men that bear the hod may wear the gown'. Reference from H. P. Smith, *op. cit.*, p. 39.
23. The translation from one to the other was very rapid. See evidence of Rev. Fuller, Vicar of St Barnabas, in *Royal Commission on the Housing of the Working Classes 1884-5*. Minutes of evidence, BPP [c. 4402], vol. XXX, p. 315.
24. See H. Warin Schupf, 'Single women and social reform in mid-nineteenth century England: The case of Mary Carpenter', *VS*, vol. XVII, no. 3, March 1974, pp. 301-18.

25. M. Shaen (ed.), *Memorials of Two Sisters: Susanna and Catherine Winkworth*, 1908.
26. Lecture to Redland Park Congregational Chapel, Bristol, by Rev. J. M. Wilson, Head of Clifton College (Bristol, 1886).
27. As a curate at St Luke's, Brighton, he had run a Men's Mutual Improvement Society.
28. D. J. Carter, *op. cit.*, p. 173.
29. See chapters XXIV–XXVIII of H. Barnett, *Canon Barnett, his Life, Work and Friends*, 1918.
30. See B. Webb, *My Apprenticeship*, 1971, p. 192.
31. H. C. A. Colville, *op. cit.*, p. 47. All details of the Mission buildings are taken from Colville.
32. See R. Nutter, 'A study of the implementation of the 1870 Education Act in Bristol, with special reference to the Newfoundland Road area' (unpub. Dip. Ed. thesis, University of Bristol, 1965).
33. H. C. A. Colville, *op. cit.*, pp. 52–3.
34. H. P. Smith, *op. cit.* (Documentary 9), p. 43.
35. D. Large and R. Whitfield, *op. cit.*, p. 6.
36. B. Atkinson, 'The Bristol Labour Movement 1886–1906' (unpub. Ph.D. thesis, University of Oxford, 1969).
37. In a sermon preached at St Agnes in May 1900. Colville, *op. cit.*, p. 24.
38. This was a repetition of the situation at Toynbee Hall where 'Barnett was anxious to keep the Settlement Movement primarily for men, fearing that men, still shy in their new role, would retire if it were captured by women'. Quoted from H. Barnett, *op. cit.*, by W. McG. Eager, *Making Men*, 1953, p. 193.
39. Quoted by H. P. Smith, *op. cit.*, p. 39.
40. *Ibid.*, p. 43.

CHAPTER 7: SOCIO-RELIGIOUS PROVISIONS FOR LEISURE 1890–1914

1. See for example, M. B. Reckitt (ed.), *For Christ and the People: Studies of Four Socialist Priests and Prophets of the Church of England between 1870 and 1930*, 1968.
2. K. Leech, 'Stuart Headlam, 1847–1924 and the Guild of St Matthew', in M. Reckitt (ed.), *op. cit.*, pp. 61–89.
3. *Report of the Bishop's Committee to Enquire into the Condition of the Poor*, 1884, p. 137.

4. General Booth, *In Darkest England and the Way Out*, 1890, pp. 35–6.
5. M. B. Reckitt, 'Charles Marson 1859–1914 and the real disorders of the Church', in M. B. Reckitt (ed.), *op. cit.*, p. 106.
6. See Reports of the New St Mission, Quaker Papers, in the 1880s.
7. C. R. Parsons recording his many years of work for temperance as a city missionary can be no more precise than the statement 'While we gathered many a trophy from the ranks of the men, the reclaimed women are few and far between', *Records of Mission Work in Bristol 1878–83*, 1883, p. 52.
8. B. Harrison, *Drink and the Victorians*, 1971, p. 321.
9. Reported in the press, *WDP*, 28 January 1895.
10. B. Harrison, *op. cit.*, esp. pp. 193–5.
11. *WDP*, 4 August 1880.
12. Walter Reid, the editor, had worked on numerous temperance publications prior to his appointment as editor of the *WDP*.
13. *WDP*, 13 October 1890.
14. In 1889–90 and 1890–1, Mr Dove Willcox was President of the Bristol Incorporated Chamber of Commerce and Shipping. He was a partner in the firm of Dove & Willcox, leather factors and importers and he had founded the Bristol Board of Conciliation and Arbitration. He was also a JP and the son of a Lancashire clergyman.
15. Annual Report 1885, New St Mission.
16. The basic moral justification of the Temperance movement was seeping away when it became clearer, from the social investigations of Charles Booth, etc. that drink was not the major cause of poverty. B. Harrison, *op. cit.*, pp. 401–5.
17. *J. W. Arrowsmith's Dictionary of Bristol* (Bristol, 1905 edn), p. 361.
18. See discussion of this point, W. McG. Eager, *Making Men: The history of boys clubs and related movements in Great Britain*, 1953, pp. 326–36.
19. *WDP*, 26 July 1881.
20. By 1890 a leader in the *WDP* (30 April 1890), entitled the 'Exhibition Era', was highly critical about whether any value at all can come 'from the maze called an Exhibition; with its claim to impart useful information in the most agreeable doses'.
21. *WDP*, 29 March 1900.
22. For a discussion of the outlook and activities of the GFS see Brian Harrison, 'For Church, Queen and Family: The Girls' Friendly Society 1874–1920', *P&P*, 61, 1973, pp. 107–38.
23. Taken from the Handbook of the Bristol Recreation Council (formed

1920) presenting a pre-war survey of juvenile recreational organizations.
24. See W. McG. Eagar, *op. cit.*, pp. 330–92.
25. *WDP*, 1 February 1869.
26. J. Latimer, *Annals of Bristol in the Nineteenth Century*, 1887, pp. 303–6.
27. For biographical details of Cossham, an Alliance candidate, see *Temperance Star*, 28 August 1868. Ref. from B. Harrison, *op. cit.*, p. 444.
28. For a discussion of the impact of the Great Exhibition in the provinces see R. J. Morris, 'Leeds and the Crystal Palace: A provincial-metropolitan link bringing education to industrial society', *VS*, vol. XIII, no. 3, March 1970, pp. 283–300.
29. C. R. Parsons, *op. cit.*, p. 59.
30. *Ibid.*, p. 58.
31. *WDP*, 26 July 1881. The Mayor and others contributed works of art, paintings and ornaments to 'fill out' and add to the workmen's exhibits. There were 2,000 exhibits in all and the Committee had insured them for the sum of £25,000.
32. See article 'A Polytechnic Exhibition in Bristol?', *WDP*, 15 October 1880.
33. A small one devoted to showing what was happening in the world of industry, science and art had been held in Clifton in 1840.
34. In the US these occasions gained cultural dimensions as they were used as meeting-places for groups concerned with academic and other kinds of cultural activities. See for example, A. W. Coats, 'American scholarship comes of age: the Louisiana Purchase Exposition 1904', *Journal of the History of the Ideas*, vol. XXII, no. 3, 1961, pp 404–17.
35. Patrick Geddes, *Industrial Exhibitions and Modern Progress* (pamphlet, Edinburgh, 1887).
36. *WDP*, 27 July 1881.
37. See prospectus of the Bristol Evening Class and Recreation Society (Bristol 1884). Prominent amongst those involved in organizing this society were the two Quaker families, the Frys and the Sturges.
38. Information from the Reports of the Evening School Committee, Bristol City Archives.
39. In the Principal's Report, SMV Technical College 1899–1900, a comparison was given between the numbers of students in 1890 and 1900.

    Students in evening classes   1889–90 = 818
                                                    1899–1900 = 1,281

> Students in day courses   1889–90 =   72
> 1899–1900 = 284

40. Annual Report of the Evening Class and Recreation Society, 1893–4.
41. For example, during the winter session 1897–8, Mr G. D. Grey gave the lecture course. Mr Grey was a solicitor, educated at Bristol Grammar School and London University; a churchman, Conservative; cultural interests, member of Somersetshire Archaeological Society.
42. *History of the Friends' First Day (Boys) School: Bristol Centenary volume 1810–1910.*
43. *Ibid.*, p. 13.
44. *WDP*, 7 July 1880.
45. H. P. Smith, *Literature and Adult Education a Century Ago: Pantopragmatics and penny readings*, 1960, p. 38.
46. *Ibid.*, p. 42.
47. See *J. W. Arrowsmith's Dictionary of Bristol*, op. cit.
48. S. A. and H. O. Barnett, *Towards Social Reform*, 1909.
49. He also ran a Working People's Meeting on Saturdays on the old Temperance entertainment lines. C. R. Parsons, op. cit., pp. 49–50.
50. For an account of the Mission, see G. F. Stone, *Bristol as it was and as it is* (reprinted articles from the *Bristol Evening News*, 1908–9), 1909, p. 231.
51. D. J. Carter, 'The Social and Political Influence of the Bristol Churches 1830–1914', 1971, p. 191.
52. W. Besant, *All Sorts and Conditions of Men*, 1898, p. 330, quoted by P. J. Keating, *The Working Classes in Victorian Fiction*, 1971, p. 95.
53. P. J. Keating, op. cit., p. 96.
54. F. J. Marquis and S. E. F. Ogden, 'The recreation of the poorest', *The Town Planning Review*, vol. III, no. 1, 1912, pp. 244–57.
55. S. A. Barnett, 'The Ideal City', c. 1893, p. 25.

CHAPTER 8: URBANIZATION AND LEISURE – THE SECULAR CULTURE OF CITY AND SUBURB

1. Different districts were physically cut off from one another by toll bridges. See *WDP*, 5 July 1870.
2. J. Strutt, *The Sports and Pastimes of the People of England*, 1801.
3. R. W. Malcolmson, *Popular Recreations in English Society, 1700–1850*, 1973.
4. *Ibid.*, p. 159.

5. *Ibid.*, p. 66.
6. K. Barker, *Entertainment in the Nineties*, 1973, p. 16.
7. Patterns of traditional behaviour were reported in the *WDP*, 3 May 1870, when a procession and effigy-burning was staged to mark the guilt of a farmer at Chipping Sodbury who cheated over corn.
8. *WDP*, 3 January 1869.
9. *WDP*, 6 December 1869.
10. *WDP*, 3 March 1870.
11. The best insights into the excitement of the streets are often found in fictional sources. See P. J. Keating, *The Working Classes in Victorian Fiction*, 1971, p. 211.
12. B. Harrison, *Drink and the Victorians*, 1971, chapters 2 and 14.
13. *WDP*, 6 May 1869.
14. K. Barker, *op. cit.*, p. 16.
15. The Rifle Drill Hall when sold in 1899 was bought by Sir W. H. Wills for an art gallery. See above chapter 3, p. 68.
16. *WDP*, 7 January 1880.
17. A. Briggs, 'Mass entertainment: The origins of a modern industry', *29th Joseph Fisher Lecture in Commerce*, 1960.
18. *WDP*, 15 April 1870.
19. *WDP*, 18 April 1870.
20. *WDP*, 12 January 1869.
21. *WDP*, 18 April 1871.
22. *WDP*, 5 July 1869.
23. *WDP*, 15 September 1869.
24. *WDP*, 5 August 1890.
25. K. Barker, *op. cit.*, p. 1.
26. *WDP*, 3 January 1910.
27. *WDP*, 15 January 1901.
28. K. Barker, *op. cit.*, p. 20.
29. E. Jackson, *A Study in Democracy: an account of the rise and progress of industrial cooperation in Bristol*, 1911, pp. 477–85.
30. *Ibid.*, p. 447.
31. H. P. Smith, *Literature and Adult Education a Century Ago: Pantopragmatics and penny readings*, 1960, pp. 37–8.
32. S. Bryher (pseud.), *An Account of the Labour and Socialist Movement in Bristol*, 1931, p. 30.
33. There was opposition in some quarters to the appointment of S. A. Barnett to a canonry at Bristol Cathedral because he opened the Whitechapel Art Gallery on Sundays.
34. H. J. Price, 'Adult Education in Bristol during the Nineteenth Century', 1965, pp. 140–4.

35. Programmes published in the *WDP*, 2 January, 30 January, 6 February 1900.
36. E. Jackson, *op cit.*, p. 488.
37. *Bristol Argus*, December 1886.
38. See N. Temperley, 'Mid-Victorian Music', 2nd Conference Report, the *Victorian Society*, 1965, p. 8.
39. E. D. Mackerness, *A Social History of English Music*, 1964, p. 112.
40. Temperley, *op. cit.*, p. 9.
41. W. S. Jevons, *Methods of Social Reform*, 1904, p. 8.
42. Mackerness, *op. cit.*, p. 165.
43. *WDP*, 24 February 1905.
44. Escott, *Social Transformations of the Victorian Age: a survey of court and country*, 1897, pp. 340–1.
45. Mackerness, *op. cit.*, pp. 153–65.
46. R. Till, *A History of Wills*, private publication, p. 40.
47. *WDP*, 23 July 1890.
48. Mackerness, *op. cit.*, pp. 165–9.
49. *J. W. Arrowsmith's Dictionary of Bristol* (Bristol, 1905 edn), p. 279.
50. Patron of this choir was Mr John Hobhouse MP. The Mayor and Sheriff were the patrons of the North Bristol choir.
51. E. Jackson, *op. cit.*, p. 479.
52. N. Elias, 'The genesis of sport as a sociological problem', in E. Dunning (ed.), *The Sociology of Sport*, 1971, pp. 88–115.
53. See J. R. Betts, 'The technological revolution and the rise of sport 1850–1900', in R. A. Smith (ed.), *History of Physical Recreation and Sport*, 1972, pp. 154–76.
54. *Bristol Argus*, November 1886.
55. *Bristol Bicycle and Tricycle Gazette* (special edn to mark 21st anniversary of the club), 1887, p. 4.
56. *WDP*, 29 March, 16 April, 14 June 1869.
57. J. R. Betts, *op. cit.*, p. 167, quotes example of the American Frederick W. Taylor, the 'father of scientific management' who was also a golf and tennis champion, and of whom it is said that he learned, through sport, the importance of methodical selection and training, the worth of time study and of standards based on rigorously exact observation.
58. *WDP*, 8 May 1900.
59. Escott, *op. cit.*, p. 195.
60. B. Harrison, 'Religion and recreation in nineteenth century England', *P&P*, no. 38, December 1967, p. 122.
61. Escott, *op. cit.*, p. 195.
62. *WDP*, 16 April 1869.

63. Though by 1900 their popularity was waning. A press report *WDP*, 9 July 1900 on the Bristol Police Constabulary Athletic Club Sports stated: 'the drawing powers of cycling and athletic festivals are not a patch on what they used to be.'
64. Quoted from H. S. Altham, *A History of Cricket*, 1962, vol. 1, p. 123.
65. *Bristol Argus*, March 1887.
66. A ladies' archery club is described in George Eliot's novel *Daniel Deronda* (1876), chapter 10.
67. *WDP*, 3 June 1890.
68. See for example the work of Thomas Wentworth Higginson, American pioneer of health and fitness, described by J. A. Lucas: 'T. W. Higginson – early apostle of health and fitness' in R. A. Smith (ed.), *op. cit.*, pp. 87–96.
69. *Bristol Argus*, March 1887.
70. *Bristol Argus*, December 1886.
71. *WDP*, 11 January 1901.
72. M. Marples, *A History of Football*, 1954, p. 127.
73. Information from Mr W. Pinnell, ex-sports editor of the *WDP*.
74. E. Dunning, 'The development of modern football', in E. Dunning (ed.), *op. cit.*, pp. 147–8.
75. H. H. Gerth and C. Wright Mills, *Character and Social Structure* (London, 1954), p. 63, quoted by E. Dunning, 'Some conceptual dilemmas in the sociology of sport', in R. Alboniro and K. Pfister-Bing (eds), *Sociologie des Sports*, 1971, pp. 34–47.
76. Escott, *op. cit.*, p. 416.
77. Examples were W. D. and H. O. Wills, which offered various benefit and welfare schemes to its workers. In 1893 the Wills Association Football Club was founded and facilities provided for cricket and tennis. At E. S. & A. Robinson, management was less paternalistic, workers organized their own cricket and football from the mid-1880s. The firm then provided better facilities for a cricket club in 1893 and a football club in 1905.
78. For conflicts between sportsmen on the Downs see report 'A Rotten Row in Bristol', *Bristol Argus*, March 1887.
79. *WDP*, 14 June 1890.

CHAPTER 9: SOCIAL DEVELOPMENT AND THE CITY

1. See H. L. Beales, 'The making of social policy', *L. T. Hobhouse Memorial Lectures*, 1941–50, 1952, no. 15.

2. Particularly of course, the studies of Charles Booth in the East End of London, and B. S. Rowntree's study of York.
3. See E. H. Phelps-Brown, *The Growth of British Industrial Relations*, 1965 edn.
4. Bentley Gilbert, *The Evolution of National Insurance in Great Britain: the origins of the welfare state*, 1966.
5. A. M. Schlesinger, *The Rise of the City 1878–1898*, 1933, p. 287.
6. See N. Elias and E. Dunning, 'Leisure in the sparetime spectrum', in Rolf Albonico and Katharina Pfister-Bing (eds), *Sociologie des Sports*, 1971, pp. 27–34.
7. See H. Jennings, *Societies in the Making: a study of development and redevelopment within a county borough*, 1962.
8. I am indebted to Professor William Ashworth for this observation.
9. Examples are gardening clubs, e.g. *WDP*, 15 August 1890; bicycling as a popular pastime, e.g. *WDP*, 2 May 1896; bird-fancying, e.g. *WDP*, 22 January 1900. In a report on the monthly meeting of the Bristol Amateur Horticultural Society, *WDP*, 5 January 1900, the idea is stated that now there is 'need for everyone to choose a hobby'.
10. C. F. G. Masterman wrote in 1909: 'Is this to be the type of all civilizations, when the whole Western World is to become comfortable and tranquil, and progress finds its grave in a universal suburb?', *The Condition of England*, 1909, p. 74.
11. See for instance N. Jacobs (ed.), *Culture for the Millions? Mass Media in Modern Society*, 1964.
12. Edward Shils, 'Mass society and its culture', in N. Jacobs (ed.), *op. cit.*, p. 1. This cultural definition can be supplemented by a political dimension suggested by C. Wright Mills. In his view mass society is 'a society in which a mass of unrelated individuals lose any effective means of criticism or influence and become easily manipulable by their rulers.' T. Bottomore, *Critics of Society: Radical Thought in North America*, 1967, p. 57.
13. Louis Wirth, 'The urban society and civilisation', *AJS*, XLV, March 1940, pp. 743–55.
14. *Bristol Argus*, November 1886, pp. 12–14.
15. G. Duby, 'The diffusion of cultural patterns in feudal society', *P&P*, 39, 1968, p. 3.
16. O. Handlin, in N. Jacobs (ed.), *op. cit.*, p. 70.
17. E. Shils, in N. Jacobs (ed.), *op. cit.*, p. 3.
18. A. Briggs, 'Mass entertainment: The origins of a modern industry', *29th Joseph Fisher Lecture in Commerce*, 1960, p. 11.
19. J. Lawson and H. Silver, *The Social History of Education in England* (London, Methuen, 1973), pp. 355–7.

20. *WDP*, 23 June 1893.
21. J. F. C. Harrison, *Learning and Living 1790–1960: A Study in the History of the English Adult Education Movement*, 1961, pp. 38–9.
22. W. S. Jevons, 'Amusements of the people', in *Methods of Social Reform*, 1904, p. 6.
23. P. Kelvin, *The Bases of Social Behaviour: an approach in terms of order and value*, 1970.
24. *Ibid.*, pp. 292–3.
25. *Self-Help* sold 20,000 copies in the first year; 55,000 by 1864; 150,000 by 1889, and about a quarter of a million by the time of Smiles's death in 1904. 'Afterword', by Royden Harrison to Sphere Books edn of S. Smiles, *Self-Help*, 1968, p. 269.
26. Brian Harrison, *Drink and the Victorians*, pp. 354–63.
27. For a detailed discussion on S. Smiles's *Self-Help* and its social impact, see K. Fielden, 'Samuel Smiles and Self-Help', *VS*, XII, no. 2 (1968), pp. 155–76.
28. Support is given to this view in an article by R. Q. Gray, 'Styles of life, the "labour aristocracy" and class relations in later nineteenth-century Edinburgh', *IRSH*, vol. XVIII, 1973, pp. 451–2.
29. Labour leaders in Bristol, educated in socio-religious educational institutions, included William Straker, Ernest Bevin.
30. R. E. Park of the Chicago School, was prepared to suggest that the most important dimension of leisure pursuits was the quest for excitement. 'Our leisure is now mainly a restless search for excitement. It is the romantic impulse, the desire to escape the dull routine of life at home and in the local community, that drives us abroad in search of adventure. Political revolution and social reform are themselves often merely expressions of this same romantic impulse.' Park, Burgess and McKenzie, *The City*, 1925, p. 117.
31. E. P. Thompson, 'Time, work-discipline and industrial capitalism', *P&P*, 38, 1967, p. 95.

SELECT BIBLIOGRAPHY

I PRIMARY SOURCE MATERIAL

(a) *Newspapers and periodicals*

Amateur Sport, 1889.
Arrowsmith's Christmas Annual, 1881.
Art Life in the West of England, June–August 1863.
Bedminster Guardian, then *Bristol Guardian*, 1897–1914.
Bristol and Clifton Almanack, 1840–1.
Bristol and Clifton Amusements, 1900–1.
Bristol and Clifton Monthly Guide, 1886.
Bristol and Clifton Monthly Social Journal, 1909–10.
Bristol Argus, 1886–7.
Bristol Bicycle and Tricycle Club Monthly Gazette, 1897.
Bristol Christian Leader, 1891–6.
Bristol Comet, January–February 1894.
Bristol Diocesan Magazine, 1900–1.
Bristol Evening News, 1877–98.
Bristol Magpie, 1883–5.
Bristol Mercury, 1870–1909.
Bristol Nonesuch News (University of Bristol Magazine).
Bristol Observer, 1883–9.
Bristol Times and Mirror, 1865–72, January–June 1873, 1874–1914.
Bristol Y.M.C.A. Monthly Record, vol. 4, 1898–9.
Bristol Young Men: being the organ of the Bristol Central Y.M.C.A., vol. 17, 1911.
Clifton Chronicle, 1852–1916.
Cliftonian, 1867–8, 1873.
Clifton Parish Church Magazine, 1899–1900.
Christian Herald, 1882.
Western Daily Press, 1858–63, 1865–73, 1875–1914.

SELECT BIBLIOGRAPHY

(b) *Guide books and directories*

J. Wright & Co., *Mathews Bristol Directory*, 1870–1910.
J. Wright & Co., *Bristol and its Environs: historical, descriptive and scientific*, 1875.
J. Baker, *New Guide to Bristol and Clifton and the Bristol Channel Circuit*, 1898.
Arrowsmith's Dictionary of Bristol, 1905 edn.

(c) *Bristol Local Collection*

The Bristol Central Reference Library contains a wide range of material. Records of the following institutions, voluntary organizations and events have been most relevant to this study.

Academy for the Promotion of Fine Arts, 1844.
Architectural Society, 1846.
Association for the Promotion of Evening Classes, 1869.
Bristol Athenaeum, 1844.
Bristol Bicycle and Tricycle Club, 1876.
Bristol Chess Club, 1860.
Bristol Evening Class and Recreation Society, 1884–95.
Bristol Educational Council, 1888.
Bristol and Gloucestershire Archaeological Society, 1876.
Bristol Housing Reform Committee, 1890.
Bristol Recreation Council, 1920.
British Association for the Advancement of Science, Bristol Meetings: 1836, 1875, 1898.
Choral Society, 1890.
Christian Social Brotherhood, Bristol Branch.
Church Congress held in Bristol, 1864.
Clifton Antiquarian Club, 1871.
Clifton Association for the Higher Education of Women, 1868.
Clifton College Scientific Society, 1871.
Clifton Conservative Club.
Clifton Cricket Club, 1830.
Clifton Improvements Association, 1902.
Exhibitions:
    Catalogues of the annual exhibition at the Academy for the Promotion of Fine Arts.
    J. B. Atkinson, *Handbook to the Bristol Exhibition of Industrial and Ornamental Art held at the Fine Arts Academy, 1861.*

Catalogue, Bristol and West of England Kennel Club Open Dog Show, 1895.
Catalogue, Bristol Dog Show, Drill Hall, 1899.
Catalogues of the Exhibition of Sporting and other dogs held 1878–6.
Industry and Fine Art Exhibition, 1893.
Clifton Grand International Bazaar, St Mary's Church, Tyndall's Park, 1896.
Gloucestershire County Cricket Club.
Library Association Conference: Bristol Meeting 1900.
Literary and Philosophical Club, 1890.
Madrigal Society, 1836.
Mechanics Institute, 1825.
Museum and Library Society, 1871.
Music Festival Society, 1873.
National Association for the Promotion of Social Science: Bristol Meeting 1869.
National Home Reading Union: Clifton Branch, 1892.
Naturalists' Society, 1875.
Orpheus Glee Society.
Philosophical and Literary Society, 1820.
Royal Sanitary Institute, 23rd Congress, Bristol 1906.
Society for Antiquaries.
Society for Bristol Gleemen.
Society for Instrumentalists.
Statistical Society: Proceedings, 1837–41.

(d) *Local Government Records*

Reports of the Town Council's proceedings, 1860–1914.
Minutes and Reports of the Library Committee, 31 March 1868–28 June 1900. Reconstituted Committee 4 June 1901 to 8 February 1907.
Minutes and Reports of Downs Committee, Private Act for Preserving Downs 1862. Reports 15 January 1868–18 March 1887.
Minutes and Reports of the Parks and Open Spaces Committee, 16 October 1877 to 10 December 1909.
Minutes and Reports of the Baths and Washhouses Commitee, 1 January 1852 to 14 April 1897.
Minutes and Reports of the Museum and Art Gallery Committee, 1901–7.

SELECT BIBLIOGRAPHY

(e) *The Quaker Papers* (Bristol City Archives)

Men's Monthly Meeting, Bristol and Frenchay: Minutes and Reports from 1869.
Women's Two-weekly Meeting, Bristol Minute Book 1755–1909.
Records of the Workhouse and New Street Mission:
  (i) Rice Committee, 17 June 1849–5 October 1849.
  (ii) Navvies Committee, 1860–63.
  (iii) New Street Mission Committee. Annual Reports and Minutes, 1868–1928. Miscellaneous information on mission and its history.
  (iv) New Street Mission Sunday School.
Records of the Friends First Day Boys' School and Adult School.
Notes on the Fry family of Sutton Benger and Bristol, 1627–1921, ed. by Marion Pease, 1951.

(f) *Clifton College Library*

Records of the St Agnes Mission.

(g) *Society of Merchant Venturers*

Private collection of the Society's records and activities. Especially useful are the records of philanthropic and educational work.

(h) *Official sources*

Census Reports, 1871–1911.
Royal Commission on the Housing of the Working Classes 1884–5.
Royal Commission on Labour 1892.
Royal Commission on the Poor Laws 1905–9.
Report of an Enquiry by the Board of Trade into Working Class Rents, Housing and Retail Prices 1908, Cd. 3864.

(i) Source material on cultural facilities from libraries in the following towns: Aberdeen, Birkenhead, Birmingham, Bradford, Cardiff, Cheltenham, Exeter, Huddersfield, Leeds, Liverpool, Manchester (Salford), Newcastle, Norwich, Nottingham, Plymouth, Portsmouth, Rochdale, Sheffield, Southampton and Stoke on Trent.

SELECT BIBLIOGRAPHY

II UNPUBLISHED SOURCES

Atkinson, B., 'The Bristol Labour Movement 1868–1906' (unpub. Ph.D., University of Oxford, 1969).
Bush, G. W. A., 'The Old and the New: the Corporation of Bristol 1820 to 1851' (unpub. Ph.D., University of Bristol, 1965).
Carter, D. J., 'The Social and Political Influences of the Bristol Churches 1830–1914' (unpub. M. Letters, University of Bristol, 1971).
Ferguson, N. A., 'Working Class Housing in Bristol and Nottingham 1868–1919' (unpub. P.D., University of Oregon, 1971, university microfilm no. 72-923).
Hewitt, F., 'Population and Urban Growth in East Bristol 1800–1914' (unpub. Ph.D., University of Bristol, 1965).
Meller, H. E., 'The Organised Provisions for Cultural Activities and their impact on the community 1870–1910: with special reference to Bristol' (unpub. Ph.D., University of Bristol, 1968).
Premble, R., 'The National Association for the Promotion of Social Science 1857–86: some sociological aspects' (unpub. M.A., University of Nottingham, 1968).
Price, H. J., 'Adult Education in Bristol during the Nineteenth Century' (unpub. M.A., University of Bristol [Institute of Education] 1965).
Roberts, E.H., 'A Study of the Growth of the provision of public facilities for leisure-time occupations, by local authorities of the Merseyside' (unpub. M.A., University of Liverpool, 1933).

III PAMPHLETS AND ARTICLES

Anon., 'Free thoughts on the Offices of Mayor, Aldermen and Common Council of the City of Bristol, with a constitutional proposition for their annihilation' (Pamphlet, Bristol, 1792).
Anon., 'Words in season to the municipal burgesses of Bristol' (Pamphlet, Bristol, 1860).
Anon., 'A Few Plain Words about Bristol: by one who has scribbled at a desk' (Pamphlet, Bristol, 1860).
Anon., 'Cry of the Poor: being a letter from sixteen working men of Bristol to the sixteen Aldermen of the city, concerning the impure air of the city, a People's Park, Free Bathing Places, Newsrooms and a Free Lending Library, No toll bridges, a Fish market, etc.' (Pamphlet, Bristol, 1871).
Barnett, S. A., articles in the *Nineteenth Century*: 'Practicable Socialism', April 1883; 'Town Councils and Social Reform', November 1883;

'University Settlements', February 1884; 'Great cities and social reforms', October 1884.
Barnett, S. A., 'The Ideal City' (Pamphlet, Bristol, n.d.).
Beales, H. L., 'The Making of Social Policy', *Hobhouse Memorial Lectures* (London, Oxford University Press, 1952).
Lord Brabazon, 'Health and physique of our city population', *Nineteenth Century*, December 1882.
Briggs, A., 'Mass entertainment. The origins of a modern industry', *29th Joseph Fisher Lecture in Commerce*, University of Adelaide, 1960.
Briggs, A., 'Historians and the Study of Cities', *George Judah Cohen Memorial Lecture*, University of Sydney, 1960.
Briggs, A., 'Cholera and Society in the Nineteenth Century', *P&P*, 19, 1961.
Conze, W., 'Social History', *JSH*, vol. I, 1967-8.
Cooke, A., 'Bristol Hovels', *Report of the Bristol Housing Reform Committee*, October 1907.
Couzen, M. R. C., 'The Plan Analysis of an English City Centre', *Land Studies in Geography*, Series B, no. 24, 1962.
Dingle, A. E., 'Drink and Working Class Living Standards in Britain 1870-1914', *EcHR* II, vol. XXV, 1972.
'Facts for Bristol: suggestions for reform on socialist principles', *Fabian Tract* no. 18, 1891.
Fisher, F. J., 'The Development of London as a centre of conspicuous consumption in the 16th and 17th centuries', *TRHS*, 1948.
Geddes, P., 'Civics as applied sociology', *Sociological Papers*, 1904.
Glass, R., 'Urban sociology in Great Britain: a trend report', *Current Sociology*, IV, 1955.
Gray, R. Q., 'Styles of life, the Labour Aristocracy and Class Relations in late nineteenth century Edinburgh', *IRSH*, 1973.
Gudge, H. G., 'W.E.A. 50 years in the life of a voluntary movement' (Pamphlet, Bristol, n.d.).
Harrison, B., 'Philanthropy and the Victorians', *VS*, 1966.
Harrison, B., 'Religion and Recreation in nineteenth century England', *P&P*, 38, 1967.
Harrison, B., 'The Church, Queen and Family: The Girls' Friendly Society 1874-1920', *P&P*, 61, 1973.
Harrison, B. and Trinder, B., 'Drink and Sobriety in an Early Victorian Town: Banbury 1830-60', *Eng. HR*, Supplement 4, 1969.
Huddleston, C. R., 'When and how Bristol got her parks', reproduced from *Bristol Evening Post*, 1937.

Jones, G. F., 'Powers of the Municipality', paper read to the Christian Social Brotherhood, Bristol Branch, 1903.

Kent, J. H. S., 'The Role of Religion in the Cultural Structure of the Late Victorian City', *TRHS*, 1973.

Kerslake, T., 'A remonstrance, chiefly of the proprietors of the Bristol Institution and the Members of the Philosophical and Literary Society in connection therewith, from a project for their annexation at some future time by the Bristol Library Society' (Pamphlet, Bristol, 1867).

Law, C. M., 'The growth of urban population in England and Wales 1801–1911', *TIBG*, vol. 41, 1967.

McGrath, P., 'Bristol since 1497', in C. M. MacInnes and W. F. Whittard (eds), *Bristol and its adjoining counties* (Bristol, British Association, 1955).

McGrath, P. (General editor), Pamphlets on Bristol published under the auspices of the Historical Association, Bristol branch. These include:

Barker, K., *The Theatre Royal: first seventy years* (no. 3, 1961).

Minchinton, W., *The Port of Bristol in the Eighteenth Century* (no. 5, 1962).

Farr, G., *The Steamship Great Western* (no. 8, 1963).

Saywell, R. J., *Mary Carpenter in Bristol* (no. 9, 1964).

Farr, G., *The Steamship Great Britain* (no. 11, 1965).

Barker, K., *The Theatre Royal 1834–1943* (no. 14, 1964).

Byard, H., *The Bristol Madrigal Society* (no. 15, 1965).

Buchanan, R. A., *Nineteenth Century Engineers in the Port Bristol* (no. 26, 1971).

Farr, G., *Bristol Shipbuilding in the nineteenth century* (no. 27, 1971).

Butcher, E. E., *Bristol Corporation of the Poor 1696–1898* (no. 29, 1972).

Large, D. and Whitfield R., *Bristol Trades Council 1873–1973* (no. 32, 1973).

Barker, K., *Entertainment in the 'Nineties* (no. 33, 1973).

Large, D. and Round, F., *Public Health in Mid Victorian Bristol* (no. 35, 1974).

McGregor, O. R., 'Social Position of Women in England 1850–1914: a bibliography', *BJS*, 6, 1955.

Mathews, E. R. Norris, 'Survey of Bristol's public libraries', paper presented to the Library Association Conference, Bristol, 1900.

Meacham, S., 'The Church in the Victorian City', *VS*, 1968.

Meller, H. E. (ed.), 'Nottingham in the 1880s: a study in social change' (University of Nottingham WEA pamphlet, Nottingham, 1971).

Minchinton, W. E., 'Bristol – metropolis of the west in the eighteenth century', *TRHS*, 1954.
'Report of the Bishop's Committee Inquiry into the Condition of the Poor' (Pamphlet, Bristol, 1884).
'Report of a Meeting held at Bristol to Promote the Establishment of a School of Science and Literature for the West of England' (Pamphlet, University of Bristol, 1874).
Taylor, L. Acland, 'Some of the Public Institutions of Bristol' (Pamphlet, Bristol, n.d.).
Temperley, N., 'Mid Victorian Music', Second Conference Report, *The Victorian Society*, 1965.
Thompson, D. M., 'The 1851 religious census: problems and possibilities', *VS*, September 1967.
Thompson, E. P., 'Time, Work-Discipline and Industrial Capitalism', *P&P*, 38, 1967.
Tuckett, R. C., 'Bristol Academy for the Promotion of Fine Arts: its foundation and history' (Pamphlet, repr. from *WDP*, 1899).
Wilson, J. M., 'The Progress of Christian Church life during the last 25 years', sermon at Redland Park Congregational Chapel (Bristol, 1886).
Wirth, L., 'Urbanism as a way of life', *AJS*, 44, 1938.
Wohl, 'The bitter cry of outcast London', *IRSH*, 13(2), 1968.
Wood, G. S., 'Real Wages and the Standard of Comfort since 1850', *JRSS*, 1909.

IV BOOKS

Albonico, R. and Pfister-Bing, K. (eds), *Sociologie des Sports*, Basle, Birhäuser Verlag, 1971.
Alford, B. W. E., *W. D. & H. O. Wills and the Development of the U.K. Tobacco Industry 1786–1965*, London, Methuen, 1973.
Altham, H. S., *A History of Cricket*, London, George Allen & Unwin, 1926.
Altick, R. D., *The English Common Reader: Social History of the Mass Reading Public*, Cambridge University Press, 1957.
Anderson, N., *Work and Leisure*, London, Routledge & Kegan Paul, 1961.
Armytage, W. H. G., *A Social History of Engineering*, London, Faber, 1961.
Arnold, M., *Schools and Universities on the Continent*, London, Macmillan, 1868.

SELECT BIBLIOGRAPHY

Arnold, M., *Culture and Anarchy* (1869) (Dover Wilson edn), Cambridge University Press, 1969.
Ashworth, W., *The Genesis of Modern British Town Planning*, London, Routledge & Kegan Paul, 1954.
Ashworth, W., *An Economic History of England: 1870-1939*, London, Methuen, 1960.
Bagwell, P. S., *The Transport Revolution from 1770*, London, Batsford, 1974.
Bamford, T. S., *The Rise of the Public Schools*, London, Nelson, 1967.
Banks, J. A., *Prosperity and Parenthood*, London, Routledge & Kegan Paul, 1954.
Barker, W. R., *History of the Bristol Museum and Art Gallery*, Bristol, 1906.
Barnett, S. A. and H. O., *Practical Socialism*, London, Longmans, 1888.
Barnett, S. A. and H. O., *Towards Social Reform*, London, T. Fisher Unwin, 1909.
Barnett, H. O., *Canon Barnett, his Life, Work and Friends*, London, John Murray, 1918.
Beaven, A. B., *Bristol Lists: Municipal and Miscellaneous*, Bristol, T. D. Taylor & S. Hawkins, 1899.
Besant, W., *All Sorts and Conditions of Men*, London, Chatto & Windus, 1898.
Beveridge, W., *Unemployment: a problem of industry*, London, Longmans, 1909.
Blackburn, H. (ed.), *Handbook for Women Engaged in Social and Political Work*, Bristol, J. W. Arrowsmith, 1881.
Booth, C., *Life and Labour of the People of London*, London, Macmillan, 1902.
Booth, W., *In Darkest England and the Way Out*, London, Salvation Army, 1890.
Bosenquet, C., *London: some account of its growth, charitable agencies and wants*, London, Hatchard, 1868.
Bottomore, T., *Critics of Society: Radical Thought in North America*, London, George Allen & Unwin, 1967.
Bowen, D., *The Idea of the Victorian Church: A Study of the Church of England 1833-89*, Montreal, McGill University Press, 1968.
Bowley, A. C. and Burnett-Hurst, A. R., *Livelihood and Poverty*, London, Bell, 1915.
Bradbury, M., *The Social Context of Modern English Literature*, Oxford, Blackwell, 1971.
Briggs, A., *Friends of the People: the centenary history of Lewis's*, London, Batsford, 1956.

SELECT BIBLIOGRAPHY

Briggs, A., *Victorian Cities*, London, Odhams, 1963.
Briggs, A. and Gill, C., *History of Birmingham*, London, Oxford University Press, 1952.
Briggs, A. and Saville, J. (eds), *Essays in Labour History*, London Macmillan revised edn, 1967.
Bryher S. (pseud. S. Bale), *An Account of the Labour and Socialist movement in Bristol*, Bristol, Bristol Printers, 1931.
Bullock, A., *Life of Ernest Bevin*, vol. I, London, Heinemann, 1960.
Burckhardt, J., *The Civilisation of the Period of the Renaissance in Italy*, London, Kegan Paul, 1878.
Burrow, J. W., *Evolution and Society: A Study in Victorian Social Theory*, Cambridge University Press, 1970 edn.
Burt, J., *The Bristol Chess Club – its History, Chief Players and Twenty-Three Years' Record of Principal Events*, Bristol, 1883.
Butcher, E. E., *Bristol Corporation of the Poor 1696–1898*, Bristol Branch of the Historical Association, The University, Bristol, 1972.
Butler, J. (ed.), *Woman's Work and Woman's Culture*, London, Macmillan, 1869.
Carpenter, M., *Reformatory Schools for the children of the perishing and dangerous classes and for juvenile offenders*, London, C. Gilpin, 1851.
Carpenter, M., *Red Lodge Girls' Reformatory School, Bristol. Its History, Principles and Working*, Bristol, 1875.
Carpenter, J. E., *The Life and Work of Mary Carpenter*, London, Macmillan, 1879.
Cave, C. H., *Bristol 1835–1935: a century of progress*, Bristol, Bristol Corporation, 1935.
Chadwick, G. F., *The Park and the Town*, London, Architectural Press, 1966.
Chadwick, O., *The Victorian Church*, part II, Edinburgh, Black, 1970.
Chapman, S. D., *History of Working Class Housing*, London, David & Charles, 1971.
Cherry, G. E., *Urban Change and Planning*, Oxford, G. T. Foulis, 1972.
Church, R. A., *Economic and Social Change in a Midland Town: Victorian Nottingham 1815–1900*, London, Cass, 1966.
Clapham, J. H., *An Economic History of Modern Britain*, 3 vols, Cambridge, Cambridge University Press, 1932.
Clark, G. Kitson, *An Expanding Society: Britain 1830–1900*, Melbourne and Cambridge, Cambridge University Press, 1967.
Clark, G. Kitson, *Churchmen and the Condition of England 1852–1885*, London, Methuen, 1973.

SELECT BIBLIOGRAPHY

Columbus, Lesser (pseud. Laurence Cowen), *Greater Bristol*, Bristol, 1893.
Colville, H. C. A., *Thomas William Harvey, Prophet and Priest*, Bristol, J. W. Arrowsmith, 1918.
Contemporary Biographies, 1898, Bristol, W. T. Pike, 1898–9.
Cottle, B. and Sherbourne, J., *Life of a University*, Bristol, J. W. Arrowsmith, 1959.
Creese, W., *The Search for Environment, The Garden City: before and after*, New Haven and London, Yale University Press, 1966.
Dunning E. (ed.), *The Sociology of Sport: a selection of readings*, London, Frank Cass, 1971.
Dyos, H. J., *Victorian Suburb: a study of the growth of Camberwell*, Leicester University Press, 1961.
Dyos, H. J. (ed.), *The Study of Urban History*, London, Edward Arnold, 1968.
Dyos, H. J. and Wolff, M. (eds), *The Victorian City: Images and Realities*, London, Routledge & Kegan Paul, 1973.
Eager, W. McG., *Making Men: The history of boys clubs and related movements in Great Britain*, London, University of London Press, 1953.
Escott, T. H. S., *Social Transformations of the Victorian Age: a survey of court and country*, London, Seeley, 1897.
Fedden, M., *Bristol Bypaths*, Bristol, Rankin, n.d.
Finer, S. E., *The Life and Times of Sir Edwin Chadwick*, London, Methuen, 1952.
Freeman, A. B., *Bristol Worthies and Notable Residents: past and present*, 2 vols, Bristol, 1907 and 1908.
Geddes, P., *Cities in Evolution*, London, Williams & Norgate, 1915.
Geddes, P. and Thomson, J. A., *The Evolution of Sex*, London, W. Scott, 1889.
Gilbert, B. B., *The Evolution of National Insurance in Great Britain: the origins of the welfare state*, London, Joseph, 1966.
Glass, D. V. (ed.), *Social Mobility in Britain*, London, Routledge & Kegan Paul, 1954.
Greenwood, T., *Public Libraries, their organisation uses and management*, London, Cassell, 3rd edn 1890.
Grosskurth, P., *John Addington Symonds: a biography*, London, Longmans, 1964.
Haggard, R., *Regeneration: being an account of the social work of the Salvation Army in Great Britain*, London, Longmans, 1910.
Handlin, O. and Burchard, J. (eds), *The Historian and the City*, Cambridge, Mass., MIT Press, 1966 edn.

SELECT BIBLIOGRAPHY

Harrison, B., *Drink and the Victorians*, London, Faber, 1971.
Harrison, J. F. G., *Learning and Living*, London, Routledge & Kegan Paul, 1961.
Harrison, R., *Before the Socialists*, London, Routledge & Kegan Paul, 1965.
Hauser, P. M. and Schnore, L. F. (eds), *The Study of Urbanisation*, New York, Wiley, 1965.
Hawkins, F. C., *History of the Clifton Rugby Football Club 1872–1909*, Bristol, Bristol Times & Mirror, 1909.
Hennock, E. P., *Fit and Proper Persons: Ideal and reality in nineteenth century urban government*, London, Edward Arnold, 1973.
Hill, O., *Homes of the London Poor*, London, Macmillan, 1875.
Hobsbawm, E., *Labouring Men*, London, Weidenfeld & Nicolson, 1964.
Hoggart, R., *The Uses of Literacy*, London, Chatto & Windus, 1957.
Holt, R. V., *The Unitarian Contribution to Social Progress in England*, London, Allen & Unwin, 1938.
Hope, E. W., *Health at the Gateway*, Cambridge University Press, 1931.
Howard, E., *Tomorrow: a peaceful path to real reform*, London, Sonnenschein, 1898.
Howarth, O. J. R., *The British Association: A retrospect 1831–1931*, London, British Association, 1931.
Hudson, T., *Temperance Pioneers of the West*, London, National Temperance Depôt, 1887.
Hutton, S., *Bristol and its Famous Associations*, Bristol, J. W. Arrowsmith, 1907.
Inglis, K. S., *Churches and the Working Classes in Victorian England*, London, Routledge & Kegan Paul, 1963.
Isichei, E., *Victorian Quakers*, London, Oxford University Press, 1970.
Ison, W., *The Georgian Buildings of Bristol*, London, Faber, 1952.
Jackson, E., *A Study in Democracy: an account of the rise and progress of industrial cooperation in Bristol*, Manchester, Co-operative Society, 1911.
Jacobs, N. (ed.), *Culture for the Millions?*, Boston, Beacon Press, paperback edn, 1964.
Jennings, H., *Societies in the Making: a study of development and redevelopment within a country borough*, London, Routledge & Kegan Paul, 1962.
Jevons, W. S., *Methods of Social Reform*, first published 1883; London, Macmillan reprint 1904.
Jones, P. d'A., *The Christian Socialist Revival 1877–1914*, London, Oxford University Press, 1968.

SELECT BIBLIOGRAPHY

Jones, G. Stedman, *Outcast London: A study in the relationship between classes in Victorian Society*, Oxford, Clarendon Press, 1971.
Keating, P. J., *The Working Classes in Victorian Fiction*, London, Routledge & Kegan Paul, 1971.
Kellett, J. R., *The Impact of Railways on Victorian Cities*, London, Routledge & Kegan Paul, 1969.
Kelvin, P., *The Bases of Social Behaviour*, London, Holt, Rinehart & Winston, 1970.
Kiernan, V. G., *The Lords of Human Kind: European atitudes to the outside world in the Imperial Age*, London, Weidenfeld & Nicolson, 1969.
Kingsley, C., *Sanitary and Social Lectures and Essays*, vol. 18 of collected works, London, Macmillan, 1880.
Knapp, J. M. (ed.), *The Universities and the Social Problem*, London, Rivington, Percival, 1895.
Knowle Cricket Club Centenary Book, 1862–1952, Bristol, 1952.
Laski, H., Jennings, W. I. and Robson W. A. (eds), *Century of Municipal Progress 1835–1935*, London, George Allen & Unwin, 1936.
Latimer, J., *Annals of Bristol in the Nineteenth Century*, Bristol, W. & F. Morgan, 1887.
Latimer, J., *History of the Society of Merchant Venturers of the city of Bristol*, Bristol, J. W. Arrowsmith, 1903.
Little, K., *West African Urbanisation: A study of voluntary associations in social change*, Cambridge, Cambridge University Press, 1965.
Lowndes, G. A. H., *The Silent Social Revolution*, London, Oxford University Press, 2nd edn 1969.
Lüsdren, G. (ed.), *The Cross-Cultural Analysis of Sport and Games*, Illinois, Stiped Publishing, 1970.
Lynd, H. M., *England in the eighteen-eighties: towards a social basis for freedom*, London, Oxford University Press, 1945.
McClelland, V. A., *Cardinal Manning: his public life and influence 1865–1892*, London, Oxford University Press, 1962.
MacInnes, C. A. and Whittard, W. F. (eds), *Bristol and its Adjoining Counties*, Bristol, British Association for the Advancement of Science, 1955.
McKechnie, S., *Popular Entertainment through the Ages*, London, Low & Marston, 1931.
Mackerness, E., *The Social History of English Music*, London, Routledge & Kegan Paul, 1964.
McLeod, H., *Class and Religion in the Late Victorian City*, London, Croom Helm, 1974.

SELECT BIBLIOGRAPHY

Malcolmson, R. W., *Popular Recreations in English Society 1700–1850*, Cambridge, Cambridge University Press, 1973.

Marples, M., *A History of Football*, London, Secker & Warburg, 1954.

Marsh, D. C., *The Changing Social Structure of England and Wales 1871–1961*, London, Routledge & Kegan Paul, 1965 edn.

Masterman, C., *The Condition of England*, London, Methuen, 1909.

Maurice, F. D., *The Life of F. D. Maurice told in his own letters, edited by his son*, 2 vols, London, Macmillan, 1884.

Mayor, S., *The Churches and the Labour Movement*, London, Independent Press, 1967.

Mills, C. Wright, *The Power Elite*, New York, Oxford University Press, 1956.

Money, A. Chiozza, *Riches and Poverty*, London, Methuen, 1905.

Mowat, C. L., *The Charity Organisation Society 1869–1913: Its ideas and Work*, London, Methuen, 1961.

Mumford, L., *The Culture of Cities*, London, Secker & Warburg, 1940.

Mumford, L., *The City in History*, Harmondsworth, Penguin Books, 1966.

Munford, W. A., *Penny Rate: aspects of British public library history 1850–1950*, London, Library Association, 1951.

Munford, W. A., *Edward Edwards 1812–1886: a portrait of a librarian*, London, Library Association, 1963.

Nettlefold, J. S., *Practical Housing*, Letchworth, Garden City Press, 1908.

Nicholls, J. F. and Taylor, J., *Bristol Past and Present*, vol. II, Bristol, J. W. Arrowsmith, 1881.

Nisbet, R. A., *The Sociological Tradition*, London, Heinemann, 1970 edn.

Owen, D., *English Philanthropy 1660–1960*, London, Oxford University Press, 1965.

Park, R. E., Burgess, E. W. and McKenzie, *The City*, University of Chicago Press, 1925.

Parsons, C. R., *Records of Mission Work in Bristol 1878–83*, Bristol, pub. priv. 1883.

Pearce, W. T. and others, *Bristol Football Club Jubilee Book 1888–1938*, Bristol, 1938.

Perkin, H., *Origins of Modern Society 1780–1880*, London, Routledge & Kegan Paul, 1969.

Phelps-Brown, E. H., *The Growth of British Industrial Relations*, first published 1959; London, Macmillan, reprint 1965.

Pimlott, J. A. R., *The Englishman's Holiday: a social history*, London, Faber, 1947.

Pollard, S., *A History of Labour in Sheffield*, Liverpool University Press, 1959.

SELECT BIBLIOGRAPHY

Pollard, S. and Crossley, D., *The Wealth of Britain 1085–1966*, London, Batsford, 1968.
Raistrick, A., *Quakers in Science and Industry*, London, Bannisdale Press, 1950.
Read, D., *The English Provinces 1760–1960: A study in influence*, London, Edward Arnold, 1964.
Reader, W. J., *Professional Men: The rise of the Professional Classes in Nineteenth Century England*, London, Weidenfeld & Nicolson, 1966.
Reckitt, M. B. (ed.), *For Christ and the People*, London, SPCK, 1968.
Redlich, J. and Hirst, F. W., *Local Government in England*, London, Macmillan, 1903.
Richter, M., *The Politics of Conscience: T. H. Green and his age*, London, Weidenfeld & Nicolson, 1964.
Robson, B. T., *Urban Growth: An Approach*, London, Methuen, 1973 edn.
Rowntree, B. S., *Poverty: a study of town life*, London, Macmillan, 1901.
Schlesinger, R. M., *The Rise of the City 1878–1898*, New York, Macmillan, 1933.
Shaen, M., *Memorials of Two Sisters*, London, Longmans, 1908.
Shannon, A. and Grebenik, E., *Population of Bristol*, Cambridge, Cambridge University Press, 1943.
Silver, H. and Lawson, J., *A Social History of Education in England*, 1973.
Simey, M., *Charitable effort in Liverpool in the Nineteenth Century*, Liverpool University Press, 1951.
Simon, B., *Education and the Labour Movement 1870–1918*, London, Lawrence & Wishart, 1965.
Smelser, N., *Social Change in the Industrial Revolution*, London, Routledge & Kegan Paul, 1959.
Smiles, S., *Self-Help*, London, Sphere, 1968.
Smith, H. P., *Literature and Adult Education a Century Ago: Pantopragmatics and Penny Readings*, Adult Education and Society Series, Documentary no. 3, H. P. Smith, 1960.
Smith, R. A. (ed.), *History of Physical Recreation and Sport*, Pennsylvania, Penn State, HPER Series no. A, 1972.
Stone, G. F., *Bristol as it was and as it is: A record of fifty years progress*, (reprinted, with additions, from the *Bristol Evening News*, 1908–9), Bristol, W. Reid, 1909.
Strutt, J., *The Sports and Pastimes of the People of England*, London, Methuen, 1903.
Sturge, E., *Reminiscences of My Life and some account of the Children*

SELECT BIBLIOGRAPHY

of *William and Charlotte Sturge, and the Sturge Family of Bristol*, Bristol, private publication, 1928.

Tarn, J. C., *Five Per Cent Philanthropy: an account of housing in urban areas between 1840–1914*, Cambridge, Cambridge University Press, 1973.

Temple, W., *The Life of Bishop Percival*, London, Macmillan, 1921.

Thomas, D. M., *Urijah Rees Thomas: His life and work*, London, Hodder & Stoughton, 1902.

Thompson, E. P., *The Making of the English Working Class 1780–1830*, London, Gollancz, 1963.

Timms, D., *The Urban Mosaic: Towards a Theory of Residential Differentiation*, Cambridge University Press, 1971.

Tovey, C., *Bristol City Library: its founders and benefactors; its present position in connection with the Library Society, etc.*, Bristol, 1853.

Veblen, T., *The Theory of the Leisure Class: An economic study of institutions*, London, George Allen & Unwin, 1925.

Vicinus, M. (ed.), *Suffer and be still: Women in the Victorian Age*, Bloomington, Indiana University Press, 1972.

Webb, B., *My Appenticeship*, first published 1962, Harmondsworth; Penguin Books reprint 1971.

Weber, A. F., *The Growth of Cities in the Nineteenth Century*, first published 1899; New York, Cornell University Press reprint, 1965.

Welton, T. A., *England's Recent Progress*, London, Chapman & Hall, 1911.

Wickham, E. R., *Church and People in an industrial city*, London, Lutterworth Press, 1957.

Wilson, J. M., *Autobiography 1826–1931*, London, Sidgwick & Jackson, 1932.

Williams, R., *Culture and Society 1780–1950*, Harmondsworth, Penguin Books, 1963 edn.

Young, A. F. and Ashton, E. T., *British Social Work in the Nineteenth Century*, London, Routledge & Kegan Paul, 1956.

Young, G. M., *Victorian England: Portrait of an Age*, London, Oxford University Press, 1937.

INDEX

Abbotsholme School, 247
Adult School Association, 190, 191, 195
Adult School Movement, 91, 190
Adult Schools, 190, 192, 193, 194
Aldermen, 21
America, 239
Anchor Society, 89
Anglican Church Extension Scheme, 143
Anglican Parochial Mission, 144–5
Anglicans, 49, 79, 123, 134, 138, 176
Anti-Corn Law League, 62
Anvil Street (Congregational Mission), 199
Arnold, Matthew, 14, 37, 39, 49, 50, 59, 248, 251
Artisan's Dwelling Act, 203
Ashley Down (County Cricket Ground), 235
Association for the Promotion of Evening Classes, 141, 143, 214
Association for the Promotion of Higher Education for Women, 51, 52, 53
Avon Gorge, 24, 25
Avonmouth, 33, 106, 210, 211, 229

Baden-Powell, R., 171
Baily, E.H., 44
Baker, W. Proctor, 176
Band of Hope Union, 124, 164, 190
Bank Holiday Act (1871), 211
Bank Holidays, 15, 166, 212
Baptist Association, 81
Baptist Mills, 143
Baptists, 79, 81, 123, 131, 138, 153, 163, 166, 194, 198, 201
Barnett, Canon S. A., 8, 9, 60, 99–100, 102, 118, 149–50, 154, 106–7, 203–4, 242, 243
Barton Hill, 194
Bath, 33
Baths and Washhouses Act (1846), 114
Baths and Washhouses Committee, 114–15
Bedales (School), 247
Bedminster, 24, 26, 30, 85, 104, 143, 146, 165, 174, 208
Bedminster Hippodrome, 208
Berkeley Benefit Societies, 209
Berkeley Square, 21, 173
Besant, W., 200–1
Bible Christians, 84, 163, 165
Bible classes, 123, 126, 127, 128, 138, 147, 159, 170, 190, 193, 198

INDEX

Birkenhead, 93, 113
Birmingham, 2, 8, 36, 41, 42, 44, 77, 96, 99, 113, 222, 240
Bishop's Committee (1884), 77
Blue Ribbon Temperance Movement, 165, 169
Board Schools, 171, 181, 182
Board of Trade Enquiry into Working Class Rents, Housing, and Retail Prices, 29, 35
Booth, Charles, 149, 162
Booth, William, 162
Borough Surveyors and Engineers, 237
Bournville, 119
Boys' Brigade, 169, 170, 171, 189
Boys' Clubs, 175, 249
Boy Scouts, 171, 172, 175
Brabham, Henry, 168, 194
Bradford, 2, 38, 80, 87, 113, 117
Brandon Hill, 118
Brislington, 24
Bristol: central areas, 30; changes in physical structure, 21; community activities, 34, 35; condition of people, 31; cosmopolitanism, 43; cultural milieu, eighteenth century, 43; docks, the, 33, 34; economic structure, 31, 35, 38, 39; growth of, 19, 20, 22, 31, 32; housing, 28, 29; migratory patterns, 32, 33; natural endowments of, 30, 31; physical condition of city (public health, etc.), 25–31; population growth, 31–3; sewerage, 27; social change in city and suburbs, 35–9; street improvements, 27, 28
Bristol Adult School Association, 190, 191, 195
Bristol Argus, 219, 226, 231, 242

Bristol Art Gallery, 66, 68, 69, 70, 93, 97
Bristol Athenaeum, 47, 63, 90, 93, 127, 128, 143, 214
Bristol Bishopric Committee, 88
Bristol Bridge, 21, 27
Bristol Cathedral, 21, 80, 203
Bristol Central Conservative Association, 89
Bristol Central Library, 66, 67, 68
Bristol Chamber of Commerce, 73, 90, 91, 180
Bristol Charity Organization Society, 204
Bristol Chess Club, 64
Bristol Children's Hospital, 89
Bristol *Christian Leader,* 197
Bristol Church Extension Commission, 89
Bristol City Mission, 81, 90, 123, 132, 138, 166, 198
Bristol Civic League, 204
Bristol and Clifton Debating Society, 57
Bristol Committee for Promoting the Better Housing of the Poor, 29
Bristol Co-operative Education Committee, 143, 156, 214, 215
Bristol Corporation of the Poor, 74
Bristol Council House, 21
Bristol and District Co-operative Society, 141, 143, 156, 215
Bristol Early Closing Association, 126–7, 143
Bristol Education Committee, 194
Bristol Endowed School, 185
Bristol Evening Class and Recreation Society (Bristol

Branch), 156, 181, 182, 184, 186, 189
Bristol Evening School Committee, 182, 185, 186, 187, 225
Bristol Free Churches, 173
Bristol Friends' Meeting House, 91
Bristol and Gloucestershire Archaeological Association, 57
Bristol Grammar School, 83
Bristol Housing Reform Committee, 29, 30
Bristol Liberal Federation, 89, 92
Bristol Medical School, 44
Bristol Microscopical Society, 45, 57
Bristol Museum, 66, 67, 68, 121, 187, 203
Bristol Museum and Library Society, 56, 57, 63, 66, 67, 90, 92, 93, 104, 106, 190
Bristol Naturalists Society, 57
Bristol Pharmaceutical Society, 57
Bristol Philosophical Institution, 40, 47, 48, 49, 51, 56, 92, 93
Bristol Recreational Council, 175, 204
Bristol Royal Infirmary, 21, 89
Bristol School Board, 53, 89, 92, 133, 143, 155, 176, 184, 185, 186, 189, 194, 204, 215
Bristol Socialist Society, 157
Bristol South Conservative Association, 89
Bristol and South Wales Union Railway, 131
Bristol Statistical Society, 25, 33, 45, 79
Bristol Sunday Society, 193, 217, 218, 245; speakers at: G. B. Shaw, Annie Besant, R. H. Haldane, Graham Wallas, 218

Bristol Tabernacle, 81, 91, 92
Bristol Temperance Society, 164, 243
Bristol Trades Council, 157, 196, 214
Bristol United Temperance Council, 164
Bristol University, 58-9, 92, 215
Bristol University College, 62, 90, 92, 143, 144, 159, 176, 179, 181, 184, 185, 199, 215, 218
Bristol University Settlement, 196, 197, 199, 202
Bristol YMCA, 90, 91, 93, 123, 126-30, 131, 141, 144, 145, 146, 147, 148, 149, 155, 161, 181, 190, 195, 218, 224, 232, 236; supporters of: Oatleys, 128, George Thomas, 130
Bristol YWCA, 173
British Association for the Advancement of Science, 45, 46, 58, 62, 67, 70, 97, 104
British Museum, 101
British Women's Temperance Society, 164
Broadmead, 91
Broadmead Baptist Chapel, 81
Broadmead Rooms, 128, 210
Broad Plain, 138, 199
Broad Plain Mission (Congregationalist), 199, 202
Broad Weir, 114
Brown, William, 101
Brunel, I. K., 25, 33
Bryce, J., 10
Bute family, 112
Butler, Josephine, 52, 54

Caldicott, Rev. J. M., 83, 176
Cambridge, 149, 153

INDEX

Cardiff, 112–13
Carpenter, Dr Lant, 43, 45
Carpenter, Mary, 137, 151
Cashmore, Hilda, 197
Castle, the, 184
Cathedral, 21, 80
Central Education Department, 182, 185
Chadwick, Edwin, 27
Chamberlain, J., 77
Chant, Mrs Ormistan, 165
Charity Organization Society, 16, 75
Cheltenham, 115
Chester, 33
Children's Employment Agency, 137
Children's Help Societies, 249
Christian Brethren, 84, 163, 198
Christian Socialist, 153, 157, 159, 161, 162, 195
Christian Socialist Guild of St Matthew, 161, 195
Church Extension Committee, 150
Church Extension Scheme, 80, 138, 143
Churchill, W. S., 238
Church of England, 44, 78, 80, 81, 122, 144, 161, 163, 164; societies, 189, 195, 196, 197, 198
Church of England Christian Social Union, 195
Church of England Temperance Society, 164
Church Lads' Brigade, 169, 171
'City Beautiful' movement, 113
City council, 97, 191
'Civic Gospel', 96
Civic gospellers (of Birmingham), 41
Civic structure, 154, 156
Civilization, 5, 6, 7, 8, 11, 12, 13, 15, 17, 40, 48, 99, 102, 237, 239, 252; 'higher', 141, 144; urban, 120, 172, 192; 'civilizing' influences, 248; 'civilizing' mission, 72, 90, 122, 126–34, 138, 163, 176, 197, 198, 199, 200, 202; 'civilizing' process, 5, 11, 15, 17, 102, 103, 218
Clare Street, 37
Clevedon, 210, 211
Clifford, Hon. and Rev. William, DD, 64
Clifton, 21, 24, 25, 36–7, 38, 39, 42, 49, 52, 75, 81, 85, 91, 110, 115, 138, 182, 228, 230
Clifton Antiquarian Club, 57, 63, 64
Clifton College, 37, 49, 57, 65, 83, 92, 118, 141, 143, 185, 223, 248
Clifton College Mission (St Agnes), 63, 136, 145, 149–60, 161, 172, 174, 199, 203, 234, 239
Clifton Exhibition, 178
Clifton High School for Girls, 51, 92, 185
Clifton Rugby Football Club, 229
Clifton Suspension Bridge, 25
'Coketown', 4
Colchester, 33
Colston, Edward, 74
Colston Commemoration Societies, 74, 77, 88
Colston Hall, 58, 93, 129, 198, 210, 218, 220, 222, 242
Colston Hall Company, 57, 220
Colston School, 57
Colston Societies, 77
Colston Society, 88
Commercial entertainment, 210, 222, 251
Community, 6, 7, 8, 9, 10, 11, 161, 207, 214, 238, 239, 246
'Community' spirit, 123, 239

298

INDEX

Congregationalist Bristol Tabernacle, 126, 138
Congregationalist Highbury Chapel, 81
Congregationalists, 79, 81, 91, 123, 138, 153, 163, 170, 194, 198, 200, 201, 202
Conservative Club, 140
Conservatives (Tories), 85, 87, 88
Contagious Diseases Act, 54
Contemporary Review, 5
Co-operative Movement, 143, 159, 189, 194, 214, 215, 251
Corn Street (Co-operative Educational Classes), 143
Cossham, Handel, 58, 177
Cotham, 24, 38, 81, 118, 138, 143
Counterslip, 166, 167
Crystal Palace, 177, 220, 222, 225, 234
Crystal Palace Orchestra, 220
Culture, 14, 40, 50, 52, 179, 237, 238, 241, 243, 246; Arnoldian vision of, 50, 54, 59, 248
Cultural activities, 217, 218, 245
Cultural diffusion, 129, 141, 150, 153, 177, 243, 246
Cultural entertainment, mass, 134-7, 139, 140
Cultural environment, 169
Cultural experiences, 1, 16, 241, 249
Cultural improvement, 200
Cultural influences, 247, 248
Cultural institutions, 245, 246, 247, 248
Cultural interests, 246
Cultural life of city, 41, 42, 45, 53, 126
Cultural pursuits, 41, 42, 47, 50, 65
Cultural 'renaissance', 48, 65, 66, 104, 141, 248

Cultural unity, 14, 15, 41, 42, 141, 150, 242
Curwen, Rev. John (Tonic Sol-fa method), 223

Daniel, H., 148
Davies, Dr (Medical Officer of Health), 28
Day Industrial Feeding School, 137
Deering, Dr, 109
Dickens, Charles, 47
District ward, 38
Dolphin Society, 88
Domestic Mission, 123
Downs, 24, 75, 116, 211, 212, 229, 235
Dowry Square, Hotwells, 29
Dublin Weekly Tract Society, 129
Duckworth, Alderman, 113
Dunfermline, 100

Easton, 22, 30, 146
Eastville, 22
Education, 43, 44, 45, 51, 52, 53, 56, 57, 58, 59, 60, 61, 62, 66, 83, 93, 96, 98, 127, 128, 137, 139, 140, 141, 143, 151, 153, 175, 176, 181, 182, 184, 185, 186, 187, 189, 217, 245; adult, 189-94, 205; facilities, 177, 182, 186; further, 238; Rev. Seyer's School, 44; Dr Swete's School, 44
Edwards, Sir George W., 88-9
Elementary Education Act (1870), 3, 56
Elementary schools, 123
Elites, 41, 56, 65, 69, 70, 71, 76, 77, 78, 84, 91, 94, 95, 245, 248;

INDEX

governing, 72, 73, 74, 76, 77, 78, 79, 80, 83, 84, 85, 90, 95; social and cultural, 128, 132, 149, 176, 178, 190; socio-economic, 17
Ellicott, Bishop of Bristol and Gloucester, 80, 138
Empire Theatre of Varieties, 212, 218
Endowed Charity Commission, 77
Endowed Charity Commissioners, 51
Escott, T. H. S., 9, 228, 235
Estlin, Dr, 44, 45, 47
Estlin, John Bishop, 44, 45, 47
Evangelical Free Church, 78, 122, 125
Evangelicalism, 43, 44, 78, 79; (Moody and Sankey), 84, 122, 147, 198
Evangelicals, 43, 44
Evening Class Association, 143
Evening classes, 181, 182, 186, 189
Evolutionary positivism, 13
Ewart, William, 101
Exeter, 107, 115

Family entertainment, 212
Fishponds, 106, 146
Floating Harbour, 33, 110, 114
Florence, 8, 41
Free Libraries and Museum Acts, 41
Free Methodists, 84, 163
Free Port Association, 73
Friendly Societies, 209, 210, 225
Friends' School, 190
Frome (river), 27

Fry, J. S., 35, 57, 132, 148, 190–1, 193
Fry, Lewis, 57, 80, 89, 90, 104, 116, 148, 176
Fry, Miss, 148, 172
Fry family, 34, 35, 57, 62, 88, 91–5, 128, 148, 193

Garden City movement, 109
Garfield, J. A., 239
Gas Workers and General Labour Union, 168
Geddes, Patrick, 7, 10, 100, 118, 180
General Educational Council, 185
Girl Guides, 175
Girls' Friendly Society, 174
Gladstone, William Ewart, 102
Gloucester, 25, 32, 80
Gloucestershire Society, 88
Glover, Rev., Dr, 83
Gore, H. H., 157
Gospel Temperance Society, 168
Gospel Temperance Union, 165
Gotch, Rev., Dr, 176
Grace, W. G., 229
Grantham Grammar School, 153
Grateful Society, 88, 89
Great Exhibition (1851), 40, 177, 212
Great George Street, 21
Great Western Railway, 22, 226
Great Western Railway Temperance Friendly Society, 164
Great Yarmouth, 33
Green, T. H., 10
Greenwood, Thomas, 101, 106
Grove, the, 209
Guild of Coopers, 21
Gymnasia, 98, 102, 121

300

INDEX

Hall of Freedom, 140
'Happy Evenings for the People', 166, 169
Harford family, 44
Harvey, Mrs, 159
Harvey, Rev. T. W., 136, 144, 152–60, 192, 193, 243, 248
Haymarket, 118
Headlam, S., 161, 163, 195
Highbury Congregational Chapel, 138, 148, 199
Hill, Octavia, 28, 172
Holiday-making, 211–12
Home Encouragement Exhibitions, 172, 173; Bedminster Home Encouragement Exhibition and Flower Show, 172; Redland and Kingsdown Home Encouragement and Flower Show, 172
Home Encouragement Societies, 172
Horfield, 211, 229
Horsfall, T. C., 120
Hotwells, 29, 139, 146
Hotwells Adult School Club, 192
Hotwells Road, 27
Housing, 119

Imperial Tobacco Company, 93
Independent Order of Good Templars, 164
Industrial Dwelling Company, 28
Industrial Exhibitions, 177, 179, 180; Brussels International Exhibition (1898), 180; Chicago Exhibition (1893), 180; Paris Exposition (1900), 180
Industrial and Fine Arts Exhibition, 66
Industrial Revolution, 1, 3, 12, 19, 24, 31, 35, 43, 227

Inskip, James, 128, 148
Inspectors of Nuisances, 237
International Herald, 140
International Working Men's Association, 140

Jacobs Wells' Road, 29
Jacobs Wells' Swimming Bath, 115
Jevons, W. S., 5, 15, 66, 220, 250
Jowett, Benjamin, 60–1, 159

Kingsdown, 21, 24, 115, 138, 199, 231
Kingsley, Charles, 16,
King Street, 56, 67
King Street Theatre, 212
Kingswood, 146
Knowle race-course, 211
Kyrle Society, 162, 172, 199

Labour and Co-operative movement, 159
Labour movement, 140, 143, 156, 157, 204, 217
Law Society, 92
Lean, Vincent Stuckey, 67, 68, 101, 106
Leeds, 2, 42, 44, 222
Leisure, 5, 7, 16, 17; activities, 217, 218, 239, 240, 251; attitudes to, 60, 61, 214, 241; experiences, 240; facilities, 7, 16, 96, 97, 98, 122, 135, 140, 163, 170, 173, 217, 239–41; patterns of city, 245; use of, 211, 240
Leonard, George Hare, 173, 199
Leonard, Robert, 127, 128, 130
Leonard, Sir Thomas, 148
Lewins Mead Chapel, 21, 43, 137

INDEX

Liberal Culture, 7, 8, 14, 51, 52, 53, 54, 56, 60, 62, 65, 70, 97, 103, 179, 201, 202, 214, 246, 247, 248
Liberal Nonconformists, 87, 89, 90, 104, 147, 163, 176, 178
Liberal party, 128
Libraries: donor of, Andrew Carnegie; 100, 101, 106; lending, 96, 97, 99, 246
Library Acts (1850, 1855, 1919), 101
Library Association, 67, 107
Library Committee, 103, 104
Library movement, 100–7, 112
Library and Museum Society, 63
Library Society, 56
Literary and Philosophical Club, 127
Literary and Philosophical Institute, 44, 127
Literary and Philosophical Society, 44, 45, 46, 47, 49, 63
Liverpool, 2, 11, 19, 26, 33, 44, 77, 80, 96, 100, 101, 110, 112, 118
Lloyd George, David, 238
Local government, 8, 97
Local Government Board, 3
London, 2, 21, 29, 43, 109, 126, 140, 149, 161, 180, 196, 213, 222
Long Ashton, 209
Lord's Day Observance Society, 78, 218
Low Countries, 15

Manchester, 2, 11, 26, 33, 42, 44, 96, 101, 110, 115, 117, 120
Mangotsfield, 24
Marshall, Mrs Alfred, 53
Marshall, J. W. D., 217
Marson, Charles, 163
Marx, Karl, 5–6

Mass media, 245
'Mass' society, 241, 242, 245, 247
Matthews, E. Norris, 106
Maurice, F. D., 151, 161
Mawson, T. H., 100
Mayor's Paddock, 114
Mechanics Institute, 47
Medical Officers of Health, 28, 237
Merchant Venturers School, 184, 185
Merchant Venturers Technical College, 186, 218
Methodist New Connection, 84
Metropolitan Early Closing Association, 126
Mill, J. S., 14
Milward, Henry, 212
Mina Road, 118, 198
'Modern' city, the, 1, 2, 3, 4, 5, 6–7, 9, 15, 76, 252; urban form, 4, 15
More, Hannah, 43
Morgan, E. T., 225
Morley, S., 61, 147
Morris, William, 7, 64
Mothers' Meetings, 133, 139
Mothers' Union, 174
Municipal Charities Trustees, 74, 77; Board of, 89
Municipal Council, 99, 110, 117, 122
Municipal Councillors: Bush family, 87; Castle family, 87; George family, 88; Lucas family, 87; Miles family, 88; Nash family, 88; Poole King family, 88; Ricketts family, 87; Terrell family, 87; Vining family, 88; Wait family, 88
'Municipal pride', 97
Municipal Reform Act (1835), 74, 85

INDEX

Museums, 102, 121, 203, 246
Music, 219–25, 251; facilities, 223; -making, 219, 222, 223, 224, 225; 'revolution', 219
Music institutions: Bohee and Livermore Troupes, 210; Bristol Madrigal Society, 49, 89, 219, originator of (E. J. Taylor), 46; Bristol Music Festival, 58; Bristol Vocal Society, 46; Butterworth's Christy Minstrels, 210; Choral music festivals, 219, 222; Choral Societies: Aeolian Male Voice Choir, 224, Bristol Cathedral Choir, 225, Bristol Co-operative Choir, 225, Bristol Harmonic Male Voice Choir, 225, Bristol South Choral Society, 225, Choral Society at the Clifton College Mission, 224, Church Choral Union, 223, East Bristol Choral Society, 224, Knowle and Totterdown Choral Society, 225, North Bristol Society, 225, Railwayman's Choir, 225, St John Choral Union, 223, Temperance Choral Society, 223, YMCA Choral Society, 225; Choral Society, 47; Classical Harmonists, 47; Empire Music Hall, 165; Monday Popular Concerts, 220; Moore and Burgess Minstrels, 210; Musical Union, 220; Music Festival Committee, 223; Music Festival Society, 89; National Co-operative Festival, 225; Orpheus Society, 47; Philharmonic Society, 47; Post Office Band, 224; Royal College of Music, 222; Royal Orpheus Glee Society, 148; Sacred Harmonic Society, 222; Society of Instrumentalists, 224; Wills' Workpeople's Band, 224
Mutual Improvement societies, 93, 126, 156, 157, 159, 190, 191

Naish, Arthur, 131
Narrow Plain, 132, 139
Nash, Vaughan, 156
National Association of Working Girls' Clubs, 174
National Commercial Travellers' League, 164
National Council of Women, 54
National Women's Co-operative Guild, 216, 217
Nettlefold, J. S., 119
Newcastle upon Tyne, 2
Newfoundland Road School, 176, 184
Nonconformist Christian Social Brotherhood, 195
Nonconformists, 43, 49, 79, 80, 122, 126, 127, 128, 134, 138, 144, 145, 147, 151, 153, 162, 164, 176, 190, 195, 196, 197, 198, 213
Norwich, 33, 46
Nottingham, 36, 80, 109, 240

Parks and open spaces, 96, 98, 99, 107, 110, 112, 117, 118; donors of: C. B. Adderley, Lord Calthorpe, Baron Masham, 113; Open Spaces and Recreation Committee, 162; public park movement, 113, 119, 121
Park Street, 21, 44, 56, 143
Parliament, 28
Parsons, C. R., 132, 198
Paternalism, 94

Paulton Harvest Home, 212
Pease, Marian, 197
Penny banks, 126
Penny readings, 125, 134–7, 145, 165, 166, 177, 245
People's Entertainment Society, 162
People's Mission, 198
People's Palace, 201, 212
Percival, Rev. John, 49, 50, 54, 58, 59, 60, 62, 64, 80, 83, 141–4, 153, 156, 157, 159, 160, 176, 182, 189, 193, 214, 243, 251
Philanthropic activity, 74, 75, 76, 77, 83, 84, 89, 90, 91, 104, 123, 138, 161, 175
Pinney family, 44, 45, 47
Pitman's Association, 186
'Pleasant Saturday Nights', 166
Pleasure gardens, 210, 211
Plymouth, 113
Politics of conscience, 10
Poor Law Amendment Act (1834), 11, 74
Popular amusements, 206–8, 210, 212, 213, 214, 217–18
Popular pastimes, 15, 16, 17, 208, 211, 225
Portishead, 33, 211
Primitive Methodists, 163
Prince's Theatre, 212
Proctor, Alderman, 75
Public Health, 8, 96, 97–8, 114
Public Health Act (1848), 28; (1875), 3
Public Health movement, 25, 237

Quaker Adult School, 91, 193
Quaker Mission, 53, 90, 91, 92, 132–4, 139, 141, 190, 194
Quaker Mission Committee, 134, 139, 168, 169, 194

Quakers, 73, 75, 79, 91, 92, 125, 130–1, 132, 136, 137, 139, 153, 163, 168, 190, 191, 192, 194, 195, 197, 200, 201
Quakers' First Day School for Men, 190; First Day School for Boys, 190
Quaker Sunday School, 91, 92, 132
Queen's Square, 118, 166, 209

Ragged schools, 123, 133, 137
Rawnsley, Rev. H. D., 150
Rechabites Order, 164
Recreation: football, cricket, 116; municipal provisions for, 107–17; parks and open spaces, 107–13; Physical Recreation Society, 235; sports grounds, 116–17; swimming baths, 113–16
Redcliff parish, 26, 138
Redland, 24, 38, 44, 81, 105, 106, 143
Redland High School, 51, 185
Redland Park, 81, 138
Redland Park Congregational Chapel, 81, 138, 153, 170
Redland Park Young People's Guild, 170, 171
Reform Act (1867), 54, 56
Regional Survey Associations, 10
Religion: development of, 77–84; growth of churches, 77–84 (*see also* individual denominations)
Religious sub-culture, 78, 84, 245
Report on the Sanatory Condition of Bristol (1846), 26
Rifle Drill Hall, 68, 69, 210
Riley, William H., 140
Riseley, George, 148, 198, 222
Roath, 112

INDEX

Robinson, Mrs Edward, 203
Robinson, E. S. & A., 93
Robinson family, 34, 93
Rochdale, 113
Roman Catholics, 79, 176
Rowntree, B. S., 12–13, 148
Royal Commission on the Health of Towns, 25
Royal Commission on the Housing of the Working Classes, 24, 29
Royal Commission on the Poor Laws, 238
Royal Family: Prince Albert, 219, 222; Prince of Wales, 211
Royal Institute of London, 44
Royal South and West of England Agricultural Show, 179

St Agnes Mission, *see* Clifton College Mission
St Agnes Mutual Improvement Society, 159, 160
St Agnes parish, 118, 145, 150, 151, 153–4, 156, 159, 160, 176, 184, 192, 193, 239, 240, 243
St Agnes Working Men's Club, 199, 248
St Augustine's Parade, 57
St Augustine ward, 85
St Barnabas parish, 150
St George parish, 30, 106
St James Back, 137, 223
St James parish, 104
St John's Ambulance class, 147, 186
St Judes parish, 132
St Lukes parish, 34
St Michael's ward, 38, 39, 135
St Paul parish, 21
St Paul ward, 85
St Philip & Jacob ward, 85, 104

St Philips Literary Institution, 104
St Philips parish, 104, 198, 199, 200
St Thomas parish, 26
Salford, 2, 96
Saltford, 229
Salvation Army, 84, 162, 169, 198, 210
Sanitary Authority, 28, 115
Sanitary Commission, 3
Scandinavia, 15
School of Science and Literature for West of England, 58, 60
Self-Help, 250
Self-improvement, 132, 140, 141, 146
Settlement movement, 196
Shaftesbury Crusade, 164, 170, 240; supporters of: Harris and Tribe families, 170
Sheffield, 2, 36, 38, 39, 44, 80, 240
Shirehampton, 106, 229
Smith, H. P., 156, 160
Smythe, Sir Greville, 113
'Social citizenship', 7, 8, 9, 10, 74, 76, 77, 86, 87, 94, 97, 98, 99, 100, 113, 115, 119, 120, 186, 195, 203, 238, 247
'Social co-operation', 150, 153, 155, 160, 163, 201, 203
Social engineering, 225
Social environment, 5–6, 7, 8, 11, 16, 35, 36, 117, 119, 122, 144, 199, 237, 238, 239, 240, 250, 251
'Social evil', 124, 125, 169
'Social evolution', 5, 6, 14, 15, 17
Social Improvement Institute, 140
Socialist ideas, 217, 218
Social problems, 11, 204
'Social question', the, 11, 12, 13, 15, 17
'Social rescue' work, 202

INDEX

Social Science Association, 11, 12, 54
Social Service League, 203, 204
Social work, 194, 195, 196, 199, 204
Society of Arts, 186
Society of Merchant Venturers, 21, 28, 36, 58, 73–7, 81, 88, 116, 181
Socio-religious activities, 90, 91, 92, 94, 104, 137, 149, 175, 177, 223, 224
Socio-religious institutions, 152, 173, 190, 203
Socio-religious organizations, 122, 146, 176, 180, 225, 236
Socio-religious work, 122, 124, 125, 126, 130, 131, 135, 137, 138, 139, 141, 146, 148, 151, 161, 181, 193, 195, 197, 200, 202, 239, 240
Solly, Rev. H., 139
Somerset, 25, 32
Southampton, 115
Southmead, 199
Spelling bees, 125, 135, 145, 177
Sport, 158, 225–37, 251; activities, 230, 233, 234; facilities, 229, 230; 'legitimate', 231; 'muscular Christianity', 146, 205, 225; organizations, 228, 229, 230, 231, 232, 233, 234, 235; organized, 225–36; papers: *Amateur Sport*, 226, *Bristol Bicycle and Tricycle Club Monthly Gazette*, 226
Sporting clubs: Clifton Rugby Football Club, 229; Cricket: Clifton Cricket Club, 229, Gloucestershire County Cricket Club, 229, Knowle and Bedminster Cricket Club, 229; Cycling: Bristol Crusaders' Cycling Club, 230, Bristol Tricycle and Bicycle Club, 227, 230, 231, 232, 235, Clifton Cycling Club, 227; Football: Aston Villa, 233, Bedminster Club, 233, Blackburn Olympic, 234, Bristol City, 233, Bristol South End, 233, Eastville Rovers, 233, Manchester United, 234, Old Etonians, 234, St George's, 233, Warmley, 233
Stapleton, 106
Stoke Bishop, 25, 93, 138
Stoke on Trent, 2
Stokes Croft, 210
Straker, William, 192–4, 217
Sturge, Elizabeth, 51
Sturge, Emily, 52, 53
Sunday schools (and Bible classes), 123, 124, 190, 191
Sunday School Union, 191
Swimming baths, 98, 99, 107; and Washhouses, 114–17; Baths and Washhouses Committee, 114, 115
Swimming clubs, 114
Symes, R. H., 75, 88
Symonds, Dr Addington, 47
Symonds, J. Addington, 40, 44, 45, 47, 48

Taylor, John, 105
Teetotalism, 165, 169, 213
Temperance Coffee Tavern (Quaker British Workman), 125, 139, 164, 168, 169, 170, 194, 200
Temperance Friendly Societies, 164
Temperance Halls, 125, 135
Temperance movement, 15, 90, 123, 124, 130, 163–9, 170, 190, 209, 243, 251

INDEX

Temperance societies, 243
Temple Meads Station, 27, 224
Temple Parish, 26, 138
Terrett, Mrs, 165
Thomas, Rev. U. R., 83, 138, 152, 153, 154, 170
Tivoli Theatre, 213
Torrens and Cross Acts (1868, 1875), 3, 28
Total Abstinence Society, 164
Totterdown, 24, 135, 146
Tovey, Charles, 56, 104
Town Council, 27, 29, 33, 67, 68, 74, 75, 85–90, 92, 96, 98, 104, 105, 106, 114, 116, 117, 118, 204, 246
Town Council Improvement Committee, 27
Town Council Library and Museum Committee, 66, 67, 68, 69
Town Planning Act (1909), 30, 98, 180
Town Planning Movement, 117–21
Towns and Cities Exhibition, 180
Townsend, Charles, 81, 89–90, 104
Toynbee Hall, 149, 154, 175, 203, 234
Trade School, 58, 181, 186
Trades Council, 29, 139, 157, 182, 218, 251
Trades Early Closing Association, 47
Trade Unions, 139, 193, 196, 210, 217, 225
Transport and General Workers' Union, 193
Tyndale Baptist Chapel, 81, 139
Tyndall Park, 138

Union Street, 91

Unitarians, 21, 81, 123, 137, 163
University of Cambridge, 42, 52, 59, 149
University Colleges in Ireland, 59
University Extension movement, 41
University of Oxford, 42, 46, 52, 59, 149, 226
Urban civilization, 237, 241, 248
Urban community, 76, 83, 86, 97, 98, 238
Urban development, 138
Urban environment, 161, 180, 239
Urban growth, 100
Urbanization, 1–4, 13, 18, 207, 213, 237, 238, 250, 251
Urban renewal, 118
Urwick, E. J., 175

Venice, 8
Victoria Rooms, 57, 219
Victoria Street, 27
Visiting Societies, 123; Diocesan Visiting Society, 123; Inner City Visiting Mission, 123
Voluntary organizations, 73, 122

Wall, J. W. H., 141, 214
Waterworks Company, 28
Wathen, Sir Charles, 66, 88, 104, 180
Wesleyan National Congress, 81
Wesleyans, 79, 81, 123, 198, 201, 202
Wesley Hall, 198
West Bristol Gospel Temperance Society, 164
Westbury-on-Trym, 25, 38
West of England College of Art, 66
Western Daily Press, 8, 79, 103,

INDEX

135, 145, 167, 176, 208, 211, 212, 222, 226, 229
Western Europe, 239
West Indian trade, 21
Weston, Joseph Dodge, 66, 75, 88–9, 90, 104, 105, 177–9, 180
Weston-super-Mare, 211
White Hart Hotel, 213
White Ribbon Temperance Army, 165, 169
Whitwill, Mark, 89, 90, 92, 104, 115, 116, 139, 146, 176, 200
Whitwill, Mark, Jnr, 180
Wilcox, Mr Dove, 166, 167, 192
Williams, Sir George, 148
Wills, E. P., 80
Wills, S. D., 148
Wills, W. D., 130
Wills, Sir W. H., 58, 68, 69, 89, 90, 101, 104, 106, 170
Wills family, 25, 34, 57, 62, 69, 81, 87, 91–5, 126, 128, 129, 148
Wilson, Rev. J. M., 65, 118, 141, 150, 155, 156, 157, 158, 176, 185, 248, 249
Windmill Hill, 184
Winkworth sisters, 28, 151
Winter Amusement Committees, 135
Wolverhampton, 2
Women, 50, 51, 52; activities of, 53, 54; education of, 51, 52, 53, 215–17; equality, 51
Women's Total Abstinence Society, 164
Woodcraft Folk, 172
Workers' Educational Association, 156, 189, 193, 194
Working Girls' Clubs, 173, 175
Working Men's Club and Institute Union, 162
Working Men's Clubs, 154, 156, 190, 192
'Workshop of the world', 3, 12

York, 12